XSLT Jumpstarter

Level the Learning Curve and Put Your XML to Work

David James Kelly

Raleigh, North Carolina

Printed in the United States of America.
ISBN-13: 978-0-913465-03-5
Printed on acid-free paper.
Book version: 1.0—May, 2015

Contents

Foreword

Think of a reservoir full of water, or a storm cloud full of static electricity. There's energy there, but it isn't doing anything. To get value from the water, you can let if fall through turbines, or pipe it into people's homes. You have to transform the potential energy to extract its value.

It's the same for data. On its own, a pile of data is just a bucket full of bits. Data only pays back when you transform it.

Maybe you convert sales data into a analysis of who bought what. Maybe you turn a production specification into a maintenance document. Maybe you turn someone's words into a book.

In the bad old days of software, this was challenge. Each application had its own ways of representing the data it consumed and the data it created. There was no real standardization. But gradually, this chaos got better. Standards emerged. And one of the most popular was XML—a text-based way of representing just about any structured data.

But we still faced the problem of turning the potential of this data into something useful. For a while, people hand-coded these solutions. But around the turn of the century life got easier—we could use the Extensible Stylesheet Language, XLST.

It worked like this: Given data in an XML document, you could write instructions in XSLT. These instructions would tell the system how to *transform* the original XML. The result could be another XML document, a spreadsheet, a webpage, or the markup for a printed book (like this one).

This is magical. Given any data, expressed in XML, you can use XSLT to transform it into something more valuable to you.

At the Pragmatic Bookshelf, we've been using an XML-based system to create our books for over 10 years. The original XML content expresses the structure of the book (here's a chapter, here's a figure, or a cross reference, or some text to make italic for emphasis). We then use XSLT to transform this content in many, many ways. We print paper books, create online PDFs. We generate epub and mobi formats for eBook readers. We create extracts and tables of contents for our online website. We reformat it for delivery to Amazon and Safari. And so on, and so on. In a very real way, XSLT is the backbone of our business.

Initially, I wrote XSLT myself. And I really enjoyed it.

Now, this is probably not something you'd hear a programmer like me say everyday. Most developers view XSLT as being a little verbose, or a little ugly. But that's because they never get beyond the surface. Underneath all the angle brackets, XSLT is actually very advanced, very powerful, and (relatively) easy-to-use.

First, XSLT is written as a series of functions. Now a function is simply something that takes an input and produces an output. In the case of XSLT, the function is a pattern that matches some parts of the input XML. A function could transform the part of a document that matches a chapter name into a new chapter in a printed book. A function could match all the item values in an invoice and output the total. And the joy of this is that each function is (largely) freestanding. You can match some part of your document, and then forget about that part of the XSLT and move on to match something else. This is wonderful, because it means that the XSLT you write will consist of lots of independent functions. When the input document format changes (and, in the real world, _everything_ changes), you'll find that updating the XSLT is a lot easier than it will be in another language.

Second, the functions in XSLT work together seamlessly. Think of formatting an invoice. You could write one XSLT function that handles the top-level work to get the invoice printed. There will then be dozens of other functions that work on specific jobs—formatting the name and address, layout out the line items, maybe calculating a total, and so on. The top-level function doesn't need to know about the lower level ones. It just all works out, like magic. Again, think how much easier this makes maintenance.

And, third, XSLT is universal. We have authors using Windows, Mac, and Linux systems. The same XSLT is used on all these platforms to reformat their books.

So, I was having a blast writing all this XSLT. But that meant I was not giving enough time to my other duties. So we looked around for someone to help.

We were lucky enough to find David Kelly. We threw him in at the deep end, handing over tens of thousands of lines of XSL code. And, in the same way you first tame a horse and then teach it to work with you, he wrestled all our code into submission, and then improved it in uncountable ways.

You couldn't ask for a better guide. But, while you're out exploring, remember to stop every now and then and think just how cool the path is. XSLT is an amazing system. I envy your journey.

Dave Thomas

The Pragmatic Programmers

The Martian language, as I have said, is extremely simple, and in a week I could make all my wants known and understand nearly everything that was said to me.

> *Edgar Rice Burroughs,* A Princess of Mars

Preface

Why a New Book on XSLT?

XSLT, or Extensible Stylesheet Language for Transformations, has been around as a specification since late 1999, and the first books about it started appearing not long after. The most well-known texts arrived in the early 2000s, providing guidance for many an XSLT novice in the duration. With the publication of XSLT 2.0, new editions arrived, and then, for a long time, the land of XSLT books has been fairly quiet.

As one of those XSLT novices back in 2004, I found that the early XSLT documentation spent much of its bulk describing elements of the language in a tone that suggested deep familiarity with the specification, but much less interest in the problems that XSLT might solve. As I dealt with the requirements for the company I worked with, I struggled to assemble the bits and pieces of XSLT into larger solutions. It was like being given a bucket of electronic components and being asked to assemble a radio without a schematic. I didn't need academic discourses, I needed to see how to apply it in real life.

Then I met other programmers who told me about similar experiences with XSLT's learning curve. An accomplished documentation toolsmith I worked with used to lament that it would be nice to have a book that showed XSLT in action on real-world problems. A college-level computer science teacher talked about the difficulty he had when he first encountered XSLT. If these folks were frustrated, pity the poor student!

Their comments made me wonder: what makes XSLT so difficult to learn?

I don't know that there's a single good answer, but here are a few guesses:

- An uncommon, verbose syntax
- The relative immaturity of the language when most of the books appeared
- A small range of applications, meaning a small audience, meaning a small support community and thin documentation.

In reflecting on these issues, it seemed to me that a book centered around the concepts involved in solving certain basic problems could go a long way toward helping people get over the big bump of the initial XSLT learning curve.

A Little about Me

I can't claim that knowledge of XSLT is my primary qualification for writing this book. As an XSLT programmer, there are a lot sharper tools in the shed! What I bring to the task is a career as a technical writer/documentation manager and software tools user/developer. If there's one thing I enjoy, it's taking complex information and making it accessible to other people. One of the most gratifying comments I hear after someone reads something I've written is, "I thought it was hard, but there's really nothing to it."

I've used XSLT for over 10 years, and I've solved some thorny problems along the way. I've used XSLT to deconstruct the DITA Open Toolkit, which turned out to be an excellent training ground (although I wouldn't recommend it to the faint of heart). Other projects took me through a conversion of markup for ancient Greek manuscripts, timesheet applications, NROFF and Wiki markup conversions, and a variety of conversions to PDF and ebook formats. Working on these complex applications taught me that XSLT is a powerful, flexible solution for manipulating XML. Once I got past the initial conceptual barriers, I found it to be a fascinating and extremely useful language.

Recently, I spent a few years working for The Pragmatic Programmers, helping with their publishing system and learning their writing methods. I have tailored this book to fit the style of books from Pragmatic Bookshelf: friendly, encouraging, and moving gently along the path from initiation toward mastery.

A Little about You!

You may be a student or a young professional who wants to tackle the wide world of XML processing, and you are looking for a "leg up." On the other hand, you may be a seasoned pro who has dealt with XML before, but you've used other tools and have found them to be less than adequate. In both cases, you've been wondering whether XSLT is a better solution—and then you've gotten stuck on its syntax. (To quote Dave Thomas in conversation, "XSLT is a wonderful functional language with a really lousy syntax.")

One thing I do know is that you'll need a few skills to get started:

- Knowledge of the major components of XML—elements (tags), attributes, comments, and so forth. Nothing exotic.

- A few basic principles of computer programming logic
- Low-level familiarity with HTML (to understand the outputs created in the examples)

You may find this book starts a little slow, although we'll get started with some hands-on examples pretty quickly. First we'll lay some groundwork, covering a lot of ground in a short time. Once we get past the conceptual introduction, there will be a good bit of juggling between describing components and showing how they work in the context of a solutions. While I present most of the code for the examples in full, I'm hoping that you'll be trying out the code yourself, working with XML examples that you process in a web browser or with a standalone XSLT processor.

And don't stop with just the examples provided in this book! I've found there's nothing more effective for learning XSLT than experimenting with it. I'm hoping you will use the examples in this book as jumping-off points for your own explorations.

So, regardless of your level of experience, I hope you'll bring curiosity and a sense of adventure to this book...and even a sense of fun as you play with the possibilities.

What You'll Need for This Book

The requirements for creating and processing XSLT are fairly simple: you can do it with as little as a text editor and a web browser. However, there are benefits to using more robust tools. The good news is that there are a lot of robust tools available at no charge.

Here's the list of what we'll use in this book:

- An XML editor, preferable one that understands the XSLT syntax
- A web browser that supports XSLT processing
- A standalone XSLT processor

I'll be recommending specific packages later in this book—we'll need to discuss what options are available, since there are many possibilities. At the moment, though, let's not worry about it—the requirements are fairly simple and will be easy to put in place when we need them.

And that's it! We'll be sticking with XSLT 1.0 for the most part, since that's what is supported by web browsers. It should be fairly easy to find tools that support the examples in this book.

About the Examples

You can find the source files for the examples at https://pragprog.com/titles/djkxsl/source_code. These are provided in a single zip file to simplify downloading. I hope you'll attempt the create the XSLT files on your own as we go through the examples—it will help with the learning process. However, the XSLT files are provided in the source files for your reference. In some cases, extended versions of the source XML files are also provided—the example XML files in the book have been kept brief for the purpose of saving pages.

A Word about the Epigraphs

When thinking about the initial effect of learning XSLT, I thought about *A Princess of Mars* by Edgar Rice Burroughs. The hero, John Carter, is suddenly transported to an alien planet with no warning; he has to learn all over how to walk, talk, and battle in a strange and hostile environment. Once he learns, he discovers that this new environment has given him extraordinary powers. The analogies to my first encounter with XSLT seemed perfect.

Hopefully your experience will be more as if John Carter had found a friendly mentor to guide him through the hazards of Barsoom.

Acknowledgments

This book has been considerably improved by the gracious help and guidance of many people. I'd like to thank David Artman, Ethan Duty, Betty Meeler, and Vladimir Uzun for the time and intelligence they contributed to the technical edit. Also many thanks to the folks at Pragmatic Bookshelf who helped steer it toward a more user-friendly experience: Jaquelyn Carter, Susannah Davidson Pfalzer, Andy Hunt, and Dave Thomas. I'm especially grateful to Dave Thomas for the broad perspective and keen insight he brought to the foreword. It's a perfect way to jumpstart this book.

And finally, to my wife and son: thank you for your patience and support through all the turmoils.

Jumpstart!

My hope is that by the end of this book, you will have gained a solid understanding of the principles of XSLT as well as a good starting toolkit for solving common problems in XML processing. The goal is to take a giant leap over the learning curve of XSLT and set you on the path toward XSLT mastery.

There's only one way to find out if it works, right? Let's get started!

"I closed my eyes, stretched out my arms toward the god of my vocation and felt myself drawn with the suddenness of thought through the trackless immensity of space."

Edgar Rice Burroughs, A Princess of Mars

CHAPTER 1

Introducing XSLT

What is XSLT? As the name says, it is an Extensible Stylesheet Language for Transformations. That tells you a lot, right? Not really. The extensible part is the least important part of XSLT, but it comes first in the acronym, so it's a little misleading

Let's turn it around a little. XSLT is a Language using Stylesheets to Transform XML into different kinds of text, and it's eXtensible. The output can be plain text, different forms of XML, HTML, SVG, or pretty much any text-based output you could imagine.

The means by which it transforms XML is called a *stylesheet.* A stylesheet is simply a collection of *templates*. And templates in turn are clusters of code that execute when a pattern at the beginning of the template matches a pattern in the XML.

A Purpose Under Heaven

Why is XSLT important? Why should we care about transforming XML into "other stuff?"

Apparently it's important enough that every major web browser out there has a built-in XSLT processor!

XSLT is important because XML is important. XML provides the structure for markup languages in data storage, documentation, and information interchange in a broad range of industries. The number of XML standards that have appeared since the late 1990s is staggering.[1] XML is used for mathematics, graphics, document contents and formatting, medical records,

1. See http://en.wikipedia.org/wiki/Category:XML-based_standards for a listing of XML-based standards. I'm especially intrigued by the "Emotion Markup Language."

Joe asks:

What browsers run XSLT?

In the following pages, we're going to work a lot with web browsers as a way to get to work quickly.

Browsers that support XSLT 1.0 include most of the usual suspects: Internet Explorer, Firefox, and Safari, among others. But be careful and test the browser for your particular use case. Different browsers have different limitations.

Here's an excellent chart showing tests for XSLT conformance for a range of browsers:

http://greenbytes.de/tech/tc/xslt/

For example, Chrome and later version of Opera contain a controversial bug/feature that prevent them from working with local XSLT files (see http://code.google.com/p/chromium/issues/detail?id=111905 for the painful details). They will run XSLT if the XSLT is running on a server somewhere, but not if the XSLT is a local file. For this reason, I do not recommend trying to use Chrome or Opera for the examples in this book—because they won't work.

If the output from the XSLT process is text only, not including any XML tags, Safari will consider the results "empty," and it won't display anything.

Firefox supports XSLT, but the stylesheet has to be in the same directory as the XML file. The examples in this book[a] are set up this way.

If you intend to serve documents dynamically, with XSLT providing on-the-fly formatting of XML documents, it's probably wise to check your stylesheets on a variety of browsers before sending them out. We'll start with processing XSLT in browsers in this book, but eventually we'll see that a standalone XSLT processor is our best bet.

a. https://pragprog.com/titles/djkxsl/source_code

broadcasting, business, sports statistics, music, and on and on. You name it, there's probably a way to get it into XML.

With all that XML around, people have to manage it and use it for something. XSLT was designed for that purpose early in the history of XML, and it's still one of the best options.

One misperception of XSLT is that it is just a glorified form of CSS. In a way, there's some truth to the perception, because one of its basic characteristics is similar to CSS: the execution of the XSLT code is dependent on the order of elements in the document being processed. In fact, you could use XSLT very much like CSS, simply making stylistic modifications to a source document without changing the order of the tags. But if you did only that, you would miss out on the distinctive power of XSLT.

The kinds of transformations XSLT can perform are practically limitless. Want to turn a numbered process list into a flowchart? Transform your XML into SVG. Want to perform calculations based on the source, set up conditional processing, rearrange the document order, access external documents, test for patterns, and perform functions like sorting and grouping? You probably won't be doing that with CSS, but XSLT is designed to make these tasks easy.

How do you know when to use XSLT instead of CSS? I can't put it more succinctly than the World Wide Web Consortium, which says, "Use CSS when you can, use XSL when you must."[2] Their reasoning is that CSS is easy to use and maintain, but XSLT provides a lot of functionality that CSS doesn't, particularly in the area of transformations.

Experts claim that XSLT is a Turing-complete language,[3] [4] meaning that it can perform any kind of function that a Turing machine can complete. Basically, it means that it's a fully qualified computer language, the same as most others, and it can probably do anything we're likely to ask of it. But what we usually use it for is—yep—turning XML into other stuff.

Presto Change-o

What does it mean to transform XML? Let's look at an example, something relatively simple. Here's an XML document that we want to turn into HTML.

Introduction/caution1.xml

```
<?xml version='1.0' encoding='UTF-8'?>
<?xml-stylesheet type="text/xsl" href="caution1.xsl"?>
<note type="caution">
  <p>
    The potential for intergalactic broadcast while
    using the <bold>AZGuard Protaxis</bold> unit
    has not yet been determined.
  </p>
  <p>
    Please avoid transmitting information that could place the
    human race at risk.
  </p>
</note>
```

Figure 1—Sample XML for conversion to HTML

2. http://www.w3.org/Style/CSS-vs-XSL.en.html
3. http://conferences.idealliance.org/extreme/html/2004/Kepser01/EML2004Kepser01.html
4. http://www.unidex.com/turing/utm.htm.

And here's what I want it to look like in a browser:

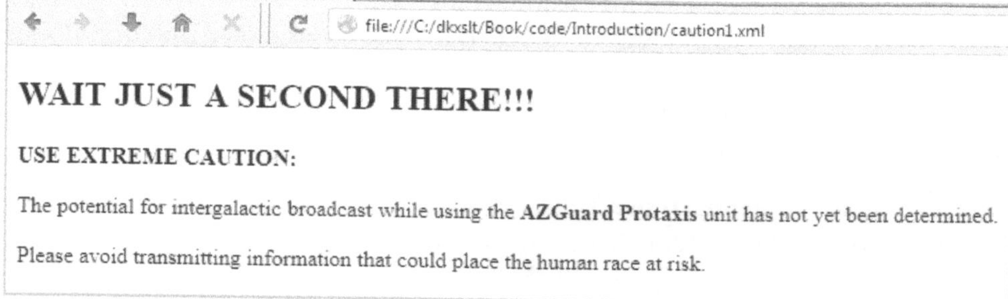

Figure 2—The HTML output in the browser

Looking a little closer, here's the HTML source for what's rendered in the browser:

Introduction/caution1.html

```
<?xml version="1.0" encoding="UTF-8"?>
<html xmlns="http://www.w3.org/1999/xhtml">
<head>
  <title>Caution!</title>
</head>
  <body>
    <h2>WAIT JUST A SECOND THERE!!!</h2>
    <h3>USE EXTREME CAUTION: </h3>
    <p>
      The potential for intergalactic
      information broadcast while using the <b>AZGuard
      Protaxis</b> unit has not yet been fully determined.
    </p>
    <p>
      Please avoid transmitting any information that
      could place the human race at risk.
    </p>
  </body>
</html>
```

Figure 3—HTML source for the browser view

So what's the magic spell that gets us from the XML to the web view? XSLT, right? Well, yes and no. At a very high level, several things have to happen to get the HTML to come out:

1. An XML parser reads in the XML and constructs a complete XML tree structure for the XSLT processor to use.

2. The XML parser reads in the the XSLT stylesheet, parses it as an XML tree, then sends it to the XSLT processor.
3. The XSLT processor moves through the XML tree and applies the appropriate rules from the XSL stylesheet to what it finds in the XML.
4. As it applies the rules, the XSLT processor assembles a tree of the output structure and content.
5. Then another part of the XSLT process, called the serializer, creates the actual output, the HTML (or whatever sort of output we're constructing) that is specified in the rules, then writes it out somewhere—a file, a data stream, or a browser.

The World of an XSLT Processor

Note in Figure 4, *The XSLT process,* that the XML parser, the XSLT processor, and the serializer are shown jammed up against each other. These parts of the processor are often lumped together under the term XSLT processor because most XSLT processors provide all three functions.

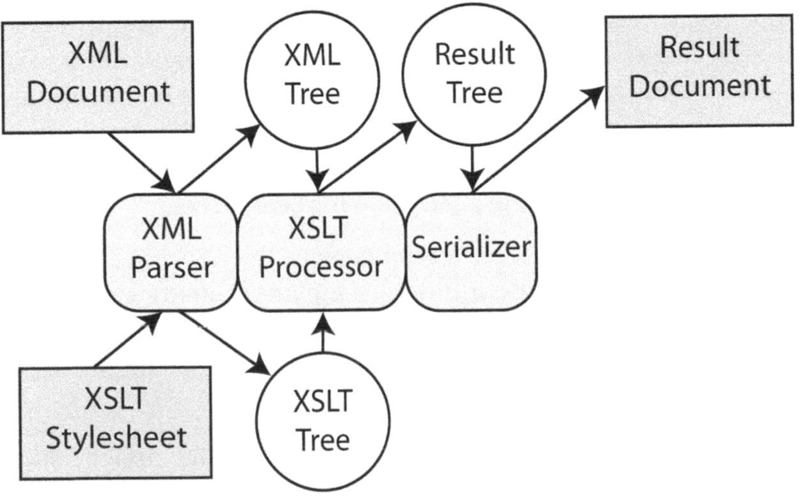

Figure 4—The XSLT process

However, the processor itself, the part in the middle, gets the result of the XML parser, which are *XML trees.* An XML tree is an abstract data representation of the XML tags and content. A visual model of an XML tree might look something like the diagram in Figure 5, *An XML document tree,* on page 6.

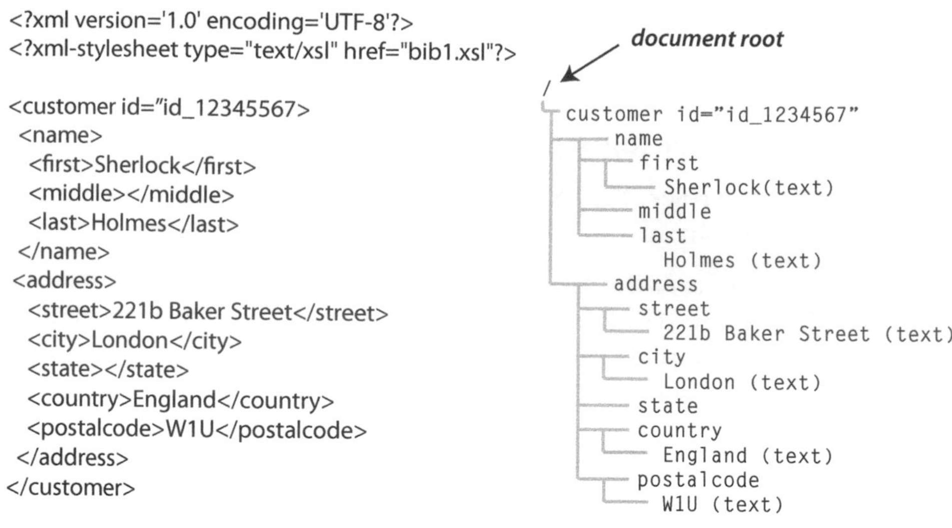

Figure 5—An XML document tree

What the XSLT processor sees is two XML trees coming at it, one from the source document, one from the stylesheet. The job of the processor is to function a bit like the slider of a zipper. But it's a funny kind of zipper. On the one side, the XML source tree zips along in the order of the original document, as you would expect. But on the other side, the XSLT processor has to rummage around and find a zipper tooth (an XSLT template) that matches the tooth on the other side (the XML node in the source).

The good news is that the order of templates in the stylesheet's tree doesn't matter to the processor. If it can find a template that matches the current XML node, executes the template, possibly creating some output. If the template also instructs the processor to zip it up another notch on the XML source tree, it zips it up another notch.

Coming out the other side of the XSLT processor, or the zipper slider in our analogy, should be a neat line of tags and/or text. This output is also formed in terms of an XML tree, which then has to be translated into tags and text by a piece of software called a serializer. That's probably way more than you need to know, because most XSLT processors have a serializer built in.

This simplified description of the XSLT process will get us through for the purposes of this book. The point is that to get our HTML output, we need XSLT, but we also need some tools to run the XSLT. We'll get to the specific tools later; for the purpose of our example, let's just look at the XSLT that the tools will run. Figure 6, *XSLT stylesheet for the caution HTML*, on page 7 shows the XSLT code that gave the browser the HTML it needed.

Introduction/caution1.xsl

```
<?xml version="1.0" encoding="utf-8"?>
<xsl:stylesheet xmlns:xsl="http://www.w3.org/1999/XSL/Transform"
  xmlns="http://www.w3.org/1999/xhtml"
  version="1.0">
<xsl:template match="note[@type='caution']">
  <html>
    <head>
      <title>Caution!</title>
    </head>

    <body>
      <h2>WAIT JUST A SECOND THERE!!!</h2>
      <p><b>USE EXTREME CAUTION:</b></p>
        <xsl:apply-templates select="p"/>
    </body>
  </html>
</xsl:template>

<xsl:template match="p[not(position() = 1)]">
  <p>
    <xsl:apply-templates/>
  </p>
</xsl:template>

<xsl:template match="bold">
  <b><xsl:apply-templates/></b>
</xsl:template>
</xsl:stylesheet>
```

Figure 6—XSLT stylesheet for the caution HTML

What can we learn about XSLT from this example?

First, you can see that XSLT is itself a form of XML. An XSLT document must be a well-formed XML document; however, unlike XML, XSLT can contain a lot of other stuff, so it can't really be validated against a DTD or schema. However, it must still fit the definition of a well-formed XML document.[5]

For another thing, an XSLT transform always has the <xsl:stylesheet> tag as its root element. The stylesheet is the XSLT equivalent of a program, and the <xsl:stylesheet> tag contains the details of the program. Later we'll see that we

5. See http://www.w3schools.com/xml/xml_dtd.asp for a short comparison between a well-formed XML document and a valid XML document.

can import multiple stylesheets into a single stylesheet, but the point is still valid: everything in XSLT takes place inside <xsl:stylesheet> tags.

Within the <xsl:stylesheet> tag, there can be a variety of other tags, but there is usually at least one <xsl:template> tag. Templates do most of the heavy lifting in XSLT.

You'll also notice that the XSLT tags (in this book) all begin with *xsl:*. This string identifies the XSLT tags as belonging to the *xsl:* namespace.[6] *Namespace* is an XML concept that we won't define here, but if you're not familiar with it, you can find a decent definition here:

http://searchsoa.techtarget.com/definition/namespace

The namespace prefix helps distinguish the XSLT nodes from nodes in other namespaces. You'll often find yourself using other namespaces in an XSLT document—in fact, the output document in the example above uses *xhtml:* as the default namespace for outputting HTML tags. You could set up a stylesheet to omit the *xsl:* prefix, but then you'd have to deal with namespace issues for other kinds of tags you might want to use. Do yourself a favor: stick with the *xsl:* prefix and don't worry about it.

In Chapter 4, *Beginning with the End: Creating Output*, on page 43, we'll have a closer look at the example we saw here. But at the moment, let's take a look at XSLT from a slightly broader perspective, starting with the XSLT processor itself—the engine at the center of everything.

XSLT Processing

Like most programming languages, XSLT is useless for anything until it executes. However, unlike a compiled language such as C, the XSLT program (called a stylesheet) does not execute itself. Instead, it relies on an external piece of software called an XSLT processor. As we saw in the example above, the XSLT processor reads in an XML file, reads in an XSLT stylesheet, and applies the code to the XML nodes as it reads its way through the XML file.

There are a number of ways to handle XML besides XSLT: brute-force programming with your language of choice, XSLT-based add-ons to other languages (such as Java's XSLT Module or JAXP, the Android XmlPullParser, and Ruby's Nokogiri parser), conversion tools, and so forth. I won't go into those except to say that many of the concepts discussed in this book will

6. *http://www.w3.org/1999/XSL/Transform*

transfer readily to those tools because they all deal with the same problem set: the structure and content of XML.

Most web browsers have built-in XSLT processors that support only XSLT version 1.0. For this reason, the XSLT covered in this book is XSLT 1.0. This version forms the basis for later versions of XSLT, so learning XSLT 1.0 is a great way to get started. If your intent is to let the browser do the processing, you're stuck with XSLT 1.0 anyway. And to tell the truth, until you need to do some pretty sophisticated programming, XSLT 1.0 will accomplish almost everything you need.

(That being said, XSLT 2.0 has some pretty cool stuff in it, and you'll definitely want to check it out at some point. In this book, though, we'll stick with XSLT 1.0.)

If you don't require a browser to do your XSLT processing, there are a variety of options. There are a number of stand-alone XSLT processors that support XSLT 2.0. Some XSLT processors even support some of the yet-to-be released XSLT 3.0. We'll cover a range of the available XSLT processors when we get ready to install a stand-alone processor in Chapter 3, *Installing, Testing, and Using a Stand-Alone XSLT Processor*, on page 31. Some are free, while others will be the subjects of extensive acquisition committee meetings. For this book, we'll go with free.

We'll eventually need a stand-alone processor for our examples because we'll want to see the interim results of transformations, not just the output renderings a browser would give.

But for the first couple of chapters, we're going to do it the easy way. We'll use a standard web browser for transformations so you don't have to install anything to get started. Just check it out and enjoy the magic.

What's in This Book

The chapters in this book are designed to orient you at a gentle pace to the new world of XSLT processing.

In Chapter 2, *XSLT in Action*, on page 13, we'll begin with an example of XSLT at work in a web browser. We'll open an XML document in a browser to see how it's rendered when it's transformed into HTML. Then we'll dig a little deeper into how the pieces of XML, XSLT, and XSLT browser all work together. This will lay the foundation for everything that comes after.

With Chapter 3, *Installing, Testing, and Using a Stand-Alone XSLT Processor*, on page 31, we'll cover the mechanics of selecting and installing an XSLT processor. Web browsers will work for a lot of the XSLT code we'll develop in this book, but we'll want to see the nuts and bolts of the XSLT transformation results, not just the pretty fonts rendered by the browser. Using a stand-alone XSLT processor gives us access to the raw output from our transforms.

When we get to Chapter 4, *Beginning with the End: Creating Output*, on page 43, we'll start getting our hands dirty with output. The purpose of XSLT is to get some kind of text output from XML (thinking of XML and HTML as forms of text). So the first thing we'll do is look at several methods by which XSLT channels text into the output results. And when we're finished, you'll be able to go through the entire basic XSLT process, reading an input file, processing it with XSLT, and getting out something completely different.

Of course, the fun doesn't end there. To add power to how we process our input, Chapter 5, *Filtering with the Identity Transform*, on page 57 introduces a technique called the Identity Transform. We'll learn a few XSLT elements along the way, and we'll put them together into a short, simple solution for transforming a document into an identical document. And what use is that? We'll find that it's a great place to start by applying small changes to the transform, so we can filter and transform the content into something subtly —or radically—different.

Until this point we'll be pretty much stuck with output appearing in the same order it occurs in the source document. That's not always what we want, and this is where XSLT begins to distinguish itself from a pure rendering transform like CSS. In Chapter 6, *Changing the Structure and Order of Content*, on page 75, we'll begin learning ways to modify the content order—omitting content, adding content, and making changes to the order of content. To get the ultimate power in modifying content order and making logical decisions about processing, we'll stretch our definition of XSLT to include a small language, a sibling to XSLT, called XPath (Chapter 7, *XPath: The Sibling Language*, on page 93). We'll see XPath in some detail—XSLT without XPath is a bit like a car without tires. We won't get far without it.

In Chapter 8, *Using XPath to Change the Order of Documents*, on page 117, we'll use XPath to solve more complicated problems of document order. While we're at it, we'll see some interesting tricks for grouping and sorting content. When we finish this chapter, we'll have a good handle on XSLT tools for reordering and restructuring content.

To add logical sophistication to our stylesheets, we'll start with values in Chapter 9, *The Value of Values*, on page 145. From there, we'll learn how variables and parameters contain values, and we'll see logical structures like

<xsl:if> and <xsl:choose> that take advantage of values to add conditional processing to the stylesheet. Using these new tools, we'll learn how to create recursive structures that enable us to do iterative processing for a variety of purposes.

By the end of the values chapter, we'll have seen most of the basics of content transformation. In Chapter 10, *Large-Scale Stylesheet Strategies*, on page 183, we'll see techniques for extending the processing scenario beyond a single stylesheet, input file, and output file. We'll learn how to organize things like sets of attributes and templates for reusability and for processing overrides. We'll also see global controls that control different aspects of our output.

Finally, with most of XSLT 1.0 behind us, we'll see strategies for troubleshooting our stylesheets. Yes, mistakes happen, and XSLT can be ridiculously unforgiving. (Did I mention hostile alien environments?) Using the knowledge we've gained from our earlier explorations, we'll follow a rational pattern for discovering where our mistakes lie. We'll also see strategies to isolate failures and prepare code for debugging.

The appendices provide a streamlined set of definitions for XSLT elements, functions, and expression operators. Since this is an introduction to XSLT concepts, the gory details of these language components are not covered in full. XSLT, being a well-established language, has its components well represented in web resources and elsewhere. The intent of these appendices is to give just enough to jog your memory for the basics.

Think of it as an orientation to a new planet. A planet is a big chunk of real estate to cover, but give it time and you'll get to know it better. Until then, hop in the speeder and take the grand tour. I think you'll like it.

Instead of progressing in a sane and dignified manner, my attempts to walk resulted in a variety of hops which took me clear of the ground a couple of feet at each step and landed me sprawling on my face at the end of each second or third hop...and so I hit upon the unique plan of reverting to first principles in locomotion, creeping.

Edgar Rice Burroughs, A Princess of Mars

CHAPTER 2

XSLT in Action

Enough preliminaries. Time to do some ground-level work.

In the following sections we're going to set up a simple stylesheet, apply it against a simple XML document, and get a simple result. In the process, we're going to do a deep dive into how the XSLT processor simultaneously handles an XSLT stylesheet and an XML document, working its way through both of them in a concerted fashion to get the final results.

Understanding how the XSLT processor moves through the XML file and matches the XML with templates in the XSLT stylesheet will be useful for understanding how the rest of XSLT works.

While we're covering these concepts, we'll look at the roles of the `<xsl:template>` tag, the `match=` attribute, and the `<xsl:apply-templates>` tag, three XSLT components at the core of XSLT.

Before we get started, though, let's get you set up with an XML editor. While most of what follows in this chapter is fairly conceptual, you might try following along with the examples on your computer. Using a good XML editor—preferably one that is aware of the XSLT syntax—will go a long way toward lightening the experience of XSLT programming.

Installing and Using an XML Editor

There are hundreds of XML editors out in the wild, many of them free. We can narrow the field a bit by establishing some criteria for a good editor for XSLT programming purposes. First of all, for this book it has to be free. Beyond that, a good XSLT editor has:

- A tag-view text editor
- XML parsing
- XML syntax highlighting
- Validation against DTDs and/or schemas

In addition, it would be nice for it to have:

- Tag folding
- Tag autocompletion
- Syntax suggestions
- XML tree view
- XSLT transform execution

Some of these terms may not be familiar to you, but as you begin to use an XML editor, you'll discover features that may be useful to you. For XSLT development, the features above are some of my favorites. We won't go into the details of what all these mean: we'll just take a look at some XML editors that have some or all of these features. It would be good to spend time with the documentation for the XML editor you choose and become familiar with its capabilities.

Following is a list of free XML editors that have most or all of these capabilities. (There are a number of excellent commercial XML editors out there, but if you're just playing around with XSLT to check it out before committing to it, you'll be fine with a free editor to get you started.) I've provided URLs to the web locations where the editor packages are available.

I have tried all of these to one extent or another, but I can't vouch for their use in a professional development environment. For the purposes of this book, though, any of these should do nicely.

WmHelp XMLPad . . . . http://www.wmhelp.com/
iOS, Windows

A surprisingly full-featured editor for XML, XSL, and related standards. You can close the "project" windows and work with loose files for this book.

XML Copy Editor . . . . http://xml-copy-editor.sourceforge.net/
Windows, Linux

Uncomplicated and to the point. Not quite as full-featured as XMLPad, but easy to use for the purposes of this book

jEdit . . . . http://www.jedit.org/
Mac OS, OS/2, Unix/Linux, VMS, Windows

A full-featured, Java-based development editor; you'll need to install the XML and XSL plugins, but that's pretty easy. The interface is a little clunkier than the other two editors on this list.

If you're not able to get one of these to work for your operating system, you might try one of the numerous other open-source XML editors available online.[1] Some very nice commercial XML editors are also available with a free, short-term evaluation license.

Once you have the editor downloaded and installed, play around with it for a while to see how it feels and whether it will work for you. You can use Figure 7, *XML for a customer*, on page 16 as an example file, if you need some XML to help you get started.

The Parts of a Transformation

To get a sense of how XSLT works on an XML document, we'll start with a small piece of XML, then apply some XSLT to it to get a result. Our example XML is a customer address. Perhaps we've been asked to make a "heat map" of where our customers live, so we need to produce a list of our customer postal codes.

Starting with XML

Let's have a look at the first XML document we'll transform with our stylesheet (see Figure 7, *XML for a customer*, on page 16). For clarity in our first example, we'll use an entry for a single customer's profile information.

The first two lines set up the file. The first line is the XML declaration. It alerts any file processor that this is an XML file, using XML version 1.0 and a character encoding of UTF-8. This is all standard XML.

The second line is more important to our XSLT interests: it instructs an XSLT processor to use a particular stylesheet if one has not already been specified. We'll take advantage of this line to run our XML and XSLT files in a web browser. This will eliminate the need, for the moment, to set up a stand-alone XSLT processor.

Now we get to the substance of the file. In our little XML file, you can see that the XML has a root tag, <customer>, which contains a <name> tag and an

1. http://en.wikipedia.org/wiki/Comparison_of_XML_editors

howitlooks/bib1.xml

```
<?xml version='1.0' encoding='UTF-8'?>
<?xml-stylesheet type="text/xsl" href="bib1.xsl"?>
<customer id="id_1234567">
  <name>
    <first>Sherlock</first>
    <middle></middle>
    <last>Holmes</last>
  </name>
  <address>
        <street>221b Baker Street</street>
        <city>London</city>
        <state></state>
        <country>England</country>
        <postalcode>W1U</postalcode>
      </address>
</customer>
```

Figure 7—XML for a customer

<address> tag. The <name> tag in turn contains three other tags, which contain text for the customer's first, middle, and last names. The <address> tag, naturally, contains additional tags for the text of the customer's address.

The structure of this file will be important for how our stylesheet transforms it, so take a little time to check it out.

Understanding the structure of the source is a good habit that we should carry over to all of our XSLT work: XSLT stylesheets work best with known XML structures. The XML source should have a DTD, schema, or other structured definition so we know what elements and attributes we'll need to deal with in our XSLT stylesheet. Without being based on a known structure, the stylesheet may encounter XML relationships that it's not set up to handle. And at that point, all bets are off.

If you're confronted with a piece of XML and don't have a DTD or schema for it, you can create one by running DTD-generating software against your XML samples. XML editing software such as oXygen and Stylus Studio often have this capability built into them, and various standalone DTD generators are available.[2]

A DTD or schema isn't a necessity for writing XSLT—you can always wing it. But it sure helps to know what you're up against.

2. http://stackoverflow.com/questions/1815216/how-to-derive-dtd-or-other-xml-spec-format-from-xml-file-samples

Setting Up an Example XSLT Stylesheet

Now let's set up a stylesheet to transform the XML into something else. Suppose we want to see only the postal codes of where our orders are going. The stylesheet might look like this:

howitlooks/bib1.xsl

```
<xsl:stylesheet xmlns:xsl="http://www.w3.org/1999/XSL/Transform" version="1.0">
  <xsl:output method="text"/>
  <xsl:template match="/customer">
        <xsl:apply-templates/>
    </xsl:template>

    <xsl:template match="address">
        <xsl:apply-templates select="postalcode"/>
    </xsl:template>

    <xsl:template match="postalcode">
       <code>
         <xsl:apply-templates/>
       </code>
    </xsl:template>

    <xsl:template match="name">
    </xsl:template>
</xsl:stylesheet>
```

That's a lot to understand right out of the box. At the moment, though, I'd like you to focus on the fact that there are four <xsl:template> tags, each with a closing </xsl:template> tag, and each opening tag has a match="something" attribute. We're going to walk through what those mean and how they work to process the XML document.

But hey, first let's see whether this thing actually works.

To run the XSLT stylesheet, let's open the XML document with a web browser. (Remember, don't use Chrome or Opera.) As we said, the second line in our XML file tells the browser what stylesheet to run against the XML.

To keep things easy, we've stored our bib1.xsl file in the same directory as the XML file, so the href= attribute in the <?xml-stylesheet> tag (in line 1 of the XML file) only gives the name of the stylesheet. All we have to do is put the path to the XML file (including the file name) into the URL area of the browser. In my case, it's *H:\ppsvn\Bookshelf\titles\djkxsl\Book\code\howitlooks*.

If you're lazy like me, and your operating system allows it, you could just drag the file icon from a file browser to the open web browser. Figure 8, *The results of our first XSLT transformation*, on page 18 shows how it looks in Mozilla Firefox.

Figure 8—The results of our first XSLT transformation

Great! That's what we wanted, all right. But how did we get it?

Following the Transformation in Detail

This example probably looks easy, but a lot of pieces had to work for us to get the result. Check it out:

1. The web browser had to know the document was an XML document. The first line in the XML file took care of that for us.

2. The web browser had to know what stylesheet to apply to the XML document. The second line took care of that for us.

3. The web browser had to know how to run an XSLT stylesheet against an XML document. Fortunately, most web browsers these days have XSLT processors built into them, which is convenient. Setting up an XSLT processor isn't difficult. (We'll do it in Chapter 3, *Installing, Testing, and Using a Stand-Alone XSLT Processor*, on page 31.) But if you're learning or just want to check out a simple piece of XSLT, bang!, it's a quick solution.

4. The stylesheet had to specify which parts of the XML document we wanted to keep, and which parts we wanted to ignore. The main body of the stylesheet, the `<xsl:template>` tags, provided those instructions to the XSLT processor.

5. Finally, the XSLT processor had to send some output to the web browser to display and tell it how to format the output. We didn't do a lot of output manipulation with this particular example—we just sent it a single line of text. But eventually we're going to need to create some complex forms of output, so it will pay us to learn a little bit about the output process and how it is controlled. We'll cover some output controls later in this chapter and more advanced output controls in Chapter 4, *Beginning with the End: Creating Output*, on page 43.

Those are background details that the browser and the XSLT processor take care of. Most of this happens automatically. For instance, we don't really need to know where the browser's XSLT processor is located and how the browser invokes it. What we're more interested in are the parts we control ourselves, in particular those <xsl:template> tags, their contents, and how they gave us our result.

So first let's look at the overall XSLT process for our example. Then let's look at some details of the <xsl:template> tag, the match= attribute, and the <xsl:apply-templates> tag.

XSLT Processing: Under the Hood

One way to think about XSLT processing is to think of the XML as a stream of coins or tokens, all sizes and shapes, and the XSLT templates as a series of slots of corresponding sizes and shapes.

Figure 9, *An XML structure matched by XSLT templates*, on page 20 shows the XML as a group of connected objects, essentially a set of connected tokens. The different parts of the XML appear in this diagram with different shapes. At the same time, the XSLT side of the figure contains slots of corresponding shapes that allow the different parts of the XML to "fall through."

A couple of things you'll note immediately:

- The stylesheet doesn't have templates for all of the XML elements.
- The templates in the stylesheet aren't structured the way the XML is structured. In fact, they aren't explicitly connected at all. We'll see the advantage of this arrangement in a moment.

To understand how our example worked, let's see what happens when we start "dumping" the XML into the stylesheet. For this analogy to work, you might think of the XML as being turned upside down, with gravity pulling the <customer> tag in first, then everything else following in *document order*. The term document order describes the order the XML is handled by the XSLT processor, and it's worth spending a little time to understand what it means.

The XSLT processor typically parses the XML document into a document tree. The document tree for our sample document would look like the diagram we saw back in Figure 5, *An XML document tree*, on page 6.

In this example, the document tree on the right is formed out of the XML document on the left. The vertical lines define the scope of the parent nodes, and the horizontal lines point to specific children of a parent node. By parent

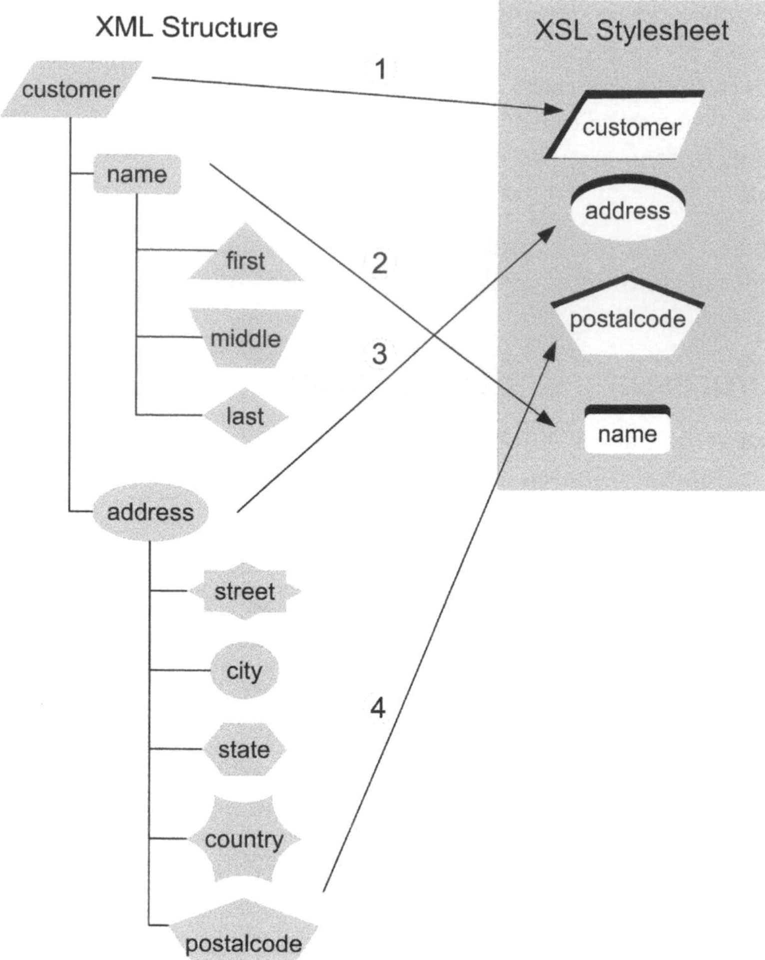

Figure 9—An XML structure matched by XSLT templates

and child, we mean simply that a parent is a tag that contains another tag, and a child is a tag that is contained by a parent tag.

The example shows that attributes are not *child nodes*. (Check out the `id="id_1234567"` attribute for the `<customer>` tag.) They belong to elements, but they aren't children of elements. It sounds like an odd distinction to make, but we'll see in Chapter 7, *XPath: The Sibling Language*, on page 93 that it has an effect when we attempt to process the children and attributes of an element.

Joe asks:

What's the difference between an element and a node?

We mention elements, attributes, and text quite a bit in this book. In the XML world, all of these things and others are referred to as *nodes*. A node is just a general term for a variety of XML object types.

When we use the word "node" by itself, we can be talking about any or all of these things (including XML comments and XML processing instructions). However, when we want to be more specific, we'll say "element node" or "text node," or just element and text.

We'll need to keep the differences between *node* and *element* in mind especially once we see the XPath wildcards for each of them. But let's not get ahead of ourselves.

Another point the example shows is that instances of text are XML nodes themselves. Text nodes are children of their containing elements, and their containing elements are their parents. The main difference between an element and a text node is that text can't have any children. Text always occurs at the end-point of the branches of the document tree—which is to say, text is always a leaf of the document tree.

Finally, notice at the top of the document tree on the right that the first node in the document is the root. (How many other trees have their roots on top?) The root node is present in every XML document, and it contains everything else, including the root element (in this case, `<customer>`).

The nodes are processed in the order they are presented in the tree part of the diagram, working from top to bottom. In document order, the order of processing is from the top branch down and to the right as far as possible, then back up to the next-topmost, unprocessed element in the tree, and so forth. Referring to the right side of Figure 5, *An XML document tree*, on page 6, the nodes are processed from the top line to the bottom line, one line at a time, in the order shown.

If the document were processed in hierarchical order, the root element in the document (`<customer>`) would be processed first, followed by the two tags at the next level in the document (`<name>` and `<address>`), followed by the third-level tags, and so forth. But that's not how it works.

It seems too sensible to be true, but every now and then there is a reassuring sense of order in XSLT.

Now let's walk through the process in detail, with our XML being dumped into the stylesheet in document order:

1. The document root and <customer> tag come first, and immediately we find a template that matches both in the stylesheet. In the XSLT, this template looks like this:

   ```
   <xsl:template match="/customer">
     <xsl:apply-templates/>
   </xsl:template>
   ```

   Great! With this match, we have changed the context for execution to the <customer> tag. The rest of the XML "falls through" into the matching template and gets processed according to the instructions inside the template. In this case, the instructions are <xsl:apply-templates>, so the XSLT processor looks for templates to match whatever comes next in the XML document.

2. Next, the processor comes to the <name> tag and finds a template that matches it:

   ```
   <xsl:template match="name">
   </xsl:template>
   ```

   Also fine—we didn't want any of the name in our report, so this template is empty. We don't do any more processing, and the <first>, <middle>, and <last> tags are forever after ignored.

3. The XML keeps streaming along, and next up is the <address> tag. Yep, we find a template that fits, so we do whatever the template says:

   ```
   <xsl:template match="address">
     <xsl:apply-templates select="postalcode"/>
   </xsl:template>
   ```

   The template for <address> has an instruction to apply templates, but it includes a qualifier, the select="postalcode". This instruction tells the XSLT processor to go off looking for templates again, but this time, it will only look for a template that matches <postalcode>.

   Since we're only interested in the postal code, we use the select= attribute to narrow the scope of what will be processed inside the <address> tag. If we left off the select="postalcode" attribute, the XSLT processor would apply templates for all of the XML that it finds inside the <address> tag.

   You can try this yourself. Going back to the stylesheet in code on page 17, delete (or comment out with the <– –> notation) the template that matches on <address>, then process the XML file again. (If your browser is still up from the first time you ran it, and the result is still visible, you can just refresh the browser.) Do you see what happens? The text goes from showing just the postal code to showing the text of the entire address.

(Be sure to undelete or uncomment the template for some of the following discussions.)

4. We sent the processor off to match against the <postalcode> tag, and now we've found it. Our stylesheet does only one thing: return the value of the <postalcode> tag. The <xsl:apply-templates> in the template for <postalcode> returns the text for us—we'll get to how that works in a short while. In the meantime: mission accomplished. We have the value of the postal code from the file.

That's the general outline of how XSLT processing works: match some XML with a template, do some work inside the template, then get instructions inside the template for what to do with the next bit of XML. It sounds simple enough, but it can do a lot of complex work with this processing pattern.

The trick here is that we don't necessarily need to know how many of a given tag there are in the XML, or in what order they occur. Because of the <xsl:apply-templates> tag, and because the templates aren't explicitly connected to each other, the XSLT processor just takes things in the order they come, and does its best to find templates to match. If it finds a match, it follows the instructions then goes to the next piece of XML; if it doesn't, the processing stops following the branch at that point in the structure of the XML, then goes on to whatever branch in the XML comes next. It's this flexibility to follow XML wherever it goes that gives XSLT a big part of its power.

XSLT Components at the Heart of the Process

We've now seen some of the core components that animate the XSLT process:

- Templates, defined by the <xsl:template> tag, contain most of the action instructions for the stylesheet.
- The match= attribute of <xsl:template> associates a template with nodes in the XML document.
- <xsl:apply-templates> and its select= attribute send the processor to find more templates and continue processing the XML document.

Let's take a look at each of these core XSLT components in more detail to understand the ins and outs of how they work.

The <xsl:template> Tag in Detail

Templates are the basic working unit of a stylesheet. As we saw, an XSLT stylesheet is made up mostly of templates. In our example, the templates were defined by `<xsl:template>` tags with `match=` attributes. These templates corresponded, in turn, to pieces of our XML file.

Templates provide three types of functions in the XSLT process, not all of which have to be present in a given template:

- The `match=` or `name=` attribute (or both) tells the XSLT process when to use the template.
- Inside the template, some additional work gets done. This work might be any of the following types of functions:
  - Creating output
  - Setting up variables
  - Performing calculations or other functions
  - Making decisions
  - And a host of others
- One or more instructions invoke other templates to process more of the XML document.

Templates can be used in other ways than just matching elements. You can call them explicitly to do work without changing the processing context, and you can specify *modes* to enable you to process a given XML element more than one way. Most of the work we'll do in XSLT takes place in templates, as we will see throughout the rest of this book.

At the moment, though, let's concentrate on the most important aspect of templates for the purposes of the XSLT process: the `match=` attribute.

The match= Attribute

The `match=` attribute is one of the primary functions that enables XSLT to handle the unpredictability of an XML document. As we saw, it provides the means for the XSLT processor to identify which template is appropriate for processing a given piece of XML.

Here are a few points to keep in mind about `match=` to keep our XSLT happy:

Matches in the XSLT occur within the current context of the XML.

A given piece of XML matches a template only when that piece of XML is within the current context of the XSLT processor. In our example, when we've already matched on the `<customer>` tag, the current context is

<customer>; when we specify <xsl:apply-templates>, the XSLT processor looks for a template that matches anything in the current context, so it will look for the attributes and immediate child elements of <customer>.

XML items within the current context include attributes of the matched element, any text immediately inside the matched element, and any elements that are immediate children of the matched element. In our example, the <name> and <address> tags are within the current context; however, the <postalcode> tag is not. If we don't match on the <address> tag at this point, the XSLT processor will never have the <postalcode> tag within its current context, and it will never get to our template that matches <postalcode>.

Using XPath in the match= attribute, you can match any part of the XML document from any other part of the XML document.

XPath? I thought we'd already mentioned all the X-languages in this book!

XPath is a language that provides a syntax for referring to the parts of an XML document. In a way, it's a lot like the syntax used for describing files in a file system, but tailored to refer to XML nodes instead.

Let's look at our example again. We wanted our stylesheet to retrieve only the contents of the <postalcode> tag. We could actually have done that much more easily if we had used the / symbol from the XPath syntax in the match= attribute. (We'll learn more about XPath in Chapter 7, *XPath: The Sibling Language*, on page 93, but for now just think about the slash acting like it does in a file path.) Using the / symbol, we can string together nodes to represent parents followed by children, followed by subchildren, like this:

```
<xsl:template match="/customer/address/postalcode">
  <xsl:apply-templates/>
</xsl:template>
```

The only thing that gets matched in this example is the <postalcode> tag, but here we are matching it when the current node is the document root. If the root contains a <customer> with an <address> inside it and a <postalcode> inside that, we have a match. And that's it! Using XPath, we could retrieve the postal code with a single template!

The / is just one of many operators and functions that XPath offers. As mentioned, it allows you to address practically any node or node set from the context of any other node. And that makes it incredibly powerful.

For the moment, the fact to take away is that XSLT is not limited to processing the XML in the order it is given. With XPath, you can turn the XML around into completely new forms. And the match= attribute, using XPath, is one of the pivotal points that helps make it happen.

When the XSLT processor matches an element, the current context changes to that element.

Only two instructions in XSLT can change the node currently being pointed to by the XSLT: the <xsl:template> tag with a match= attribute, and an instruction called <xsl:for-each>, which we will see later.

For this reason, the match= attribute is absolutely necessary for the XSLT processor to work its way through the XML file in the order of the XML nodes.

You could explicitly change the context by means of XPath within other instructions, but that would go against the design principles of XSLT. In general, it's best to use the combination of <xsl:apply-templates> and <xsl:template match="some-tag"> to allow the XSLT processor to follow the order of the XML nodes as they occur in the file, because who knows what shape those XML files are going to be in.

The <xsl:apply-templates> Instruction

We've seen that the central processing model in XSLT is to match XML, do some work, then keep going through the XML. The primary means by which the processing "keeps going" is by the use of the <xsl:apply-templates> instruction.

When the XSLT processor encounters <xsl:apply-templates>, it uses its current position in the XML to look for what XML node is next for it to process. It then looks at what templates are available in the stylesheet to see whether there is a match for the next XML node. If it finds a matching template in the XSLT, it applies it to that node. And that's all perfectly straightforward.

It turns out that <xsl:apply-templates> comes with a few zingers. But that's what we're here for, right?

As we did with the match= attribute, we'll list some points to remember about <xsl:apply-templates>.

Used without modifiers, <xsl:apply-templates> tells the XSLT processor to find a match for the next XML node of *any type*, looking for any template available.

The plain old <xsl:apply-templates> is indiscriminate: it takes any XML that comes its way and uses any template match it can get its hands on. This is useful when you have no idea what's coming, and you want to handle all of it.

The select= attribute limits the scope of what <xsl:apply-templates> instruction processes.

What if you don't want to handle all of the XML that comes along?

select= specifies the XML node or *node-set* that will be processed. (A node-set is a related group of nodes—not necessarily in the same relationship as they appear in the source document.)

The node or node-set specified by select= need not be within the current context, depending on how the XPath statement is set up.

In our example, once we matched on <address>, we only wanted to match on the <postalcode> tag and ignore the rest of the elements at that level. In that case, we used the select= attribute to narrow down what we wanted to match within that context.

Going back to our coins and slots, think of the select= attribute as a "hole-maker" that stamps a slot only for the shapes of tokens we're interested in. Items that don't match the slots we've stamped out at that point don't make it through. They get discarded into that bin at the bottom where the bent coins, slugs, and foreign look-alikes fall out. For our needs, they're worthless.

The mode= attribute allows you to create multiple templates that match the same element, with each template doing different work.

The mode= attribute on <xsl:apply-templates> says to match only on templates that also have a mode= attribute with the same name.

A common example of how this is used is when creating a table of contents for a document. Templates without nodes might be used to process the body of the document, but templates for the table of contents need to operate on the same set of XML tags. To operate on the XML for the table of contents, you would create the instruction <xsl:apply-templates mode="contents"/> where you wanted the table of contents inserted. Then you would create a separate set of templates with the mode="contents" attribute on <xsl:template>. These templates would match the elements to be represented in the table of contents.

We'll see examples of the mode= attribute at work once we get far enough along to create more complicated stylesheets.

<xsl:apply-templates> invokes XSLT's hidden *default templates*.

Here we dip into one of XSLT's dirty little secrets: in addition to the templates that are explicitly defined in our stylesheet, XSLT handily (and at times confusingly) includes something called *built-in template rules* or *default templates*. These hidden templates are always included by default when the XSLT processor runs.

Referring back to our example, if you match on <postalcode> and then use <xsl:apply-templates>, you might think there are no further templates to process anything within the <postalcode> tag, so nothing is going to happen. Well, you would be wrong (but not alone by any means!).

The built-in template rules say to the processor, if you find an element and you can't find a template, run *<xsl:apply-templates/>* on that element's children. If you find any text, send it to the output and keep going.

These rules mean that sometimes we get results we might not expect. For example, suppose we had put this in our sample stylesheet:

```
<xsl:template match="name">
  <xsl:apply-templates/>
</xsl:template>
```

The contents of <name> are <first>, <middle>, and <last>; since we don't have any templates that match these tags, that <xsl:apply-templates> should be ineffective, right? Ah, but don't take my word for it, go ahead and alter the sample stylesheet by adding <xsl:apply-templates/> into the last template, then process the XML again. What we'll see is something like:

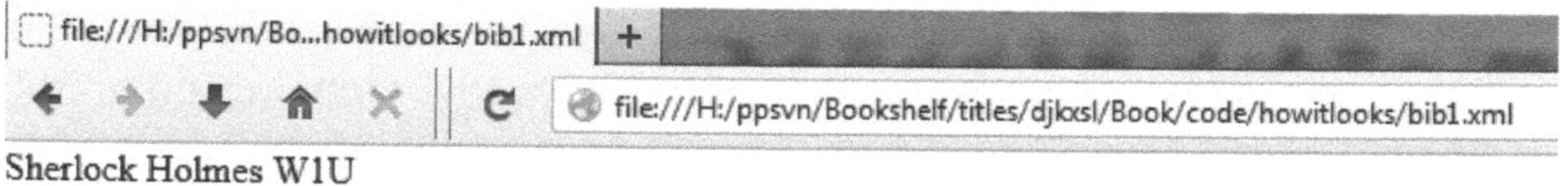

Possibly useful, but it's not what we said we wanted. The contents of <name> come through, including the text of all its descendants, because of the default template rule. To prevent the unwanted content, we have to stub out that branch of the XML by matching it at the top (<name>) and purposely omitting <xsl:apply-templates>.

This a case where XSLT tries to be a little too helpful behind the scenes, but, to be fair, it's also a useful feature if we want to get all the text from a complex bit of XML, and we don't want to have to write templates for every element.

We can override the default templates by creating our own templates that explicitly match on the same things as the default templates. By creating templates for text nodes and for all of the elements we're likely to find in an XML document, we can control all the XSLT operations and not have to worry about unexpected XML content leaking through into our output.

> But sometimes that's easier said than done! We'll see a couple of safeguards in Chapter 11, *Troubleshooting*, on page 217 that will help us control any "overlooked" XML nodes.

And that's the <xsl:apply-templates> instruction. It provides the gravity for our stream of tokens, to keep the flow going through our XSLT machine. Get used to the look of it, because we're going to use this one a lot.

What We Did

That was a lot of work to get a one-word result. We had a lot of new concepts to deal with, so we can't expect to have gotten a whole lot done to begin with. The nice thing is that with these concepts under our belts, we've laid the groundwork for a lot of what we're going to see going forward.

We went into a good bit of detail about how the XSLT processor handles an XML file and its related XSLT stylesheet. The important concept to take away here is how the XSLT processor coordinates between XSLT stylesheet templates and the current context of the XML file. There's a lot more to XSLT than that, but this is the basic process that makes XSLT go.

Our example XSLT code was relatively simple. It contained a template that matched the root element of the XML file, which gave the stylesheet an entry point into the document. It contained a template that matched one of the root element's child elements, but then did nothing. And it matched another child element and rendered the text inside it by using a hidden feature of XSLT, a built-in template rule.

The example demonstrates some of the basic working principles behind XSLT. The good news is that you'll probably need to read this chapter only once. It's a conceptual framework, but it will be helpful for understanding many of the ideas that follow. The other good news is that while the example in this chapter may have been simple, XSLT has a rich and subtle array of controls that will be needed for some of the ridiculously complex XML we're likely to encounter in the real world. These controls will be the subject the rest of this book.

As a matter of fact, it was the only kind of logic that could be brought to bear upon my problem.

— *Edgar Rice Burroughs,* A Princess of Mars

CHAPTER 3

Installing, Testing, and Using a Stand-Alone XSLT Processor

XSLT processors are the engines that drive XSLT transformations. Without an XSLT processor of some sort, XSLT stylesheets accomplish nothing.

We can do a limited amount of work with the XSLT processors that are built into web browsers, but once we get beyond HTML and text, we're going to want to see results that the browser may not be able to display. For example, while developing an XSLT stylesheet, we might occasionally make a mistake (yes, it happens). We'd like to see the results for troubleshooting, but the erroneous results may not be displayable in a browser. Also, getting the browser to display XML is not always as simple as it sounds.

In this chapter we're going to cover:

- Which XSLT processors are available
- How to install the Saxon XSLT processor
- How to test the processor
- Typical methods of using the processor

What Processors Are Out There?

Different people have implemented XSLT processors based on their own needs or the needs of the communities they serve. There are only a few XSLT processors in widespread use, so choosing between them isn't difficult.

The differences between XSLT processors are fairly moderate. In general, an XSLT processor is required to support, at a minimum, the specification for whatever XSLT version it claims to support, although complete support for the specification isn't always a given. In addition, XSLT processors usually offer extensions to the

XSLT instruction set, with each processor differing in what it supports. Performance is another area where the processors differ (sometimes dramatically). The execution platform varies from processor to processor (although two of the most popular, Xalan and Saxon, work with Java). And finally, the amount of ongoing support for the different processors varies widely.

In the following entries, I list the major XSLT processors currently available, with a few notes about each.

Saxon . . . . http://saxon.sourceforge.net/

- Supports XSLT 1.0, 2.0, and much of 3.0 (as currently defined)
- Available in open-source and commercial versions
- EXSLT and Saxon XSLT extensions supported in commercial versions
- Supported on Java and .NET
- A client edition adds XSLT 2.0 support to browsers
- Actively supported by Michael Kay, who edited the XSLT 2.0 specification

Xalan . . . . http://xml.apache.org/xalan-j/index.html

- An open-source XSLT processor supporting XSLT 1.0
- Implemented in C++ and Java
- Actively supported by the Apache community

libxslt . . . . http://xmlsoft.org/XSLT/

- libxslt is a free library for the C language
- Implements most of the EXSLT extension library[1] as well as a subset of Saxon's XSLT extensions
- Considered one of the faster XSLT processors

XT . . . . http://www.blnz.com/xt/index.html

- Supports XSLT 1.0 only
- Java-based
- Advertises itself as "fast"
- No updates since 2005

Altova RaptorXML Server . . . . http://www.altova.com/raptorxml.html

- Supports XSLT 1.0, 2.0, and a subset of 3.0, as well as other XML-related processing specifications
- Only available under commercial license

---

1. http://www.exslt.org/

MSXML http://msdn.microsoft.com/en-US/data/bb190600.aspx

- Windows-only application
- Supports XSLT 1.0 and 2.0
- Intended for use with Visual Basic, C, C++, or scripting languages

System.Xml in the .NET Framework . . http://msdn.microsoft.com/en-us/library/2bcctyt8.aspx

- Windows-only application
- Supports XSLT 1.0
- Intended for use with managed code targeting the .NET Framework in C#, Visual Basic, J#, managed C++, or other managed languages

Xuriella . . . . http://common-lisp.net/project/xuriella/

- A Lisp-based XSLT processor
- Supports XSLT 1.0

Web browsers http://www.w3webtutorial.com/xslt/xslt-browser-support.php

- Supported by Safari, Chrome, Firefox, Opera and Internet Explorer
- Typically support only XSLT 1.0—with limitations

In this book, we're going to install a version of the Saxon processor that supports XSLT 1.0. We'll use the free, open-source version. I've used Saxon and Xalan extensively, and both give excellent support for the XSLT 1.0 specification. However, Saxon is more actively supported, and it offers a broad range of possibilities for expanding your processor functionality once you progress beyond the confines of XSLT 1.0. The home edition of Saxon gives an excellent stepping-off point if you later find you need additional functionality from your XSLT processor.

Although we show how to install the Saxon processor in this book, you're welcome to explore and install any other XSLT processor you find convenient. The examples in this book should all run the same with any processor that supports XSLT 1.0. Also, you can later swap out processors when you get ready for real-world implementations.

Installation

In this section, we're going to download and install Saxon 6.5.5. This is not the latest and greatest from Saxon, but it is the last version that supports XSLT 1.0 and not 2.0. Running an XSLT 2.0 processor against an XSLT 1.0 stylesheet is possible, but it opens up the possibility of inconsistencies when the XSLT 2.0 processor runs in "backwards compatibility mode." So we'll use a straight XSLT 1.0 processor to keep things simple.

To run Saxon 6.5.5, we'll also need to have Java installed and available in our Path environment variable. And, naturally, you'll need to follow the Java installation instructions for the operating system you're running for these exercises. However, once Java is installed, the installation for Saxon is a breeze.

Installing Java for the Saxon XSLT Processor

Chances are you already have Java installed on your computer. It seems like everything uses Java these days. To check whether you have Java installed and called out in your Path environment variable, open a terminal window and enter `java -version` at the command prompt.

You should get a message back telling you which version of Java you have installed. The version of Saxon we'll be using is fairly old, and it is advertised to be compatible with Java JDK 1.2 through 1.5, but it works in Java 1.6 (Java SE 6) just fine, and I suspect it will be fine with later versions of Java as well.

You may get a message to the effect `'java' is not recognized as an internal or external command, operable program or batch file`. If you get this, you need to install Java and get the path to it into your Path environment variable. Rather than repeat the installation procedures for Java here, you can go to the web page at http://www.oracle.com/technetwork/java/javase/downloads/index.html and follow the instructions from that point. Select the latest version labeled "JDK," and that should give you what you need.

Once you get Java set up, you'll need to set your Path environment variable to include the path to the Java executable. The executable is located in the JDK folder for the version of Java that you installed. (You do remember which directory you installed Java in, don't you?) For example, I installed Java SE 8 in `C:\Program Files\Java` on my machine. Within that folder, I find the `java.exe` file for the JDK located in `C:\Program Files\Java\jdk1.8.0_05\bin`. This is the path that I put into my Path variable. (Yours will likely differ from mine).

For additional information on setting the Path environment variable for Java, take a look at http://java.com/en/download/help/path.xml.

If you're running Java 1.4 or later, you shouldn't have any problems. With earlier versions of Java, you need to specify additional files for classpaths on the command line.[2] Let's make all of our lives easier and assume that you're not using an ancient version of Java.

Again, once Java is installed, you can check the installation by opening a new terminal window and entering java -version. (Don't use a terminal window that was open before you changed the path, because it won't pick up the change.) Now you should see the Java version message smiling back at you, similar to mine:

```
C:\>java -version
java version "1.8.0_05"
Java(TM) SE Runtime Environment (build 1.8.0_05-b13)
Java HotSpot(TM) 64-Bit Server VM (build 25.5-b02, mixed mode)
```

We've set the table for installing Saxon. Now—just one more package to install.

Getting and Installing Saxon 6.5.5

To get Saxon 6.5.5:

1. Visit the Saxon XSLT and XQuery Processor page here:

   http://saxon.sourceforge.net/

2. On this page, scroll down to the "Older Products" section and find the "Saxon 6.5.5" section.
3. Click on the link labeled "Download (3265 Kbytes)." This will take you to the Sourceforge download page, and your download should start automatically after a few seconds.

Install Saxon 6.5.5 as follows:

1. Create a folder for your Saxon installation. You might want to create a general Saxon folder, and within that a folder for the specific version you're installing. In my case, I created a folder called Saxon, then a folder within it called Saxon6-5-5.
2. Locate the downloaded .zip file for the Saxon 6.5.5 installation file. Using a zip application of your preference, unzip the file to the destination directory you just created.
3. Check the destination directory to make sure the files are present. Your directory should look something like Figure 10, *Directory content for installed Saxon files*, on page 36.

---

2. http://saxon.sourceforge.net/saxon6.5.5/index.html

Name	Date modified	Type	Size
doc	5/28/2014 2:08 PM	File folder	
samples	5/28/2014 2:09 PM	File folder	
saxon.jar	11/24/2005 10:45 ...	Executable Jar File	560 KB
saxon-jdom.jar	11/24/2005 10:45 ...	Executable Jar File	17 KB
saxon-xml-apis.jar	11/24/2005 10:45 ...	Executable Jar File	65 KB
source.zip	11/24/2005 10:55 ...	Compressed (zipp...	682 KB

Figure 10—Directory content for installed Saxon files

And that's it. Saxon is now ready to process XSLT. Now all we have to do is construct a command line to make it go.

Testing

Before we launch into the heart of our story, let's make sure the XSLT processor is working. We're not quite ready to demo in front of the CEO.

To test the processor, you'll need an XSLT stylesheet and an XML file to work on. I've placed a couple of files on the website for this book that you can test with. Download the files from the two following links and save them together in the same directory somewhere on your computer:

- http://media.pragprog.com/titles/djkxsl/code/standalone/streamline.xsl
- http://media.pragprog.com/titles/djkxsl/code/standalone/accounts.xml

In case you can't get to the files, here is the text of the XSLT file:

standalone/streamline.xsl

```
<xsl:stylesheet xmlns:xsl="http://www.w3.org/1999/XSL/Transform" version="1.0">
  <xsl:template match="/accounts">
    <accounts>
      <xsl:apply-templates/>
    </accounts>
  </xsl:template>

  <xsl:template match="account">
    <xsl:element name="account">
      <xsl:attribute name="id">
        <xsl:value-of select="@id"/>
      </xsl:attribute>
      <xsl:attribute name="name">
        <xsl:value-of select="name/first"/>
        <xsl:text> </xsl:text>
        <xsl:value-of select="name/middle"/>
        <xsl:text> </xsl:text>
```

```
        <xsl:value-of select="name/last"/>
      </xsl:attribute>
      <xsl:apply-templates select="transactions"/>
    </xsl:element>
  </xsl:template>

  <xsl:template match="transactions">
    <xsl:apply-templates/>
  </xsl:template>
  <xsl:template match="transaction">
    <xsl:element name="transaction">
      <xsl:apply-templates/>
    </xsl:element>
  </xsl:template>

  <xsl:template match="date">
    <xsl:element name="date">
      <xsl:value-of select="month"/>
      <xsl:text> </xsl:text>
      <xsl:value-of select="day"/>
      <xsl:text>, </xsl:text>
      <xsl:value-of select="year"/>
      <xsl:text> </xsl:text>
      <xsl:value-of select="time"/>
    </xsl:element>
  </xsl:template>

  <xsl:template match="amount">
    <xsl:element name="amount">
      <xsl:value-of select="."/>
    </xsl:element>
  </xsl:template>

  <xsl:template match="product">
    <xsl:element name="product">
      <xsl:value-of select="."/>
    </xsl:element>
  </xsl:template>
</xsl:stylesheet>
```

And here is the content of the XML file:

standalone/accounts.xml

```
<?xml version='1.0' encoding='UTF-8'?>
<accounts>
  <account id="100007">
    <name>
      <first>Jorge</first>
      <middle>Luis</middle>
      <last>Borges</last>
    </name>
```

```
    <transactions>
      <transaction id="TR-765432198">
        <date>
          <year>1984</year>
          <month>June</month>
          <day>6</day>
          <time>12:00:00</time>
        </date>
        <amount>$14.99</amount>
        <product>B-5643A</product>
      </transaction>
      <transaction id="TR-654321987">
        <date>
          <year>1966</year>
          <month>July</month>
          <day>23</day>
          <time>23:47:12</time>
        </date>
        <amount>$12.95</amount>
        <product>A-2345B</product>
      </transaction>
    </transactions>
  </account>
</accounts>
```

Once you've got that, use the following steps to run the test:

1. Open a terminal window on the computer.
2. Change directories to the directory containing the two files you downloaded.
3. Enter the following at the command line. (Note that the line return in the command line is artificially placed to take into account the width of this book. Don't enter a line return within the command line text.)

   ```
   java -jar [absolute path to the saxon.jar file/]saxon.jar  -o output.xml
        accounts.xml streamline.xsl
   ```

   You'll need to supply the absolute path to the saxon.jar file that we placed during the installation procedure. For example, I use the following:

   ```
   java  -jar C:/Saxon/Saxon6-5-5/saxon.jar -o output.xml accounts.xml streamline.xsl
   ```

   The -o output.xml option tells the processor to send the output to a file called output.xml, in the same directory where it is currently processing. multiple_accounts.xml is the name of the XML file we want to process, and streamline.xsl is the name of the file containing our stylesheet. (We'll use this same stylesheet and XML file in a later chapter, but at the moment, don't worry about the details. We're just proving high-level functionality in this step.)

4. When the command executes, you should see something like the following in the terminal window.

```
H:/djkxsl/Book/code/standalone>java -jar C:/Saxon/Saxon6-5-5/
     saxon.jar -o output.xml accounts.xml streamline.xsl

H:/djkxsl/Book/code/standalone>
```

   Which is to say that you see nothing. And that's a good thing. If there were a problem with our setup, we'd be seeing error messages instead of a blank line. (And if you are seeing error messages, don't panic. We'll address some of the gotchas in *What if It All Goes Wrong?*, on page 39.)

5. To double-check that the processor ran properly, go to the directory containing the XML and XSL file, and find the file called output.xml. Opening this file, you should see something like the following:

standalone/output.xml
```
<?xml version="1.0" encoding="ISO-8859-1"?><accounts>
  <account id="100007" name="Jorge Luis Borges">
      <transaction>
        <date>June 6, 1984 12:00:00</date>
        <amount>$14.99</amount>
        <product>B-5643A</product>
      </transaction>
      <transaction>
        <date>July 23, 1966 23:47:12</date>
        <amount>$12.95</amount>
        <product>A-2345B</product>
      </transaction>
    </account>
 </accounts>
```

   If your output.xml file contains this content, you're golden. You can skip over the next section and keep going. If you're running into problems, go on to the next section and let's see if we can sort them out.

What if It All Goes Wrong?

In the world of software, things sometimes go wrong. Hard to believe, I'm sure…

In the case of our installation and test of the XSLT processor, the number of things that might go wrong is fortunately not that large. The following sections list some of the main issues you're likely to encounter, with suggestions for fixes.

Java doesn't run.

Still getting 'java' is not recognized as an internal or external command, operable program or batch file? Are you sure you set the Path environment variable correctly? Check the path to the java.exe file.

To check what the Path environment variable is set to, open a terminal window and do one of the following, based on your operating system:

- In Mac OSx, Unix, or Linux, enter echo $PATH.
- In Windows, enter set Path.

In the Path variable, is there any other Java path that precedes the Java path you intended to point to? If so, does that path point to a directory containing java.exe? The Path variable only uses the first instance of paths that point to executables of the same name. You may need to clean up your Path variable.

Saxon does not run.

If Java is running, but Saxon does not run when you enter the command line above, you will get an error message like this:

```
Error: Unable to access jarfile C:/Saxon/Saxon6-5-5/saxon.jar
```

Check again. Is the saxon.jar file in the location you specified on the command line? If so, something may be wrong with the the installation. You might try installing the Saxon files again.

Does the error message mention some other jar file as missing? If so, you may be using Java 1.3 or earlier, in which case you'll want to install a later version of Java.

The source XML and/or XSL stylesheet file is missing.

If you get a message reading Source file account.xml does not exist or Stylesheet file streamline.xsl does not exist, check the directory where the command prompt is located. (In OSx, Unix, and Linux, enter pwd; in Windows, enter echo %cd%.) Is the current directory for the command window the same as where the files exist? If not, change the directory to where the files exist.

The output file cannot be created.

You might get a message along these lines:

```
Error
Failed to create output file: H:\djkxsl\Book\code\standalone\output.xml
(The process cannot access the file because it is being used by another process)
Transformation failed: Run-time errors were reported
```

If you have the output.xml file open in an editor application, the file may be locked so Saxon can't write to it. Close the file and try again.

Once we get beyond these issues, if you are still having problems, it might be best to get online and post your problems to a support community for your operating system or computer. Java and Saxon are relatively easy, but—what was that we started with? "In the world of software, sometimes things go wrong." Too true, too true...

Using the Command Line

Before we move along, let's go over the command line so you have a little more understanding of how it works. That way you can adapt the command line to your circumstances.

Take a look again at the example I entered for the Saxon test command line:

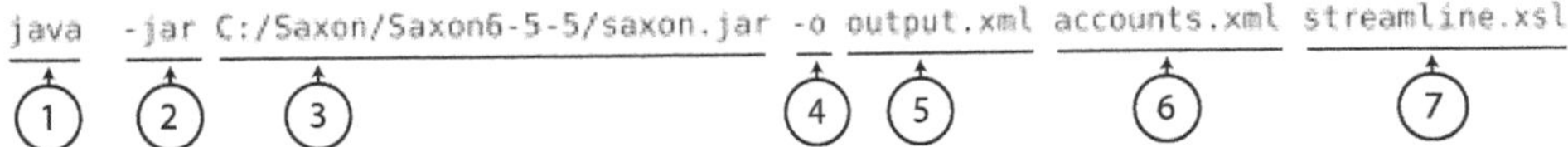

The numbered parts of the command line in this diagram are as follows:

① The command used to execute Java. The file location for the java executable must be contained in the Path environment variable for this to work.

② The label or switch for the option that specifies where the saxon.jar file is located. If you later find that you need to list other .jar files, you would provide them, separated by spaces, after this option label.

③ The absolute path to the saxon.jar file.

④ The option switch for the output option. An output file name must be given if you use this switch.

If you leave off this option, the output will be directed to the terminal window where you enter the command. If you're processing a really long XML file—just sit back and enjoy the fireworks.

⑤ The path and name of the output file. If you just give a filename, the file is created in the directory where you are executing the command. You can also use a relative or absolute path to place the output file somewhere else.

⑥ The name of the input file. This is a required entry. As with the output file, you can use a relative or absolute path along with the filename. (If the path or filename contains spaces, try enclosing the complete path and filename in quotation marks.)

⑦ The name of the file containing the XSLT stylesheet. Again, relative and absolute paths can be included.

The command line can get tedious if you move between a lot of different XSLT files, like we're going to do in this book. If you get tired of typing the absolute path to the Java executable, you could create a command script (specific to your operating system, of course) that allowed you to abbreviate what you have to enter for the execution.

There are a variety of things you can do with the command line that go beyond what we need for this book. You can invoke Saxon from within another program, for instance. You can set up the command line to use classpaths rather than the absolute path to the saxon.jar file. There are good reasons for all of these variants, but you'll have to discover your own particular needs as you grow in your experience with XSLT. For a good summary of how to invoke Saxon, and all things Saxon-related, I recommend looking at the Saxon documentation, available on the Saxonica website.[3]

What We Did

For a short chapter, we covered a lot of ground. We had a look at the list of available XSLT processors and settled on using Saxon 6.5.5 for this book. We installed Java, installed Saxon, and tested it. Those of us who weren't so lucky had to do a little troubleshooting. (Sorry about that!) And then we had a look at the command line for executing the XSLT processor, trying to give ourselves a little flexibility for ease of use down the road.

So now we're set! We're able to process XSLT two different ways: with a qualified web browser, or with a standalone XSLT processor. I always like to use the standalone processor, but there's no denying that a web browser is much easier. However, as we get into some more complex situations with XSLT processing, we'll want to use the standalone processor almost exclusively.

Now let's put our spiffy new processing tools to work. In the next part of this book, we're going to look at XSLT from the perspective of how it solves certain classes of problems. We'll see how to control output, how to change the order and structure of documents, and how to use values for decisions, selections, and other kinds of control. We'll take a look at more large-scale issues such as grouping, sorting, and stylesheet organization. And finally, we'll encounter some strategies for the inevitable and necessary topic of troubleshooting XSLT.

Ready to jump in?

---

3. http://www.saxonica.com/documentation/documentation.xml

During the early years of the discovery of this ray many strange accidents occurred before the Martians learned to measure and control the wonderful power they had found.

Edgar Rice Burroughs, A Princess of Mars

CHAPTER 4

Beginning with the End: Creating Output

Output is what it's all about. In Chapter 2, *XSLT in Action*, on page 13, we saw how the XSLT processor finds XSLT templates to match against the elements in an XML document. But what can we do in the templates once they match an element? In almost all cases, the goal is to create output.

To craft the output to our needs, we're going to need controls over how we create it. Our output file might be XML very similar to what we started with, or it might be a massive reconstruction to convert it to something that bears little resemblance to the original. It might be HTML, or maybe even another XSLT stylesheet. We might want to add or subtract content, or we might want to use the document data to do calculations and make decisions about how to modify other data. Yes, we can do all that.

How are we going to do all that?

It turns out there are a number of different ways for XSLT to output data, and the different methods are appropriate to different situations. In this chapter we're going to learn some of the patterns for creating different kinds of output. We'll learn new instructions as well as check back on the `<xsl:apply-templates>` instruction. We'll find subtle differences between the different instructions used to control output.

The methods of getting output that we'll cover in this chapter include:

- Getting text out of nodes in the source document
- Adding literal text
- Adding elements and attributes to the output as static text
- Dynamically adding element and attribute names and values during runtime

There are a few other types of output to learn, but we'll save those for later. First let's get comfortable with the basic output methods.

Reaping the Flow: Built-in Template Rules

As we've seen, one way of getting text out of an XML file is to use the <xsl:apply-templates> instruction and rely on the built-in template rules to retrieve the text that is in the XML source document.

Let's set up a simple XML document and XSLT template to retrieve its text. Here's the XML:

handlingcontent/caution1.xml

```
<?xml version='1.0' encoding='UTF-8'?>
<?xml-stylesheet type="text/xsl" href="caution1.xsl"?>
<caution type="Intergalactic">
  <paragraph>The potential for intergalactic broadcast while using
    the <product>AZGuard Protaxis</product> unit
    has not yet been determined.</paragraph>

  <paragraph>Please avoid transmitting information that could place
    the human race at risk for alien invasion.</paragraph>
</caution>
```

Figure 11—Example XML for a cautionary note

Here's the stylesheet that will give us all the text in the <caution> tag:

handlingcontent/caution1.xsl

```
<?xml version="1.0" encoding="utf-8"?>
<xsl:stylesheet xmlns:xsl="http://www.w3.org/1999/XSL/Transform" version="1.0">
<xsl:template match="/caution">
  <xsl:apply-templates/>
</xsl:template>
</xsl:stylesheet>
```

Since the <?xml-stylesheet/> processing instruction in the XML file points to the XSLT stylesheet, we could just open the XML file in a browser to see the results. Remember that the XSLT stylesheet should be in the same directory as the XML file for our examples.

Here's the result we should see: an unformatted string that concatenates all the text in the file:

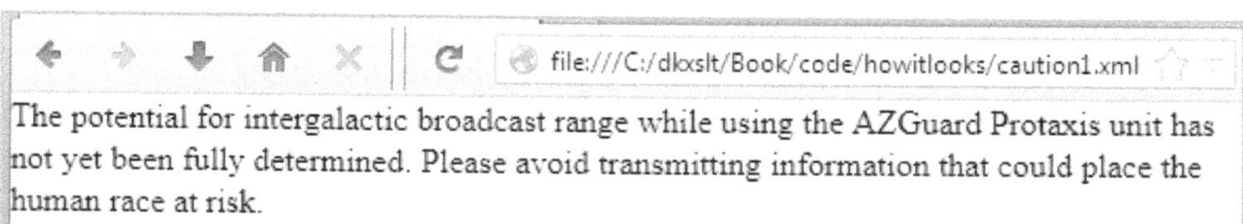

We've seen this before, and it's not particularly useful. This is a good way to get the text out in the order it appears in the document, if that's all we're interested in. All we need to do is create a template to match something and put an <xsl:apply-templates> in it. It will retrieve all the text in the element we matched, including the text of any descendant tags.

If there are no descendant tags, this is a safe way to output the text, but usually we're going to need more than that. We're going to want to format the text, add stuff to it, maybe even leave things out. Let's see if we can get some help with that.

Fine Tuning the Output with <xsl:value-of>

We'll heed the famous admonition of *The Elements of Style* by Strunk and White: "Omit needless words." Instead of using <xsl:apply-templates> and the indiscriminate reaping machine of the default template, let's use something a little pickier: <xsl:value-of>. With this tag we can limit what we output more precisely.

<xsl:value-of> returns a value based on the expression in its attribute. The contents of the select= attribute could be an XML node or node-set, in which case the value returned might be the text content of the XML node or nodes. It could be the value of a variable (we'll get to variables later, but they're pretty much what you might think they are). It could be some static text or a number that we supply directly in the attribute. Or it could be the result of a complex expression, in which case what it returns could be a carefully tailored value. In all cases, though, <xsl:value-of> returns either a string or a number.

If we place static text in select=, it needs single quotes around it or we'll get a syntax error.

Unlike <xsl:apply-templates>, <xsl:value-of> doesn't kick off any additional processing. What you specify in select= is what you get, and it ends there. As we said, it's a bit more precise than <xsl:apply-templates>.

To see an example in action, we'll continue using the XML document in Figure 11, *Example XML for a cautionary note*, on page 44.

Suppose we have a couple of hundred products, each with a library of caution statements, and we want to make sure all the products have the correct caution statements. We want to know which products are mentioned in various caution statements. So all we need from the XML file is the value of the type= attribute and the text of any <product> tag.

When we match on the <caution>, we can get the text of the type= attribute with <xsl:value-of select="@type">. (The @ symbol before a node name means that the node is an attribute. To select an attribute, you always have to use @ before the attribute name.)

That just leaves the value of the <product> tag. We match on <paragraph> but this time we need to prevent the output of the <paragraph> text, since we don't want it. We do this by using the <xsl:apply-templates> tag with a select= statement that doesn't select for text. Instead, it selects only for the <product> tag, like so: <xsl:apply-templates select="product">. By defining what we want to select, we avoid invoking the default template for text.

All we need now is a template for <product> that outputs its text (line 9), and we have what we wanted:

handlingcontent/caution2.xsl

```
1  <?xml version="1.0" encoding="utf-8"?>
2  <xsl:stylesheet xmlns:xsl="http://www.w3.org/1999/XSL/Transform" version="1.0">
3    <xsl:template match="caution">
4      <xsl:value-of select="@type"/>
5      <xsl:apply-templates select="descendant::product"/>
6    </xsl:template>
7
8    <xsl:template match="product">
9      <xsl:value-of select="text()"/>
10   </xsl:template>
11 </xsl:stylesheet>
```

(We'll get more details about the text() function later in the book, but at the moment all we need to know is that it returns the text of a selected element —in this case, the current element.)

Change the XML file to point to the new caution2.xsl filename, then display the XML file in a browser again. The output now looks like this:

<xsl:value-of> has allowed us to fine tune the output, giving us only the parts we need.

Of course, to do that we had to step away from using the bare <xsl:apply-templates> instruction. We'll find in XSLT that we often have to trade off between giving explicit instructions and allowing the templates to work in a more functional, take-it-as-it-lays method. Our working methods will be determined by what we're trying to accomplish.

When outputting text, as we've done here, one thing to keep in mind: if the current content contains several text nodes that are separated by other nodes (such as elements or comments), <xsl:value-of> selects only the first node it finds. For example, in the following:

```
<p>Here is a point that <emph>must</emph> be emphasized!</p>
```

If our template matches on the <p> tag and contains <xsl:value-of select="text()">, our result will be "Here is a point that". So you'll need to exercise caution with this one.

You could also say <xsl:value-of select=".">, but like <xsl:apply-templates>, this approach gives the contents of all the elements contained. That dot in the select= attribute means to return the value of everything in the current context element—and that includes all of its children. That might even be what we want, but we need to be careful with using the dot.

<xsl:value-of> was just what we needed to get a specific slice of data out of our XML file. But you probably noticed that the output isn't exactly user friendly. The values of the type= attribute and <product> tag are run together, and we don't have any indication of what type of data each part represents.

It looks like we need to add some text to the output to indicate what the output is about. Fortunately, the next section shows a couple of ways to do that.

More Is Better: Supplying Our Own Text

As we saw in the last section, the content inside the tags isn't always enough to construct our output. XML content is sometimes terse because the document *structure* is intended to convey information to supplement the content. The structure of XML allows the XSLT to derive clues about the content, and with the help of those clues, the XSLT can supply additional text as needed. In our example, our clues were that the content we wanted was in the type= attribute and the <product> tag.

XSLT recognizes a certain rule for outputting things from the templates:

If it's in a template and it's not recognized as an XSLT node, it goes into the output.

We can output raw text pretty much anywhere within an <xsl:template> tag (as long as it doesn't screw up the syntax of any other tagging), but it's our responsibility to ensure that the text is valid within the structure of our output.

We could code XSLT to output <h2></h2>WAIT JUST A SECOND..., and the XSLT processor would be as happy as a clam. On the other hand, the browser would just snicker.

Raw text anywhere: that's cool. And, of course, with great power comes...great potential for screw-ups.

Let's go back to that output for the note type and product and add a little text to it, to give the output values some context. Here's what we're looking for:

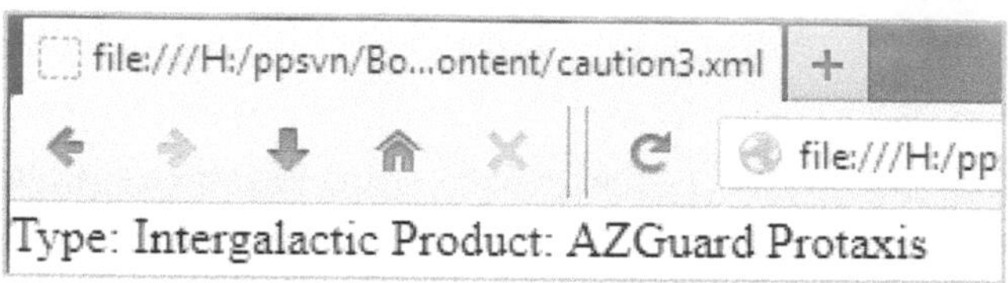

You can probably figure this one out yourself:

handlingcontent/caution3.xsl

```
Line 1 <?xml version="1.0" encoding="utf-8"?>
       <xsl:stylesheet xmlns:xsl="http://www.w3.org/1999/XSL/Transform" version="1.0">
         <xsl:template match="caution">
            Type:
     5     <xsl:value-of select="@type"/>
           <xsl:apply-templates select="descendant::product"/>
         </xsl:template>

         <xsl:template match="product">
    10     Product:
           <xsl:value-of select="text()"/>
         </xsl:template>
       </xsl:stylesheet>
```

Just add the text in lines 4 and 10, and we're good to go.

A point worth mentioning here: whitespace can be a little tricky. We now have spaces between the words because the text lines contain line returns, and the XML parser by default collapses any whitespace in text to a single space. That worked out fine this time, but it may not always be what we want. We'll see controls for whitespace in Chapter 10, *Large-Scale Stylesheet Strategies*, on page 183.

I said you can add text anywhere inside a template as long as it doesn't mess up the XSLT tagging syntax. That's easier said than done, and it reinforces the need for having a good XML editor that is XSLT-aware. It will keep you out of all sorts of syntactical nightmares. But, in the absence of an XSLT-aware editor, here are some places you should avoid adding text:

- Inside the <xsl:choose> tag, except inside the <xsl:when> and <xsl:otherwise> tags. (We cover <xsl:choose> in *Variation on a Theme #4: Changing One Word to Another*, on page 69.)
- Before the <xsl:param> tag inside a template. (See *Parameters and xsl:call-template*, on page 160 for more about <xsl:param>.)
- Between an <xsl:element> tag and an <xsl:attribute> tag. (We'll get to these tags shortly in *Adding Elements and Attributes Dynamically*, on page 52.)

(We haven't learned about these instructions yet, but since we're on the subject, you are now forewarned.)

These are the most common areas you might be tempted to place text but shouldn't. There are others, but you'll learn about those places as you learn more about XSLT in general.

We still have a presentation problem. We're only seeing the text output in the browser. We don't have any HTML formatting in our output for the browser to interpret, so everything is still just text stretched out on a single line. If we had more than one caution in our file, we would need a way to output the results in a more readable format.

It's time to stop dilly-dallying around. Let's output HTML.

Adding Tags and Attributes as Text

The ability to add raw text means we can also form elements and attributes by simple text entry, just using the standard angle brackets and attribute_name="" as needed.

For our example, we'll use this source markup as our source document:

handlingcontent/caution4.xml

```
<?xml version='1.0' encoding='UTF-8'?>
<?xml-stylesheet type="text/xsl" href="caution4.xsl"?>
<caution>
  <paragraph>The intergalactic broadcast range of
    the <product>AZGuard Protaxis</product> unit
    has not yet been determined.</paragraph>

  <paragraph>Please avoid transmitting information that could place
    the human race at risk.</paragraph>
</caution>
```

When we output the XHTML content, we might want to match on the <caution> tag and add a couple of other pieces of formatted text to draw attention to the cosmic consequences of the note, as in Figure 12, *The formatted caution Sstatement*, on page 50.

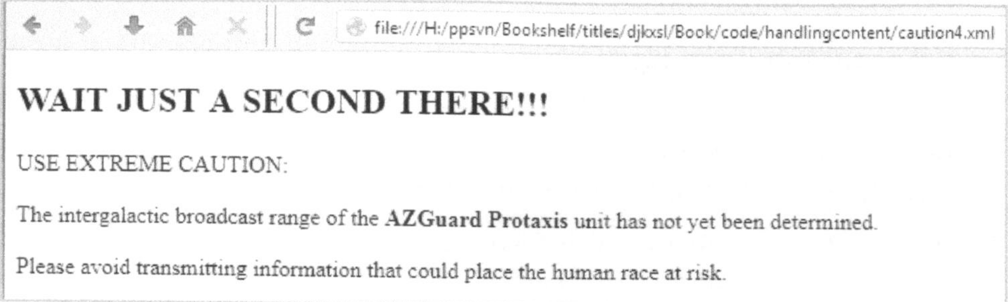

Figure 12—The formatted caution Sstatement

The additional text and formatting we supply helps to label and draw attention to the original content. (It may be a teensy bit heavy-handed in this case.)

Where did that extra text and formatting come from? Let's look at the stylesheet that gave us the output:

handlingcontent/caution4.xsl

```
<?xml version="1.0" encoding="utf-8"?>
<xsl:stylesheet
  xmlns:xsl="http://www.w3.org/1999/XSL/Transform" version="1.0"
  xmlns="http://www.w3.org/1999/xhtml">

  <xsl:template match="/caution">
    <html>
      <head><title>Caution!</title></head>
      <body>
        <h2>WAIT JUST A SECOND THERE!!!</h2>
        <p> USE EXTREME CAUTION:</p>
        <xsl:apply-templates/>
      </body>
    </html>
  </xsl:template>

  <xsl:template match="paragraph">
    <p><xsl:apply-templates/></p>
  </xsl:template>

  <xsl:template match="product">
    <b><xsl:apply-templates/></b>
  </xsl:template>
</xsl:stylesheet>
```

The <xsl:stylesheet> element in line 4 contains an attribute that declares the XHTML namespace as the stylesheet's default namespace. Once we do that, we're free to add XHTML tags inside the templates without referencing their namespace any more. We could specify the namespace on individual tags, but that gets tedious and repetitive. So we declare a default global namespace so we can use the XHTML tags without a URI prefix. We declare it using the xmlns= attribute on the <xsl:stylesheet> element. That way, the processor understands that any tag without a namespace prefix inside the templates belongs to this default namespace.

Do You Have Anything Else to Declare?

As you can see, the xmlns:xsl= attribute in line 4 of the XSLT example specifies a prefix for the XSL namespace, so we use xsl: as a prefix in our XSLT stylesheet.

If we needed to output multiple namespaces, we would declare the namespaces in the <xsl:stylesheet> tag, similar to how we declare the xsl: namespace. We would also need to include the namespace prefix with the appropriate tags inside the templates to avoid collisions between namespaces.

Until you start using multiple namespaces, you can get away with just using a default namespace, the way we have it set up here for XHTML.

When you do start using multiple namespaces, you'll want to check out some of the output controls, including exclude-result-prefixes=, which we cover in Chapter 10, *Large-Scale Stylesheet Strategies*, on page 183

In line 6 of our example, we matched on the <caution> tag. Inside that template, we added some HTML tags and some literal text that we wanted to output.

Since <caution> is the root element of the XML document, we put all the top-level HTML tags inside the template that matches on the <caution> element. This arrangement illustrates one of the basic principles of XSLT stylesheet design. Since the XSLT processor uses the templates to match the structure of the XML document, try to design your XSLT templates to take advantage of the XML structure when planning your output.

For example, instead of placing "USE EXTREME CAUTION:" in the template that matches on the root element, <caution>, we could have created a template to match only the first paragraph of the XML, then added "USE EXTREME CAUTION:" in that template. But then we would have had to create another template to match all the other <paragraph> tags in the document, so they would not contain "USE EXTREME CAUTION:". Instead, we stick the one-time warning in the top-level template with all the other one-time set-up tags. We'll find ourselves asking many similar questions about content placement as we encounter more complicated patterns of mapping XML source to our required output.

What about attributes? Suppose our example needs us to output something like <p class="caution">. Could we just add it into the text for the <p> tag and hope it comes across, like this:

```
<p class="caution">
  USE EXTREME CAUTION:
</p>
```

You bet your sweet bippy (as they once said in a remote and colorful past). Just pop in the attribute and its value as static text, and we're good to go.

Other than setting up the namespace, there's no big trick to using text for output elements and attributes. As far as using them for creating static output, they're relatively straightforward. The main thing you have to watch out for is making sure the order of the output creates valid syntax for the type of output you are creating. It's sometimes easy to match on an element and create a block-level piece of output (like a <p>) and find out that its parent element is also a block-level element that added a <p>—so now we've got a <p> inside a <p>, and that won't work. Sometimes this situation means that we need to change the order of how things are output—a topic we'll deal with in detail in Chapter 6, *Changing the Structure and Order of Content*, on page 75.

What we've seen here is how to create elements and attributes in static form, which is fine when we know what they're supposed to be in advance. But what if we don't know exactly what element or attribute to use? What if we don't know the value that needs to be supplied for the attribute? Suppose we can only find those values at runtime, by testing other parts of the document or by using values supplied by the process that kicks off the XSLT processor? These are all perfectly valid questions. And, fortunately, XSLT has answers.

As we'll see in the following section, XSLT provides the <xsl:element> instruction, <xsl:attribute> instruction, and the *attribute value template* as ways to dynamically create element names, attribute names, and attribute values during runtime.

Adding Elements and Attributes Dynamically

Now we've got to add a couple more XSLT instructions to our toolbox: <xsl:element> and <xsl:attribute>.

Often we won't know what to name an element or attribute until we have gathered some information at runtime. Maybe when we match an element, we'll need to place a new wrapper element around the content, and the name of that element will depend on some value that was passed in at runtime, or on the context structure, or on the contents of the text itself.

Consider a set of part numbers that previously have been contained in a <partno> tag, and the prefix was contained in an attribute (for example, <partno prefix="EVG">7891-1246<partno/>). The customer is now doing a big data migration, and for the sake of efficiency and clarity, the <partno> tag is going away. We now need the part number to be tagged with the part number prefix so the tag will no longer need the attribute. We create a template to match on <partno> and then create an element whose name is the value of the attribute:

handlingcontent/partno1.xsl

```
Line 1 <xsl:template match="partno">
     2   <xsl:element name="{@prefix}">
     3     <xsl:value-of select="."/>
     4   </xsl:element>
     5 </xsl:template>
```

If our input is <partno prefix="EVG">7891-1246</>, our output is now <EVG>7891-1246</EVG>. Using this template, source tags with different prefixes will be output with different tag names.

Let's take a look at how we got that, one step at a time:

1. In line 1, we matched on <partno>.

2. In line 2, we created an open tag for the element. The element is named with the value of the prefix= attribute.

   The @ symbol means that we're looking for an attribute; the name of the attribute is what follows the @. And those curly braces ({}) represent what we call the *attribute value template*. The attribute value template places the value of its contents into the output. Think of them as meaning "the value of" whatever they contain.

   We'll use the curly braces a lot—the attribute value template is the preferred way to get dynamic values into attributes in the output document's elements.

3. In line 3, we output the value of the current context, which is the part number itself. From the paragraph above, the part number is 7891-1246.

4. In line 4, we close the <xsl:element> tag. In the output, this creates the closing tag for the new element we've created.

And that's it! The <xsl:element> instruction captures the appropriate new tag name based on the value of the prefix= attribute.

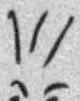

Joe asks:

What's the big deal with xsl:element?

Isn't it possible to accomplish the same thing as <xsl:element> by creating the element's angle brackets with text, then putting the name of the tag inside the two angle brackets?

Sure, you could do that by using XML character entities in place of the angle brackets, sort of like this:

```
&lt;<xsl:value-of select="@prefix"/>&gt;
```

Of course, we'd have to set up a similar statement for the closing tag, so we'd be duplicating effort. Never a good programming practice, if we can help it. And what happens when we try to add an attribute to the element using the <xsl:attribute> instruction? Nothing—the XSLT processor doesn't recognize that we've created an element, so it can't add an attribute to it. Of course, we could set up an attribute dynamically using text the same way we did with the element, but at that point we're pretty much reinventing the wheel. And the <xsl:element> tag comes with a set of attributes we'll find useful, such as the namespace= and use-attribute-sets= attributes.

The bottom line is, yes, we could do it by hand, but it's easier to use the tool provided by XSLT. Use the tools the way they're intended, trim your nails, keep your nose clean, and don't cheat. All good rules to follow.

We haven't done an example with <xsl:attribute> yet, so let's check it out. The best use of <xsl:attribute> is to create attribute names dynamically, as we did with <xsl:element>. One reason to do that might be to base an attribute name on the value of content elsewhere in the document.

Suppose we're converting some XML for a customer. The input looks like this:

handlingcontent/employees1.xml

```
<?xml version='1.0' encoding='UTF-8'?>
<?xml-stylesheet type="text/xsl" href="employees1.xsl"?>
<employees>
  <person>
    <name>David James Kelly</name>
    <id>emp-123456789</id>
    <employee-type>permanent</employee-type>
  </person>
  <person>
    <name>Sherlock Holmes</name>
    <id>temp-9876754321</id>
    <employee-type>consultant</employee-type>
  </person>
</employees>
```

The customer wants to tighten that up a bit so the <person> tag contains a single attribute and the <id> and <employee-type> tags go away. The name of the attribute will be based on the employee type, and the value of the attribute will be the ID number. That way, the <name> tag can also be eliminated, so the content of <person> is simply their name. Here's a way to handle that:

handlingcontent/employees1.xsl

```
<?xml version="1.0" encoding="utf-8"?>
<xsl:stylesheet  xmlns:xsl="http://www.w3.org/1999/XSL/Transform"  version="1.0">
 <xsl:output indent="yes"/>

<xsl:template match="employees">
  <employees>
    <xsl:apply-templates select="person"/>
  </employees>
</xsl:template>

<xsl:template match="person">
  <person>
    <xsl:attribute name="{employee-type}">
      <xsl:value-of select="id"/>
    </xsl:attribute>
    <xsl:value-of select="name"/>
  </person>
</xsl:template>

</xsl:stylesheet>
```

And our output is the required, beautifully terse XML that we expect:

handlingcontent/employees1-output.xml

```
<?xml version="1.0" encoding="UTF-8"?>
<employees>
   <person permanent="emp-123456789">David James Kelly</person>
   <person consultant="temp-9876754321">Sherlock Holmes</person>
</employees>
```

<xsl:element> is usually required only when the element needs to be dynamically generated. But you'll use the <xsl:attribute> instructions and attribute value templates quite frequently, as they give great flexibility in processing values for output attributes. <xsl:attribute> works best with the <xsl:element> tag. You can save yourself a lot of aggravation by using these the <xsl:element> and <xsl:attribute> instructions as partners.

What We Did

Now we're getting somewhere. We learned the basics of putting together a stylesheet in Chapter 2, *XSLT in Action*, on page 13, and in this chapter we've covered a pretty large chunk of what's involved in getting output with XSLT. Specifically, we learned how to:

- Output data as we find it by means of the built-in template rules
- Select the value of specific elements by means of <xsl:value-of>
- Use text to supply additional elements, attributes, and text where we want to add them into the output
- Supply elements and attributes with names and values generated on the fly using <xsl:element> and <xsl:attribute>

There's a lot of power in that short list, and you'll find that you use these techniques on a constant basis as you develop XSL stylesheets. None of it will go to waste.

But at the moment, let's move on to a completely different technique: the identity transform. This technique is also about output, but it introduces a whole different way to think about providing a filter between the input and output. It also introduces us to ideas about the relationships between different templates and how they match on content. With the identity transform, we start putting together stylesheets to accomplish some pretty powerful transformations.

"You have been with us a few days, yet during that time you have by your prowess won a high position among us."

> *Edgar Rice Burroughs,* A Princess of Mars

CHAPTER 5

Filtering with the Identity Transform

We've seen how to get some basic output from the XSLT, but we haven't done much with it. In this chapter, we'll look at how to start manipulating the output with a simple, powerful technique called the *identity transform.*

In its simplest form, the identity transform is a stylesheet that consists of a single template. The template is written so it can match any node in the document, create an identical instance of that node in the output, then apply templates in such a way that it calls itself again. With just this one template, the stylesheet works its way through the entire XML document and creates an output document that is identical to the input document.

The output file is identical to the input file? I mean, what's the point of that, right? But its usefulness down the road might be a little surprising. For example, we can create additional templates that provide exceptions to the identical copy, so we can create output with subtle changes from the input—like changing the name of one element in the document. Or we can make changes that give us radical, global changes from the input—like stripping out all the XML tags, or stripping out all the text.

The identity transform provides a starting point for solving a variety of interesting problems. But before we get to those problems, let's get a handle on how the basic identity transform works. We'll learn a couple of new XSLT tricks before we start making variations on the theme of the identity transform. After that, we'll take a look at just a few of the variations that can be made on our "identity transform" theme:

- Remove all the tags
- Remove all the text
- Uppercase or down-case text

- Create an obfuscator, where text is translated to nonsense, preserving the structural and content qualities of the output while keeping the content unreadable
- Change specific tags or text

That's all interesting and useful, so let's get started.

Output Equals Input: the Simplest Identity Transform

The simplest version of the identity transform is a single template that makes an identical copy of everything in the source XML:

to-identity/identity.xsl

```
Line 1 <?xml version="1.0" encoding="utf-8"?>
     2 <xsl:stylesheet xmlns:xsl="http://www.w3.org/1999/XSL/Transform" version="1.0">
     3   <xsl:template match="@* | node()">
     4     <xsl:copy>
     5       <xsl:apply-templates select="@* | node()"/>
     6     </xsl:copy>
     7   </xsl:template>
     8 </xsl:stylesheet>
```

Figure 13—Stylesheet for the Identity Transform

That's it. You can run a document of a million XML nodes through this stylesheet, and the output will be the same as the input.

So what's going on here? How does a single template perform such a magical trick? We saw some of the stylesheet structures in Chapter 2, *XSLT in Action*, on page 13, but there are some new things, too.

First, the `match=` attribute in line 3 includes @* and *node()*, separated by a pipe (|) character. The @ at the beginning of a string signifies an attribute. For instance, you would refer to an `id=` attribute by saying *@id*. In this case we add the asterisk (*) wildcard to get it to refer to *all* attributes.

The *node()* is a kind of wildcard itself: it tells the `match=` attribute to match any and all XML nodes in the current context. "All nodes" means text, elements, comments, and processing instructions. Pretty much everything except attributes.

The | character represents a union of node sets, although it is sometimes thought of as a logical OR. It is used between XPath statements that return node sets, and it acts to combine those node sets. This means that the `match=` attribute in line 3 says, essentially, "Match all nodes or attributes found in the current context."

There is also an or operator that is used in expressions, but that one is used as part of an expression to return a Boolean value.

A Walk through the Identity Transform's Operations.

To follow what happens when this stylesheet meets an XML document, let's take a look at a new bit of XML:

to-identity/bibliography.xml

```
<?xml version='1.0' encoding='UTF-8'?>
<?xml-stylesheet type="text/xsl" href="bibl.xsl"?>
<bibliography id="i54321">
  <book>
    <author>
      <given>David</given>
      <family>Kelly</family>
    </author>
    <title>XSLT Jumpstarter: Level the Learning Curve
      and Put Your XML to Work</title>
  </book>
</bibliography>
```

The XSLT processor looks in the stylesheet for matches starting from the XML document's root node. In our example, it matches the root node in the XML because our template matches any and all nodes in the current context with that node() wildcard.

Great, we're in. But what happens next?

Line 4 contains a single XSLT instruction: <xsl:copy>. This instruction tells the XSLT processor to make a copy of the current node, and that's it. So we copy the root node into the output and keep going.

Next, line 5 tells the XSLT processor to apply any templates, within the current context, that match any XML elements defined by the select= attribute. In this case, the contents of the select= attribute look exactly like the contents of our original match= attribute. The <xsl:apply-templates> instruction is telling the XSLT processor, "Go find any templates that provide a match for attributes or nodes in the current context," and the match is provided by the match statement at the head of the same template.

Since the <xsl:apply-templates> tag is inside the <xsl:copy> instruction, the results of applying any subsequent templates will also be inside the node that we just copied. That's as it should be for our example, but make a note: by moving the <xsl:apply-templates> tag outside the <xsl:copy> tag, we could change the structure of the output document—and there may be times when you need that.

So far, the stylesheet has processed the root node, <bibliography> and created a copy of it. Note that the XSLT processor has only output the opening tag at this point. It won't create the closing tag for <bibliography> until it reaches the closing tag of <xsl:copy> in the template.

Then, when the processor reaches <xsl:apply-templates>, the select= attribute tells it to apply any template that matches any XML attribute or node in the current context. In the XML, there is one attribute, id="i54321". So the XSL processor looks for a template to match that attribute.

Well, since there's only one template in the stylesheet, it doesn't have to look far. And since the template matches any attribute or node, it matches our particular id= attribute. So the template starts over again: the <xsl:copy> instruction copies the attribute and its value, the <xsl:apply-templates> tag keeps up moving through the XML..

This time there are no more attributes to match, so the <xsl:apply-templates> instruction matches on the next item in the XML document, in document order. The next thing is the <book> tag, so that gets matched and copied. Then the <author> tag. Then the <given> tag, and then the "David" piece of text.

There's no more text to copy, nor any other XML elements inside <given>, so the XSL process begins to unwind—remember, we've been executing the <xsl:apply-templates> tag and haven't reached the closing </xsl:copy> tag yet. The processor reaches the end tag for <given>, so the end tag for <xsl:copy> kicks in and outputs </given>. The processor moves on to the next tag (<family>), the processor finds the match for it with the node() part of match="@* | node()" in line 3 of Figure 13, *Stylesheet for the Identity Transform*, on page 58, and the process continues.

You get the pattern. This goes on and on until the end of the document is reached. The template for the identity transform uses a pattern in which it calls itself to continue processing, and it continues processing until it runs out of XML nodes and attributes. It's just a quiet, efficient little copying machine.

The result is a fine, upstanding replica of the XML file we started with.

Why Use an Identity Transform?

What was the point of all that? How useful can a copy be?

It turns out the identity transform has a lot of uses. Sometimes we want to make a copy of a document with just a slight variation—changing British spellings to American spellings, for instance. Sometimes we want to make a copy of only some parts of a document while discarding other parts. I once needed to show all the tags and structure of a document that was causing me problems, but the content was proprietary, so I couldn't share it. I used an identity transform with slight variation to translate all letters and numbers to Xs, and off it went.

To make the point, let's try a few variations of our own. In the following sections we're going to:

- Remove all tags from a document
- Remove all text from a document
- Uppercase a specific word in the document
- Change all instances of one word to another word

We'll find that the identity transform serves as a starting point for a lot of helpful purposes. And with each new function we demand from the identity transform, we'll also learn some new XSLT techniques.

Variation on a Theme #1: Removing All Tags

One variation on the identity transform occurs when we want to remove all the tags from the document. It sounds a bit drastic, but it does happen: you might want to run the text through a voice translator, for instance, or you may need to prepare the text for an audio transcription. You may simply want a list of text values in a file for parsing by some other software that works better with text than with XML.

In any case, stripping the tags out is a piece of cake. We'll just need to add one template to act as an exception to the template that copies everything.

Let's start with an XML file that will run nicely in a browser (see Figure 14, *XSLT Code for an Acknowledgements Web Page*, on page 62

Sure, it's XHTML, but that's XML, too, so it works.

Notice that the second line of this XML file points to identity.xsl. If you open this file in a browser (and the identity.xsl file is in the same directory as the XML file), the stylesheet in identity.xsl is invoked. This stylesheet contains the identity transform, so the output looks like Figure 15, *The Output from the Identity Transform in the Browser*, on page 62.

The XSL stylesheet transforms the XML into a perfect copy of itself, as we saw in the previous section. The resulting XHTML appears in the browser with all the text formatted as it should be.

to-identity/acknowledgement1.xhtml

```
<?xml version='1.0' encoding='UTF-8'?>
<?xml-stylesheet type="text/xsl" href="identity.xsl"?>
<html xmlns="http://www.w3.org/1999/xhtml">
  <head>
    <meta http-equiv="Content-Type" content="text/html; charset=UTF-8" />
    <title>Acknowledgements</title>
  </head>
  <body>
    <h1 class="acknowledgements" id="d24e12098">Acknowledgements</h1>
    <ul>
      <li>Mary Shelley</li>
      <li>E.A. Poe</li>
      <li>Jules Verne</li>
      <li>Sir A.C. Doyle</li>
    </ul>
  </body>
</html>
```

Figure 14—XSLT Code for an Acknowledgements Web Page

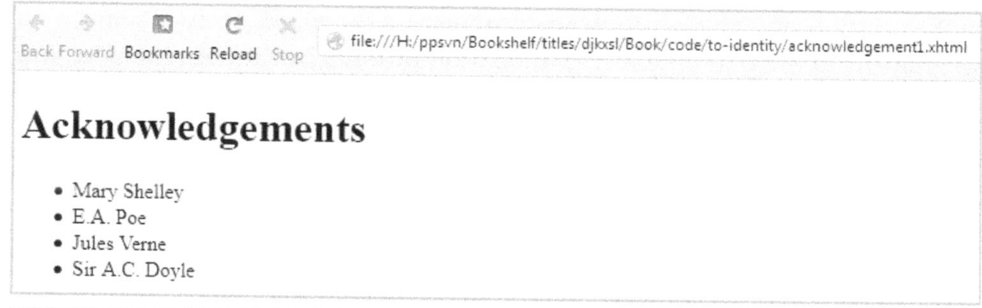

Figure 15—The Output from the Identity Transform in the Browser

Suppose we want to count the number of words in the text, or we need a version to give to someone who will read it for an audio book. All we want is the text. To get that, we'll make our transformation a copy operation, but with a slight difference from the identity transform: it will drop all the tags during the copy process.

So let's modify our identity transform to get that working (see Figure 16, *A Stylesheet to Strip Tags from XML*, on page 63.

It's similar to the identity transform, but with a difference. Check out the differences between this piece of code and Figure 13, *Stylesheet for the Identity Transform*, on page 58. As you can see, the first template looks like to-identity/acknowledgement2.xsl

```
Line 1 <?xml version="1.0" encoding="utf-8"?>
-      <xsl:stylesheet xmlns:xsl="http://www.w3.org/1999/XSL/Transform"
-        version="1.0">
-        <xsl:template match="/ | text()">
5          <xsl:copy>
-            <xsl:apply-templates select="* | text()"/>
-          </xsl:copy>
-        </xsl:template>
-
10        <xsl:template match="*">
-            <xsl:apply-templates select="* | text()"/>
-        </xsl:template>
-
-      </xsl:stylesheet>
```

Figure 16—A Stylesheet to Strip Tags from XML

the identity transform, but with a change to the match= and select= attributes. And then we've added a second template that matches on the asterisk (*), but doesn't make a copy of anything.

(If you want to learn more about wildcards right this red-hot minute, you can skip ahead to *Wildcards and General Representations for Nodes*, on page 97 —but come back straightly.)

We use * instead of node() because node() includes text nodes, and we want to distinguish between text nodes and element nodes. The * matches only elements, not text nodes. So we split up that node() from the previous example into * and text().

Let's go through it in detail to understand what we've accomplished, and how it works.

In line 4 of our tag-remover, we're now matching on the document root ("/") or any text node ("text()"). Before, we used *node()* to represent the root node, element nodes, and text nodes, because we wanted to treat all those kinds of nodes the same way—we just wanted to copy them. Now we want to treat the element nodes differently, so we discard *node()* from the match and we substitute / and *text()*. These are the two kinds of nodes we want to continue copying.

We've also discarded the @* from the match, because if we're not going to copy elements, we certainly don't need to copy attributes. And since there is nothing inside an attribute, we don't need to process them, either.

In line 6, our <xsl:apply-templates> tag has a new select= value. It includes *text()*, but it also includes *, the two of them separated by a pipe. As we mentioned, the * is a wildcard for XML elements. So now we're telling the XSL processor, "Apply any templates that match the element nodes or text nodes that you find within the current context."

In the last version, we had only one template. In this version, we have two templates. Now, when the XSLT processor finds an element in the document, it will find the new template in the stylesheet that matches elements (the one on line 10). And when it processes that template it won't have the <xsl:copy> instruction. Instead, it finds only the <xsl:apply-templates> on line 11.

The XSLT processor goes off and finds a template to match whatever it finds next—element or text node. If it's a text node, the XSLT processor finds a matching template on line 4. If it's an element, the match is with the template on line 10, which doesn't perform a copy—so the element is stripped. The templates continue churning through the XML document, as before, as long as the XSLT processor continues to find matches.

With the tags stripped out, you'll see this in the browser:

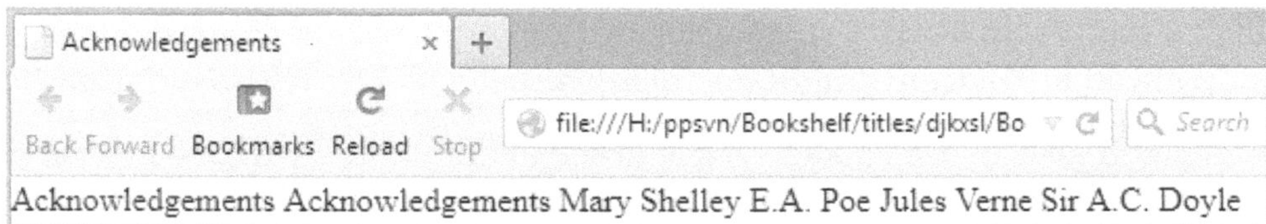

Success! None of that extraneous XHTML formatting for us.

Okay, that was fun. We did something interesting with the identity transform. And now there shouldn't be many surprises when we see the template that strips out text in the next section.

Variation on a Theme #2: Omitting Content

In an inverse situation from stripping out tags, suppose we need to strip out the text from a document. Maybe we need help troubleshooting our markup, but the content is confidential. Maybe we want to set up a template for use by other systems (or even human beings). We'd like a general method to remove all the text from the document. That sounds like a variation on the identity transform, to me.

Before I show you my answer, can you give it a try? I'll give you a hint: you're going to need to use *, @*, and text() in your matches, and you're going to

Template Matching as Functional Programming

Comparing the simple identity transform with this example, you can see that we haven't really given the XSLT processor many instructions of what to do. We've described conditions under which the XSLT processor is to take actions (with the match= attributes). In one condition we've told it to make a copy of an element then keep processing, and in another condition we've told it just to keep processing. We know nothing about when those conditions will arise, so we haven't specified any order in which to handle those conditions.

This sort of programming is called *declarative* or *functional* programming. In the first stylesheet we only had one condition; in the second stylesheet we defined two conditions, and related actions. We haven't actually told the XSLT processor *how* to do its work—and in fact, different XSLT processors will accomplish these instructions in different ways.

This type of programming provides numerous advantages over old-school, *imperative* programming where you have to tell the computer how to do its work. Given the complexity and unpredictability of XML, it's the perfect approach for XSLT.

want a template that doesn't copy the text. It's not that different from the example in Figure 16, *A Stylesheet to Strip Tags from XML*, on page 63.

How did it work for you? Here's what I did:

to-identity/acknowledgement3.xsl

```
Line 1 <?xml version="1.0" encoding="utf-8"?>
-      <xsl:stylesheet xmlns:xsl="http://www.w3.org/1999/XSL/Transform"
-        version="1.0">
-        <xsl:template match="/ | * | @*">
5          <xsl:copy>
-            <xsl:apply-templates select="* | @* | text()"/>
-          </xsl:copy>
-        </xsl:template>
-
10        <xsl:template match="text()">
-            <xsl:apply-templates select=" * | @* | text()"/>
-        </xsl:template>
-
-      </xsl:stylesheet>
```

Figure 17—A Stylesheet to Strip Text from a Document

See the difference? In line 4, we've removed text() and added * and @* so the elements and attributes get copied. And in line 10, we've matched on text() in the template that doesn't do any copying. So now the elements and attributes are output, but the text is not. If you're processing the file in the browser, you should see a list of bullets, but nothing else.

In both templates we've used `<xsl:apply-templates>` with `select=` attributes that direct the XSLT processor to look for templates that match elements, attributes, or text. Only the `match=` values and the `<xsl:copy>` tags are different between the two templates.

You'll also note that in line 6 we aren't selecting for the root element (/) any more. We already matched the root the first time through the template, and since there's only one root, we don't have to select for it any more.

We've taken the identity transform a little way down the road, but there's lots more. For instance, suppose we want to keep the tags *and* the text, but we need to alter the text a little. That sounds like another variation on the identity transform waiting to happen.

Variation on a Theme #3: Using a Function to Uppercase the Text

Leaving out content was simple. Let's take a look at something a bit harder: changing the text content. Because, you know, writers, editors, marketing gurus, management, customers, and standard committees always seem to be changing their minds about how to say things. Chances are you're going to need to do a variety of things with content: add it, remove it, tweak the case, swap words, the works.

In this section, we're going to make one particular kind of change: we're going to change words in a certain tag to be all uppercase letters.

As part of the solution, we'll learn a new type of XSLT mechanism: the XSLT *function*. An XSLT function is an operator that performs some work and returns a value. See *Functions*, on page 109 and Appendix 2, *Function and Expression Operator Reference*, on page 245 for more of the lowdown on functions.

XSLT 1.0 has only a few rudimentary functions for string manipulation. The good news is that the available functions are adequate for most problems, if we apply the right techniques.

Here's the current problem: we have an XML file full of terms that are used in a technical document. One of the sections is called *admonitions*, which contains all the standardized terms for warnings, dangers, cautions, and the like. We might have several files like this, one for each language the document is translated into. (We'll only deal with the English language, since the principle here will be the same for all languages.) An abbreviated version of the file looks like this:

to-identity/uppercase1.xml

```
<?xml version='1.0' encoding='UTF-8'?>
<?xml-stylesheet type="text/xsl" href="identity.xsl"?>
<terms>
<proprietary>
  <product>FabBooster</product>
  <feature>Sir Prize</feature>
</proprietary>
<admonitions language="en-us">
  <term name="caution">Caution</term>
  <term name="warning">Warning</term>
  <term name="danger">Danger</term>
  <term name="uh-oh">Now You've Done It</term>
</admonitions>
</terms>
```

And, just to satisfy our curiosity, if we run this file against the identity transform and view it in the browser, the output will look like this:

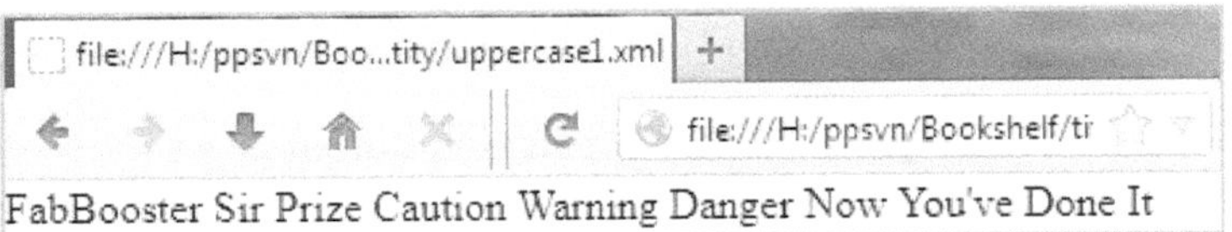

All that looks fine, but today just isn't our day. The manager from tech pubs comes along and says, "We need the admonitions always to be in uppercase so it will get people's attention. What can you do?"

No problem. We have the identity transform and a function called translate() to take care of it.

The XML file has two areas where <term> is used, so we'll need to be careful —if we uppercase all of those proprietary terms, someone will pitch a fit about it. So in this example, we'll need a way to make a template that selects for an element that has specific ancestors. (This is another example of how we tell XSLT what we want done, but not necessarily how to do it.)

As we've done before, let's have a look at the solution then talk about why it worked (see Figure 18, *Uppercasing Admonitions*, on page 68). We point our XML file to this stylesheet, and the result make the tech pubs manager happy (see Figure 19, *The Uppercased Output*, on page 68) to-identity/uppercase2.xsl

```
1  <?xml version="1.0" encoding="utf-8"?>
2  <xsl:stylesheet xmlns:xsl="http://www.w3.org/1999/XSL/Transform" version="1.0">
3    <xsl:template match="/ | * | @*">
4      <xsl:copy>
5        <xsl:apply-templates select="* | @* | text()"/>
6      </xsl:copy>
7    </xsl:template>
8
9    <xsl:template match="admonitions/term/text()">
10     <xsl:value-of select="translate(.,'abcdefghijklmnopqrstuvwzxyz',
11          'ABCDEFGHIJKLMNOPQRSTUVWXYZ')"/>
12   </xsl:template>
13 </xsl:stylesheet>
```

Figure 18—Uppercasing Admonitions

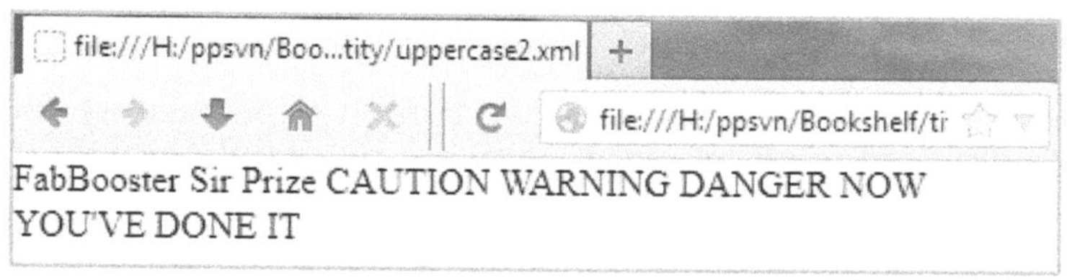

Figure 19—The Uppercased Output

The first template is the spitting image of the identity transform we ran in Figure 17, *A Stylesheet to Strip Text from a Document*, on page 65, where we completely omitted the text. It's the second template where things take a completely different turn.

Starting at line 9, the template looks similar to before, but with a difference: we've added information about the context of the text that we're looking for. Instead of saying that we just want all text, we're now saying that we want text that is in a <term> tag, and that tag has to be inside an <admonitions> tag. This type of arrangement is called an XPath node test, and it gets used in a lot of places in XSLT stylesheets. For the moment, though, all we need to know is that by matching on *admonitions/term/text()*, the only text this template will match will be the admonitions terms, not the proprietary terms.

We've matched our terms in the admonitions area, but now what do we do with them? The broken line of code that ends in line 11 appears to do the job, but what the heck's with all that alphabet soup?

First, we have the <xsl:value-of> instruction, which we've seen before. It's just going to give us the value of whatever is specified by the select= attribute. In this case, the attribute contains an XSLT function that will give us a value.

The translate() function takes three arguments, like so:

```
translate(string, string, string)
```

The first argument is the string to be translated. The second argument is a string containing the list of characters to be found in the first string. And the third argument is a list of characters to be substituted for the characters specified by the second argument. The position of the substitute character in the third argument matches the position of the selected character in the second argument. In our example, any *a* in the first argument will be replaced by *A*, any *b* by *B*, and so forth. The translation works only by single characters; you can't substitute *AA* for *a*, for instance. (You'll need another trick for that!)

Given the match in line 9 and the translation in line 11, our work is done. Everything is copied exactly the way it is except for text nodes that are within <term> tags inside the <admonitions> tag. Just the way we want it. So it's time to move on to the next example, right?

Well, wait a second. What about those text tags that aren't in the admonitions section? We don't have a template that matches any other text() nodes, so how did the text get processed into the result document?

Ah, our old friend the default template raises its hand in the back of the room. We always forget the quiet ones who do their work behind the scenes, don't we?

Variation on a Theme #4: Changing One Word to Another

We've seen the identity template make some pretty sweeping changes, but how about changing just a single word in a particular element?

You've seen it happen before. The Marketing department has decided at the last minute that *Vorblatz* is not a great name for the company's outstanding new feature. Now they want to call it *ForeKast*. Vorblatz appears throughout the text, within different XML elements, like <p>, <div>, and <note>. And to make matters worse, the feature code can't change in the database, so any <part-number> tag still needs to start with the prefix *Vorblatz*.

We could have easily handled this with a regular expression, but since the substitution is dependent on the XML tags, it's useful to have an XML-context-aware solution. There's nothing for it but to write a stylesheet to handle that little problem. Let's check it out, then figure out how it works:

...And May the Best Match Win

What would have happened if we had our template that matched admonitions/term/text() and another template that matched only text()? Both templates match text nodes—who wins?

In all cases, the template that provides the most specific match to a given node will take priority over less specific matches. In this case, the text inside admonitions/term would get the match with the admonitions/term/text() template.

In some cases, priority between the matches can't be resolved. In these cases, the XSLT processor will flag the ambiguity, and it will be up to us to create more distinction between the matches. We'll probably use XPath statements and expressions to do so—we'll learn these as we go along.

All of which is to say, we can set up a number of parallel templates with similar, but slightly different matches, and the XSLT processor sorts it all out for us.

to-identity/change-text1.xsl

```
<?xml version="1.0" encoding="utf-8"?>
<xsl:stylesheet xmlns:xsl="http://www.w3.org/1999/XSL/Transform" version="1.0">
  <xsl:template match="/ | * | @*">
    <xsl:copy>
      <xsl:apply-templates select="* | @* | text()"/>
    </xsl:copy>
  </xsl:template>

  <xsl:template match="text()">
    <xsl:choose>
      <xsl:when test="contains(.,'Vorblatz') and not(parent::part-number)">
        <xsl:value-of select="substring-before(.,'Vorblatz')"/>
        <xsl:text>ForeKast</xsl:text>
        <xsl:value-of select="substring-after(.,'Vorblatz')"/>
      </xsl:when>
      <xsl:otherwise>
        <xsl:copy>
          <xsl:apply-templates select="* | @* | text()"/>
        </xsl:copy>
      </xsl:otherwise>
    </xsl:choose>
  </xsl:template>
</xsl:stylesheet>
```

That's a lot of new pieces to learn, but you'll find that you use this technique to solve a lot of different problems in XML manipulation. So let's check it out.

First, we see that the first template repeats our basic identity transform pattern. This is starting to feel like *Groundhog Day.*[1]

But what happens inside the template at line 9 is a pattern we haven't seen before. Here we encounter an <xsl:choose> tag, and within that tag we do several new things.

With <xsl:choose>, all sorts of new programming possibilities open up. The <xsl:choose> instruction can make choices based on different conditions that you set within test= attributes. The <xsl:choose> instruction can contain two types of XSLT instructions:

- <xsl:when>, of which there must be at least one. We can add as many of these as we need inside the <xsl:choose>. The test= attribute is required; it contains an expression that evaluates to a Boolean *true* or *false*.

  When the expression evaluates to *true*, the XSLT processor executes the contents of the <xsl:when> instruction *as long as no previous <xsl:when> instruction evaluates to true.* The trick to the <xsl:choose> instruction is that only the first <xsl:when> that evaluates to true is executed; after that, the XSLT processor skips to the next instruction after the closing <xsl:choose/> in the template.

- <xsl:otherwise>, which is optional. The contents of this instruction are executed only if none of the previous <xsl:when> instructions are executed.

  If <xsl:otherwise> is not present and none of the <xsl:when> instructions are true, nothing gets executed inside the <xsl:choose> instruction.

In our example, the <xsl:when> has a test= expression that is slightly complicated. Basically, it's saying, "If the current context contains the string *Vorblatz*, and the parent element is *not* a <part-number> tag, evaluate to true."

The first part of the expression, *contains(.,'Vorblatz'),* is a function. We saw a function before when we did our uppercasing transform, but that was the translate() function, and it returned a string. The contains() function simply returns a boolean value, true or false, based on its arguments.

contains(.,'Vorblatz') has two arguments: the first argument represents the string in which we will search for the target. In this case, the string is represented by the period (.), which is a shorthand way of saying "the current context." Our context is the text matched by the template.

---

1. http://en.wikipedia.org/wiki/Groundhog_Day_%28film%29

The second argument follows the comma and gives the target string that the processor looks for inside the first argument. Here the target is 'Vorblatz'. (The single quotes tell the XSLT processor that the argument is a literal string.) If *Vorblatz* occurs inside the current text, the first part of the overall expression is true.

The second part of the expression, which appears after the and, is also a function, the not() function. If the expression inside the not() function is true, the value of the function is false, and vice-versa. There's nothing tricky about it. In this case, the expression inside the function is parent::part-number. And guess what: this is another piece of XPath that we're using inside XSLT. The parent:: is an *axis* that points to the parent node of the current context, and the part after it says what sort of node that parent is expected to be. (An axis is one of thirteen types of directional pointers in XPath that we'll learn about later.)

Add it up, and the test= attribute gives a condition that must be true for the <xsl:when> instruction to execute: "If the current context (which is text) contains the string *Vorblatz*, and the parent element is *not* <part-number>, evaluate to *true*." Just what we said we needed.

So what happens when it's true? Let's take a look at those three lines of code inside the <xsl:when>:

```
Line 1 <xsl:value-of select="substring-before(.,'Vorblatz')"/>
     2 <xsl:text>ForeKast</xsl:text>
     3 <xsl:value-of select="substring-after(.,'Vorblatz')"/>
```

We want to replace "Vorblatz" with "ForeKast," so we need to do some slicing and dicing on the text string. We'll output the text before "Vorblatz," then we'll substitute "ForeKast," and then we'll output the text after "Vorblatz."

To get that output, we need two more functions: substring-before() and substring-after(). We use the <xsl:value-of> instruction to—you guessed it—output the value of whatever is selected by the select= attribute. In line 1, the substring-before() function starts with its first argument (again, in this case, the period (.), then it returns everything from the first argument that appears before the first occurrence of the second argument ("Vorblatz"). So part one of our fiendish plot of slicing and dicing is accomplished.

In part two of the plot (line 2), we simply use the <xsl:text> instruction to output, literally, whatever its contents are. <xsl:text> preserves whitespace inside it, however many leading or trailing spaces, however may line returns. But it's also a good way to omit unwanted whitespace. Since we're taking everything before and after "Vorblatz", all we want to substitute is "ForeKast". We use

<xsl:text> because without it we might get some extra spaces or line returns. Extra whitespace probably wouldn't matter, but let's be precise and not introduce any trouble we don't want.

Finally, part three happens in line 3. The substring-after() function works just like the substring-before() function, except it takes everything in the string after the first occurrence of the second argument.

And now the <xsl:when> instruction has done the substitution we wanted.

If the string doesn't contain the forbidden "Vorblatz," we have our <xsl:otherwise> instruction to take care of it. Check out its contents starting at line 16 in code on page 70. Look familiar? Yep. All we're doing is copying the string as is, because it doesn't need any further manipulation. Our work here is done.

This type of substitution can be placed in a template of its own and called from other templates as well—the example in *xsl:message*, on page 232 shows a more convenient (and advanced) form than what is shown here. But hey—we're still learning.

What We Did

We could play with variations on the identity transform for a long time and not exhaust the possibilities. As it happens, we'll see it again when we start doing recursive templates. For now, though, we've covered a lot of ground, so let's do a recap to see what we've learned.

- We learned the basic pattern of the identity transform.
- We learned how to create templates to process exceptions to the identity transform, relying on more specific matches than those in the core identity transform template.
- We learned new tokens we can use in the match attribute, including wildcards for referencing the root (/), elements (*), and attributes (@*). We also learned about using the pipe (|) for a node-set union operator in match statements.
- We learned what functions are, and we learned about a few of them: translate(), contains(), not(), substring-before(), and substring-after().
- We learned new elements:
  - <xsl:copy>, to output a copy of the current context
  - <xsl:text>, to output text with control over the whitespace

  - <xsl:choose>, a structure for making conditional branches to the execution of a template
  - <xsl:when>, whose test= attribute specifies a condition for execution of the contents of the <xsl:when> tag
  - <xsl:otherwise>, which acts as an optional catch-all for the <xsl:choose> if none of <xsl:when> conditions are true
- We learned about matching on the most specific pattern when the same node type is matched in different templates.
- We learned how to extend the identity transform pattern to do special processing on specific nodes or node types when the rest of the XML can be copied verbatim.

One thing we didn't do was to set up special processing for two or three different elements or node types at the same time. I'm sure you can imagine how it would be done, though, right? Extra templates, new match statements for the nodes we're interested in, and off it goes.

Why not give it a try? For instance, if I told you that the space in "Sir Prize" was a mistake and needed to be removed at the same time you were uppercasing the admonitions, what would you do? Sounds like a substring function or two might be in order, what do you think? Go for it!

The identity transform allows us to do a lot of processing with a minimal set of tools, but it's not always going to be that easy. Sometimes we're going to need to do major overhauls on the original document to get our desired output. So it's time to start moving into some heavy lifting: the wonderful world of reorganizing XML. The output order often strays from the order of the source XML document, and reorganizing all that content can become amazingly complicated.

I was not yet familiar with all the weapons, but my great familiarity with similar earthly weapons made me an apt pupil, and I progressed in a very satisfactory manner.

> *Edgar Rice Burroughs,* A Princess of Mars

CHAPTER 6

Changing the Structure and Order of Content

One of the trickier parts of using XSLT is creating an output document in which the order of the content is significantly different than the order of the source document. The more difference in order between input and output, the more complex the stylesheet. Yep, that means we're about to hit one of the hard parts.

Operations we might want to perform on the order of our content include:

- Flatten the structure
- Deepen the structure
- Add structure to flat lists
- promote child elements to siblings
- Change the order of tags

Methods we'll use to reorder the content include:

- The careful matching and selection of elements in the xsl:template's match= attribute and the xsl:apply-templates's select= attribute
- The use of the <xsl:element> tag to create new elements where we need them
- The use of the XPath syntax, which will allow us to address any part of an XML document from any other part of the document. (We won't learn all of XPath in this chapter, but we'll get a heavy dose of it in the next chapter.)

As mentioned, we're approaching some difficult parts, so the examples will take longer to cover. We'll divide this subject into two chapters: one without

XPath, and one with XPath, and they'll be separated by a chapter on XPath. When we come back to the subject of re-ordering content, we'll have a shiny new set of XPath tools.

First, let's flatten out some excessively structured XML.

Tidying Up Verbose XML

It's a common problem: the data coming at you is a wonderful, complete resource chock full of informational goodness, but it's so overloaded with structure and data, it's completely inaccessible to the average reader. Maybe it's something like this:

orderorder/accounts.xml

```
<?xml version='1.0' encoding='UTF-8'?>
<accounts>
  <account id="100007">
    <name>
      <first>Jorge</first>
      <middle>Luis</middle>
      <last>Borges</last>
    </name>
    <transactions>
      <transaction id="TR-765432198">
        <date>
          <year>1984</year>
          <month>June</month>
          <day>6</day>
          <time>12:00:00</time>
        </date>
        <amount>$14.99</amount>
        <product>B-5643A</product>
      </transaction>
      <transaction id="TR-654321987">
        <date>
          <year>1966</year>
          <month>July</month>
          <day>23</day>
          <time>23:47:12</time>
        </date>
        <amount>$12.95</amount>
        <product>A-2345B</product>
      </transaction>
    </transactions>
  </account>
</accounts>
```

You can find a longer version of this code with multiple <account> tags in http://media.pragprog.com/titles/djkxsl/code/orderorder/multiple_accounts.xml if you want to try it yourself. Download the file, put it in a directory, then in the same directory create an XSLT file called streamline.xsl. We'll fill out this XSLT file in the following sections.

Take a look at the XML file: that's a lot of tags for a little information. It's great to have that level of granularity in some cases, but in others we probably don't need separate entries for month, day, year, and time of day. If our main interest is in listing transactions for an account, we might be able to simplify the structure to make sorting and data identification a lot easier. Let's see how we might map this data to a simpler form of XML:

```
<accounts>
  <account id="123457" name="Jorge Luis Borges">
    <transaction id="TR-765432198">
      <date>June 6, 1984, 12:00:00</date>
      <amount>$14.99</amount>
      <product>B-5643A</product>
    </transaction>
    <transaction id="TR-654321987">
      <date>July 23, 1966, 23:47:12</date>
      <amount>$12.95</amount>
      <product>A-2345B</product>
    </transaction>
  </account>
</accounts>
```

Ah, much better. This is easier to read, and the data more to the point of our interest.

So what did we need to do to get the simpler form? Once thing we need to do is move the name elements into a single attribute for the <account> tag. Another is to remove the <transactions> tag entirely. And the third thing is to concatenate all those date elements into a single value for the <date> tag. These actions are typical methods of simplifying XML data structures.

Let's tackle this one template at a time.

Moving Element Values into Attributes

First we need an entry point into the file, so we'll set up a template to match on <accounts>. Inside that template, we'll output the <accounts> tag the same as it was in the source, then we'll instruct the processor to apply templates, like so:

```
<xsl:template match="/accounts">
  <accounts>
    <xsl:apply-templates/>
  </accounts>
</xsl:template>
```

We're processing the next set of tags inside the <accounts> tag, so what's the next template we need to build? See if you can get ahead of me on this one.

```
<xsl:template match="account">
</xsl:template>
```

Right. But we need some content in this one. Taking a look at the output we wanted, we know that the <account> tag we output is going to look a little different than the tag we started with. In particular, that name= attribute needs to be constructed from the contents of the <name> tag. To do this, we're going to use the <xsl:element> tag along with the <xsl:attribute> tag to create the new name= attribute. Then, to fill in the value of the attribute, we'll need to get the parts of the name from the <name>. The construction of this element and attribute looks like so:

```
<xsl:template match="account">
  <xsl:element name="account">
    <xsl:attribute name="name">
      <xsl:value-of select="name/first"/>
      <xsl:text> </xsl:text>
      <xsl:value-of select="name/middle"/>
      <xsl:text> </xsl:text>
      <xsl:value-of select="name/last"/>
  </xsl:attribute>
</xsl:element>
```

Figure 20—The template for creating <account>

Since our current context is <account>, we can refer to the descendants of that tag with the path syntax we mentioned in Chapter 2, *XSLT in Action*, on page 13. That's how we can get the values of the first, middle, and last names. Notice, too, that we have to add the spaces between the parts of the name ourselves, using the <xsl:text> tag. And all of it gets wrapped up nicely into the name= attribute in our output.

Did you also remember to put the id= attribute from the original back into the <account> tag in the output? How about adding the <xsl:apply-templates> tag to keep the process flowing? If you remembered all that, your template probably looks a good bit like the one in Figure 21, *The Account Template with the id Attribute*, on page 79.

We added the select="transactions" to the <xsl:apply-templates> tag because we had already processed what we wanted out of the <name> tag and we didn't want to process it again.

We've got that. Now need to remove that useless <transactions> tag.

```
<xsl:template match="account">
  <xsl:element name="account">
    <xsl:attribute name="id">
      <xsl:value-of select="@id"/>
    </xsl:attribute>
    <xsl:attribute name="name">
      <xsl:value-of select="name/first"/>
      <xsl:text> </xsl:text>
      <xsl:value-of select="name/middle"/>
      <xsl:text> </xsl:text>
      <xsl:value-of select="name/last"/>
    </xsl:attribute>
    <xsl:apply-templates select="transactions"/>
  </xsl:element>
</xsl:template>
```

Figure 21—The Account Template with the id= Attribute

Flattening the Structure of the Source

This one is relatively easy—we saw clues about how to do this in Chapter 4, *Beginning with the End: Creating Output*, on page 43.

We're going to discard the <transactions> tag. So, just like we did with the <name> tag earlier, we can forget the template to match on <transactions>, right? We're only interested in the <transaction> tags, after all...

Okay, I thought I'd try to sneak one past you. Yes, we do need a template to match on <transactions>, even if we're not keeping it, because we need to process its descendants. The template is dead simple, though, because we're not going to create any output for the <transactions> tag itself:

```
<xsl:template match="transactions">
  <xsl:apply-templates/>
</xsl:template>
```

And, *voilà*, we took a whole layer out of our XML hierarchy. Now we will process the individual <transaction> tags, and the new ones we create will be the immediate children of <account>. Nothing to it. That's the whole secret of taking a layer out of the structure: just process the tag, but don't create anything for it.

We could also have made <xsl:apply-templates select="transactions/transaction"/> above, omitting the template for transactions completely. That would work here—but if we had more elements types inside transactions, we'd be better off doing it the way we did it here. Also, by omitting the transactions part from the match for the transaction template, we've allowed <template> to be matched in contexts other than <transactions>, if they exist.

Next, we need to tighten up that <date> tag. We'll need to rearrange the contents a bit, but that shouldn't be a problem. Let's have a look.

Merging Elements Up into Higher Elements

Another method of streamlining XML is to merge a group of lower-level elements into a higher-level element, like we did with the name= attribute. This type of merging is not necessarily great for storing data, but it's often used for presenting strings of related text in HTML and other output.

There's nothing fancy about creating the new version of the <transaction> tags. The template for this tag will look a fair bit like our template for <account>, except the parts of the date will need to be rearranged a bit, and they will go into the <date> element rather than an attribute. We'll also need to preserve the <amount> and <product> tags in the <transaction> tag.

One thing you might notice is that this part of the example does not really introduce any concepts you haven't already seen. So before I present the final solution, why not try your hand at it and see what you come up with.

Here's what I've got:

orderorder/streamline.xsl

```
<xsl:stylesheet xmlns:xsl="http://www.w3.org/1999/XSL/Transform" version="1.0">
  <xsl:template match="/accounts">
    <accounts>
      <xsl:apply-templates/>
    </accounts>
  </xsl:template>

  <xsl:template match="account">
    <xsl:element name="account">
      <xsl:attribute name="id">
        <xsl:value-of select="@id"/>
      </xsl:attribute>
      <xsl:attribute name="name">
        <xsl:value-of select="name/first"/>
        <xsl:text> </xsl:text>
        <xsl:value-of select="name/middle"/>
        <xsl:text> </xsl:text>
        <xsl:value-of select="name/last"/>
      </xsl:attribute>
      <xsl:apply-templates select="transactions"/>
    </xsl:element>
  </xsl:template>
```

```
  <xsl:template match="transactions">
    <xsl:apply-templates/>
  </xsl:template>

  <xsl:template match="transaction">
    <xsl:element name="transaction">
      <xsl:apply-templates/>
    </xsl:element>
  </xsl:template>

  <xsl:template match="date">
    <xsl:element name="date">
      <xsl:value-of select="month"/>
      <xsl:text> </xsl:text>
      <xsl:value-of select="day"/>
      <xsl:text>, </xsl:text>
      <xsl:value-of select="year"/>
      <xsl:text> </xsl:text>
      <xsl:value-of select="time"/>
    </xsl:element>
  </xsl:template>

  <xsl:template match="amount">
    <xsl:element name="amount">
      <xsl:value-of select="."/>
    </xsl:element>
  </xsl:template>

  <xsl:template match="product">
    <xsl:element name="product">
      <xsl:value-of select="."/>
    </xsl:element>
  </xsl:template>
</xsl:stylesheet>
```

As you can see, we've flattened the date considerably by concatenating the values inside a singe <date> tag. We used <xsl:value-of> to get the contents of the different date-related fields, but we could have used <xsl:apply-templates>—the default template would have picked up the text values for us. You'll also notice that the values in the output date field no longer match the order of values in our input document. Sweet!

Changing Elements from Children to Siblings

Sometimes we'll need to move content out of its parent tag so it either follows or precedes the parent. Let's take a case where we have a list of configuration values in pairs, with one value as an attribute of a parent element, and one value as the text of a child element, as in Figure 22, *XML with code Attribute*, on page 82.

```
<productlist>
  <product code="AZ123">
    <name>Wayback Machine</name>
  </product>
  <product code="BY234">
    <name>Sonic Screwdriver</name>
  </product>
  <product code="CX345">
    <name>Light Saber</name>
  </product>
  <product code="DW456">
    <name>Tricorder</name>
  </product>
</productlist>
```

Figure 22—XML with code= Attribute

What we'd like to do is get this into a simple HTML definition list, like this:

```
<dl>
  <dt>AZ123</dt>
  <dd>Wayback Machine</dd>
  <dt>BY234</dt>
  <dd>Sonic Screwdriver</dd>
  <dt>CX345</dt>
  <dd>Light Saber</dd>
  <dt>DW456</dt>
  <dd>Tricorder</dd>
</dl>
```

The two lists are structurally different: in the first list, the product name is a child tag, in the second, the product name follows the product code as a sibling. In our typical template arrangement, we would be tempted to do this for processing the <product> tag:

```
<xsl:template match="product">
  <dt>
    <xsl:value-of select="@code"/>
    <xsl:apply-templates/>
  </dt>
</xsl:template>
```

We would then create a template for <name>, which would wrap the <dd> tag around the contents of the <name>...

But that won't work! The processing for <name> would make <dd> a child of <dt>, and that would be an unfortunate mistake. What we want is more like Figure 23, *Moving the <dd> Outside the <dt>*, on page 83.

```
<xsl:template match="product">
  <dt>
    <xsl:value-of select="@code"/>
  </dt>
  <xsl:apply-templates/>
</xsl:template>
```

Figure 23—Moving the <dd> Outside the <dt>

The <xsl:apply-templates> tag is still operating within the context of the <product> tag, so it will still apply templates that match the children of <product>. But the structure of the output will be different, because now we've moved the <xsl:apply-templates> tag outside the <dt> tag.

We now add another template that matches on <name>:

```
<xsl:template match="name">
   <dd>
    <xsl:apply-templates/>
   </dd>
  </xsl:template>
```

Now that <xsl:apply-templates> in the previous template finds the <name> tag and sends the processor to our second template. The second template places <dd> tags around the content of <name> and outputs it following the <dt> created by the first template.

It's a subtle move, but it's another fine arrow in the quiver of methods for manipulating structure. In complex templates, you may find it helpful to spend a little time analyzing the structure of your output versus the structure of your input to ensure that the templates are indeed creating output in the right place.

For myself, I can say that this particular arrow once helped me solve a long, difficult puzzle in reconfiguring a lengthy set of stylesheets in the DITA Open Toolkit.[1] As a result, I was able to allow customers to create landscape-oriented pages at any point in their PDF documents—something that apparently had not been done before. All from such a simple move!

Wrapping Tags in Other Tags

We actually saw this technique in the sections *Adding Tags and Attributes as Text*, on page 49 and *Adding Elements and Attributes Dynamically*, on

1. http://ditaopentoolkit.org/

page 52. To summarize what we did there: you can add elements as text or add them dynamically using the <xsl:element> tag.

In some cases we want to add a known element, in which case it's fine to use a text-based element. In other cases, we might not know the name of the element beforehand, in which case we'll need to use the <xsl:element> tag to generate the element with a name we derive from the situation.

In some cases, the new element might be wrapped around one or more elements we're inheriting from the source document. In a case like this, we'll want the new element to be wrapped around the code that generates the existing element(s). For example, suppose we have this:

```
<customer name="Edgar Allen Poe">
  <street>203 Amity Street</street>
  <city>Baltimore</city>
  <state>Maryland</state>
  <zip>21233</zip>
</customer>
```

Let's create a <name> tag, then wrap all those loose address elements in an <address> tag at the same level as <name>. All of it should still be contained in the <customer> tag. Give it a try—I suspect you've got this one already. Create an XML file with the contents shown above, then create an XSLT file with a stylesheet. Using our command-line approach (Chapter 6, *Changing the Structure and Order of Content*, on page 75), run the XSLT file against the XML file and see if you can get the following:

```
<customer>
  <name>Edgar Allan Poe</name>
  <address>
    <street>203 Amity Street</street>
    <city>Baltimore</city>
    <state>Maryland</state>
    <zip>21233</zip>
  </address>
</customer>
```

One way to do it is like this:

orderorder/customer.xsl

```
<xsl:stylesheet xmlns:xsl="http://www.w3.org/1999/XSL/Transform" version="1.0">
  <xsl:template match="/customer">
    <customer>
      <name><xsl:value-of select="@name"/></name>
      <address><xsl:apply-templates/></address>
    </customer>
  </xsl:template>
```

```
  <xsl:template match="street">
    <street><xsl:value-of select="."/></street>
  </xsl:template>

  <xsl:template match="city">
    <city><xsl:value-of select="."/></city>
  </xsl:template>

  <xsl:template match="state">
    <state><xsl:value-of select="."/></state>
  </xsl:template>

  <xsl:template match="zip">
    <zip><xsl:value-of select="."/></zip>
  </xsl:template>
</xsl:stylesheet>
```

Did you try it? The output won't look exactly like what we are after, but that's just a matter of line indents and line returns. The structure of the XML is what we're after, and that looks right on target.

Later we'll learn a shortcut so all those templates for the different address elements can be rolled into one, but this will work for now.

As you can see in this example, the beginning and end tags surround the <xsl:apply-templates/> tag, enclosing the various existing tags as we had hoped.

What if we wanted to add a new tag between two tags instead of enclosing tags? Suppose we took our result XML and wanted to add <occupation> between <name> and <address>? We'd just put the additional tag between the <xsl:apply-templates> elements that process the other tags, making sure NOT to wrap the new element around anything else. In this instance, we know the customer's occupation ("mad poet"), so we do it the easy way. The template that matches on <customer> would now look like this:

```
<xsl:template match="/customer">
  <customer>
    <xsl:apply-templates select="name"/>
    <occupation>mad poet</occupation>
    <xsl:apply-templates select="address"/>
  </customer>
</xsl:template>
```

Then we would have templates matching <name> and <address> to fill in the rest of the tags. Go ahead and try this: whatever name you gave to your output file in the exercise above, use it as the input file for another XSLT transform you write. (You can do this kind of chaining of output files to input files all day—and sometimes there are good reasons for doing so, as we'll see in a later chapter.) Add the <occupation> tag, keeping all the other tags. Bonus points if you invert the order of the address elements!

There's no big deal to adding tags to the output. Think about where you want the new tag and what it wraps around (or doesn't), then create related tags around, inside, above, or below the new tag so it appears where you want. Sounds easy, right?

Good—because now we're going to move on to something a little trickier. Adding structure to a flat list of elements.

Adding structure to flat lists

I see it all the time: someone uses Microsoft Word without applying styles to anything. Section titles, figure titles, even the chapter headings are default paragraphs formatted to look like headings. Then the culprit, er, poor soul comes to me asking to convert it to an ebook. Sure, I can save the Word file as XML, but then I just get a long string of <p> tags. In the resulting ebook, all their lovingly hand-crafted headings look just like standard paragraphs.

Good thing I've got XSLT to whip it into shape.

Looking beyond my little problems, you're undoubtedly going to encounter data that needs additional structure imposed on it. A legacy file of undifferentiated tags is a common problem. They might be things you want to keep in the same order, but with different tags wrapped around them, or you might want to untangle unnecessary layers tags. Or we might need to move content so it's better organized for a given audience.

In the following sections, and in Chapter 8, *Using XPath to Change the Order of Documents*, on page 117, we'll see how to deal with all these types of problems.

Play It as It Lays

In this approach, we're going to address that problem I mentioned earlier, the undifferentiated <p> tags. This example addresses a more general situation: the order of the tags is okay, but we'd like to get them into a more appropriate structure.

Examples, Bad and Good

First, let's have a look at the drek...um...source file our associate has gifted us with:

orderorder/badlist.xml

```
<document>
 <p font-size="14pt" font-weight="bold">Grizzlies and People</p>
 <p font-size="10pt" font-weight="regular">Since the Ice Age,
   man has feared the great denizens of the north. But why is that?</p>
  <p font-size="12pt" font-weight="bold">Horribleness</p>
  <p font-size="10pt" font-weight="regular">Grizzlies are so horrible,
    they are named <emph>Ursus horribilis</emph>. 'Nuff said?</p>
  <p font-size="12pt" font-weight="bold">Largeness</p>
  <p font-size="10pt" font-weight="regular">Male grizzlies can average
    900 pounds and 9 feet tall. That's a lot of bear to feed, and they
    don't mind a little human in the diet!</p>
  <p font-size="12pt" font-weight="bold">Aggressiveness</p>
  <p font-size="10pt" font-weight="regular">Grizzlies are too large to
    escape danger by climbing trees; instead, they stand their ground.</p>
  <p font-size="10pt" font-weight="regular">All that being said,
    humans are still more dangerous than grizzly bears!</p>
</document>
```

That's pretty gnarly. In a well-structured XML file, we would like to see something more like this:

orderorder/grizzly-output.xml

```
<?xml version="1.0" encoding="UTF-8"?>
<chapter>
  <title>Grizzlies and People</title>
  <p>Since the Ice Age, man has feared the great denizens of the north.
    But why is that?</p>
  <section1>
    <title>Horribleness</title>
    <p>Grizzlies are so horrible, they are named <emph>Ursus horribilis</emph>.
      'Nuff said?</p>
  </section1>
  <section1>
    <title>Largeness</title>
    <p>Male grizzlies can average 900 pounds and 9 feet tall. That's a lot of bear
      to feed, and they don't mind a little human in the diet!</p>
  </section1>
  <section1>
    <title>Aggressiveness</title>
    <p>Grizzlies are too large to escape danger by climbing trees; instead, they
      stand their ground.</p>
  </section1>
  <p>All that being said, humans are still more dangerous than grizzly bears!</p>
</chapter>
```

Figure 24—The Output We Want for the Grizzly Essay

One advantage of XML like this is that it's much easier to maintain. Imagine someone confronted with the XML file in the first example, trying to put in all the font styles, sizes, and weights for each paragraph. Crazy talk!

Another advantage is that the structure is more explicit. Look at that last <p> tag in the first example. Does it belong to the secondary heading or the top heading? Who knows? When we restructure the XML, we're going to have some difficulties sorting it out.

But that's the hand we've been dealt, so let's get to work.

Starting with a Conceptual Approach

Before we leap into writing the stylesheet, let's take a little time to think through how we're going to approach this one. In general, a little advanced planning can go a long way toward resolving the problems.

What we need is a way to focus on the <p> tags that are headings, wrap some heading tags around those, and then within the heading tags, process only the following <p> tags that are actual text tags belonging within that section. That means we also have to keep track of what "this section" means.

We can select the <p> tags that follow a <p> tag with the font size of 12pt, for instance, but how do we know when to stop? To do that, we will want to check whether the text <p> tag in question comes after the <p> tag for our heading, but not after the <p> tag for the next heading. That means we'll somehow need a way of keeping track of which <p> tag with font-size="12pt" is which.

To do all this, we're going to introduce several new XSLT mechanisms and make use of them. Here's a quick rundown of the tools we'll need:

[ ]

: The square brackets [ ] create what is called a *predicate*. Predicates are added to node names to refine the description of the nodes being referred to. For example, if we want to select a <p> tag, but we only want the <p> tags where font-size="12pt", we can refine our selection like this:

```
<xsl:apply-templates select="p[@fontsize='12pt']"/>
```

We can enter a variety of expressions inside the predicate. For instance, you could just put the name of a node to test for its existence. (For instance, we would write @font-size for the font-size= attribute). If the XSLT processor finds a node where the expression evaluates to *true*, then the node is selected. You'll find predicates to be extremely useful, especially in a problem like our list of identical elements with small differences in attributes or contents.

not()

not() is an XSLT function. We ran into not() functions in the section *Variation on a Theme #3: Using a Function to Uppercase the Text*, on page 66 earlier in this book.

generate-id()

The generate-id() function has a single purpose: it generates a unique value for an XML node when the document is processed. Every node in document generates a different value. The node for which the value is given is defined by an expression inside the parentheses. If the parentheses are empty, the current node is used.

Using generate-id() gives us a way to identify any given XML node in the document with a unique value. We can use these values for id= attributes or as a means to locate and track a specific node in relation to the current context. We'll learn more about functions and values in Chapter 9, *The Value of Values*, on page 145.

<xsl:variable>

Speaking of values, <xsl:variable> provides a means to name and define or derive a value. That's the easy definition, and the only thing we'll need to know for our current exercise. Again, we'll learn more about it in Chapter 9, *The Value of Values*, on page 145.

following-sibling

following-sibling is an *axis* (plural: *axes*), a directional pointer used in XPath expressions. Let's not worry too much about what axes and XPath mean at the moment. Let's first just talk about siblings.

You know about siblings, right? In XML, as in life, they have the same parent. In an XML hierarchy, siblings are nodes (usually elements) at the same level in the XML hierarchy, and all within the same parent tag. They make a cozy little family all hanging out together.

When the current context is one of those siblings, the following-sibling axis tells the XLST processor to look for XML sibling nodes that follow the current node. We'll see an example of this in action in the example solution that follows.

following-sibling and other axes are used in much the same places as functions, except that they return XML nodes or node-sets rather than values. For our example, think of it as selecting a set of <p> tags after the current <p> tag. We can also modify following-sibling to be more specific about what it selects.

preceding-sibling

Yep, similar to following-sibling, except that it selects sibling nodes that precede the current node within the same parent.

Breaking up a list like this is a thorny problem, but we've got the tools—and by the end of this example, we should know how to use them.

Writing the List-Buster: Part 1

We're going to transform the bad example into the good example. Let's take the problem one template at a time.

First, let's do the obvious part: we'll convert that <document> tag to a <chapter> tag:

```
<xsl:template match="/document">
  <chapter>
  </chapter>
</xsl:template>
```

We want everything else to go between the <chapter> tags. Let's ask: what else do we need at the top level? Well, the chapter title, right. So we add an <xsl:apply-templates> that selects specifically for that <p> tag with the font-size of 14pt. Remember how to select for an attribute and its value? Give it a try and see if you can get only the title. Remember, you'll need a template to partner with the <xsl:apply-templates> tag.

After the title, we need something that will pick up that one text paragraph that occurs before the <p> tag with font-size="12pt". This one's a bit tricky. Take a look at those extra tools I gave you earlier and see what you can come up with.

Figure 25, *Templates for the Title and First Paragraph*, on page 91 shows what I've got so far:

Let's go through this in a bit more detail to see how it works. We're seeing a couple of new tricks here that we need to understand.

First, in line 3, we see that we've applied templates to select <p> tags, but we've also added a predicate. The predicate ensures that we select only <p> tags where the font size is 14pt. In line 9 we've created the corresponding template, which wraps the <title> tag around the text of the selected paragraph. Cool, there's our chapter title.

Next, in line 5 and the preceding line, we've got a more complicated predicate. Here we're trying to select that <p> tag that comes immediately after the one with font-size="14pt", but before the one with font-size="12pt". We want this

```
<xsl:template match="/document">
  <chapter>
    <xsl:apply-templates select="p[@font-size='14pt']"/>
    <xsl:apply-templates select="p[@font-size='10pt'
      and not(preceding-sibling::p[@font-size='12pt'])]"/>
  </chapter>
</xsl:template>

<xsl:template match="p[@font-size='14pt']">
  <title>
    <xsl:apply-templates/>
  </title>
</xsl:template>

<xsl:template match="p[@font-size='10pt'
  and not(preceding-sibling::p[@font-size='12pt'])]">
  <p>
    <xsl:apply-templates/>
  </p>
</xsl:template>
```

Figure 25—Templates for the Title and First Paragraph

paragraph to be at the chapter level and not within any of the <section1> tags we're going to create. Two things we know about it is that it has a font-size of 10pt and it comes before any <p> tag with a font size of 12pt. We convert that knowledge into a logical expression in the predicate:

```
select="p[@font-size='10pt' and not(preceding-sibling::p[@font-size='12pt'])]
```

Here we are adding a couple of logical constructs to our list of tools. First: the expression within the predicate contains an *and* operator, which works like a normal logical AND operator in any language. Both sides of the *and* have to be true for the expression to be true.

Second, we have the not() function. The contents of this function test whether the <p> tag currently selected has a preceding sibling <p font-size="12pt">. If it *doesn't* have such a sibling, then the not() function evaluates as true, and bingo!, we have the paragraph that comes before the other headings. That's what we were after.

We still need to get the remaining paragraphs into their own section headings, but to do that, we'll need to learn a little more about XPath than we've seen so far. So we'll take a break, go through a chapter on XPath, then return to the Grizzly essay problem.

Take a look back at Figure 24, *The Output We Want for the Grizzly Essay*, on page 87. Give the XSL stylesheet a try, and play around with some of the select= statements to see the effect, comparing it to the original output. It's fine if you break it. Just put it back the way it was before and try something else...

As you check out the new functions, also think about how we have used them to make a more complex re-ordering of our original document. The more we learn about XSLT, the more you should be seeing the kinds of possibilities there are for making the XML do the sorts of circus tricks that you may be asked to perform. We're beginning to see that the XML is not just dead, flat text in a file any more. We're starting to make it come alive.

What We Did

Don't get too excited, though—we still have a lot ahead of us. So far we've only changed the structure and order of the content while keeping the output content fairly close to its original order in the source document.

But we still did a lot of work:

- moving an element into a parent's attribute
- removing a level from the source
- merging several elements into a higher-level element
- changing elements from children to siblings
- wrapping tags in other tags
- adding structure to a flat list without rearranging the elements

In the last section we added a lot of new XSLT functionality to our knowledge base. We'll spend a little more time with some of these in subsequent chapters. Especially the part of the next chapter covering XPath axes will help us a lot when we get back to our restructuring project. For now, let's take a little break and get acquainted with the XPath language. XPath is essential to any complex XSLT reordering solution.

So let's bring it on.

...taking a great diamond from her hair she drew upon the marble floor the first map of Barsoomian territory I had ever seen. It was crisscrossed in every direction with long straight lines, sometimes running parallel and sometimes converging toward some great circle.

— *Edgar Rice Burroughs,* A Princess of Mars

CHAPTER 7

XPath: The Sibling Language

XPath: Mapping XML All Over the Place

So what the heck is XPath? We've heard about it, and we know it's supposed to help us with rearranging document content, among other things.

XPath is a language used to reference parts of an XML document. It's seldom used by itself; mostly it's used in conjunction with languages like XSLT and XQuery. XSLT uses it in the attributes of its instructions to return XML nodes or values. For example, we could use it in the select= attribute of the <xsl:value-of> tag to get the content of a node that is somewhere distant from the current node, or we could use it in an expression to count nodes and compare that count to some other value.

The great thing about XPath is that it can refer to just about any node or node-set in the XML document from the context of any other node in the document. Or to put it more bluntly: XPath gives you access to *everything* from *anywhere*.

Now, that's power!

Since this book is not specifically about XPath, we'll only have time for a quick introduction. The introduction should be enough to give you the flavor of it, and hopefully spur you to explore it further.

To learn more about XPath (after reading the admirable introduction that follows, of course!), check out the online information for it at one of these links:

- http://www.w3schools.com/xpath/default.asp
- http://www.w3.org/TR/xpath/

Joe asks:
But What Is XPath, Officially?

XPath is short for XML Path Language: it's a language designed for addressing nodes in an XML document. It isn't really used by itself, but it's used in the context of other languages. Currently it exists as a recommendation of the World Wide Web Consortium (W3C).[a] Version 1.0 of the recommendation was published in 1999 and has not been modified since. (There is also an XPath 2.0, as of 2010, but we won't be using that in this book.) The good news is that it's a language with a very stable syntax.

Another piece of good news is that XPath is also used in XQuery, XPointer, and XLink, among others, which are systems or languages that process XML in different ways. It can also be used in the Domain Object Model (DOM) of XML-based languages like XHTML, and it can be used in JavaScript[b] and other languages that recognize the XML Domain Object Model. So once you learn a little XPath, you'll be dangerous on a lot of fronts.

a. http://www.w3.org/TR/xpath/
b. https://developer.mozilla.org/en-US/docs/Introduction_to_using_XPath_in_JavaScript

XPath in a Thimble

Before we lose track of the forest for the trees, let's take a high-level look at the major functional areas of XPath:

- The Data Model
- Location Paths
- Expressions
- Functions

After the high-level look, we'll dive a good bit deeper into each area, particularly location paths.

The Data Model
: The data model describes the parts of the XML that we want to address: XML nodes like elements, attributes, text, comments, and so forth. XPath offers a vocabulary for describing these parts, including some wild-card naming conventions. We'll use the data model as a way to describe the parts of the XML we want to address or retrieve.

Location Paths
: Location paths are the directions for getting from the current context node to one or more nodes. Location paths can include the following parts:

- An XPath *axis* can represent different directions in the XML, but instead of north, south, etc., we can point to a child, parent, ancestor, descendant—we can even point to "here." XPath includes 13 axes.
- *Node tests* represent the type or name of the destination: *school, church, gas_station, home.* These example destinations could be the names of element nodes in our XML. We'll use the node names from the XML source document's data model in this part of a location path.
- *Predicates* appear at the end of a location path and are contained in square brackets ([]). Predicates act as filters that describe important distinctions about the destinations we are interested in.

Functions

We've discussed functions before (*Variation on a Theme #3: Using a Function to Uppercase the Text,* on page 66): functions are instructions that return values. For quick reference, the XSLT 1.0 functions are listed in Appendix 2, *Function and Expression Operator Reference,* on page 245.

If we were using a mobile device, functions might perform like some of the extra tools in an online map application. For instance, if you want to find the closest restaurant with a five-star bathroom, the application would need a function that returned the distance to each restaurant and compared them, and another function to determine how many stars each bathroom is rated. In XSLT, we'll use functions in a lot of places, even outside of XPath.

Expressions

Expressions are logical arrangements of language elements that are interpreted and evaluated by the XSLT processor to return a value.

In a match= attribute, you might use an expression inside a predicate on the <note> element, like this:

```
<xsl:apply-templates match="note[@type='caution'
   or contains(text(),'caution')]"/>
```

The equals sign (=) and the word *or* are *tokens* or parts of the XPath expression syntax. For a list of tokens used in XPath expressions, see *Expression Operators,* on page 250.

In XSLT, we use expressions for selecting nodes, for specifying tests for conditional processing, and for creating text, among other things.

We're about to embark on a lengthy tour of these four XPath components to give you a working vocabulary for putting together more complex XSLT stylesheets. It's a big chunk, but we're going to need it. Right about now I'd grab a caffeinated beverage, shut the door, and hide the clock. This won't hurt a bit. Trust me! ;-)

The Data Model

The XPath data model is a formal way to describe the parts of the XML source that we want to address. We'll need this for just about everything we do in XSLT.

The following table showing the kinds of nodes in the data model. The table also shows how these node types are referenced in the `match=` attribute in XSLT. (Although they're shown in `match=` attributes for convenience, we can use these representations in other parts of an XSLT stylesheet as well.)

Root node	`match="/"`	The root node is the top-level position in the XML tree, even above the root element. Everything else in the document is a descendant of the root node.
Element nodes	`match=` "*element_ name*"	Elements are what we have been calling tags. In some conditions you may also have to include the element's namespace to fully represent the element.
Attribute nodes	`match=` "@*attribute_ name*"	Attributes belong to elements, but they are not children of elements. Attributes provide additional information about the element it belongs to. Attributes have names and values. They also have namespaces.
Text nodes	`match="text()"`	Any group of contiguous characters (including whitespace) within an element's beginning and ending tags is considered a text node. Two pieces of text separated by an element, empty or otherwise, are considered to be two text nodes. A text node is always a child of the element that contains it; also, text nodes can't have children.

Processing instruction nodes	match= "processing-instruction()"	Processing instructions provide special instructions directly to the XSLT processor; otherwise, they are ignored by the XSLT. We won't go into processing instructions in this book—their function depends on the XSLT processor being used.
Comment nodes	match= "comment()"	XML comments (represented as <- - (some content) - ->) are nodes that may or may not be recognized by specific XML parsers. The XSLT processor will not be able to retrieve the text of the comment node if it is not passed along by the XML parser being used.
Namespace nodes	match= "@xmlns: *namespace_ prefix*"	Namespace nodes define the XML namespaces for an element. Namespace nodes occur in document order before attributes nodes. For more curious information about namespace nodes, refer to http://www.w3.org/TR/xpath/#namespace-nodes. All that being said, namespace nodes are seldom referenced in XSLT.

Table 1—Node Types in the XPath Data Model

Wildcards and General Representations for Nodes

We've learned there are general expressions for node types *text()*, *comment()* and *programming-instruction()*. Are there equivalent ways to name element and attribute nodes?

Indeed there are, and as in other languages we call them *wildcards*. For our purposes, we will consider wildcards as part of the data model.

Just to keep things interesting, wildcards don't all take the form of *node-type()*. The following table shows all the XPath wildcards. For completeness, the table in Table 2, *Wildcards for Nodes*, on page 98 includes some wildcards we've already covered, because they tend to get used in similar ways.

The differences between node(), *, and text() can sometimes be tricky. The thing to remember is that node() contains everything covered by * and text() (and more!), whereas * covers only XML elements and text() covers only text.

With the use of wildcards and general expressions, we can be more expressive about describing which parts of the XML document we want to select. Of

Wildcard	Represents...	Selects...
*	Elements	All elements within scope of the specified context. For example, * selects all the child elements in the current context. Note that it does not select the attributes of those elements, and it does not select the text of those elements. (But watch out for the built-in template rule for text! (We covered this in *Reaping the Flow: Built-in Template Rules*, on page 44.)
@*	Attributes	All the attributes of the specified context. The context has to be an element for this wildcard to select anything, since only elements have attributes.
node()	Nodes	All the nodes in the specified context. This includes elements, attributes, text, and the others. This wildcard gets used a lot when you want everything in all or part of the source document.
text()	Text	Text nodes in the current context. Note that attributes, comments, and processing instructions do not contain text nodes, they only contain string values. Elements are the only nodes that contain text nodes.
comment()	Comments	All comments in the current context.
processing-instruction()	Processing Instructions	All processing instructions in the current context.

Table 2—Wildcards for Nodes

course, with great power comes great...complexity, right? And it's only going to get more interesting when we add location paths.

Location Paths

Location Paths tell the XSLT processor where to look in the data model and what kinds of nodes to look for in that location. Location paths can be defined by three subcomponents, *axes*, *node tests*, and *predicates*, which we briefly introduced earlier.

Before we jump in, let's look at a full-blown location path so we have a clue what we're talking about when we discuss the parts. Here, for instance, is a location path that tells the XSLT processor to look for <p> tags at any level below the current context, and with font-size="10pt":

```
descendant::p[@font-size = '10pt']
```

The *descendant::* part is the axis, which in this case says to look at any level below the current context in the hierarchy. The *p* part is the node test—it just says to look for a <p>. And the part in square brackets is the predicate. In this case the predicate contains an expression that narrows down what sort of <p> tag we're looking for. You could imagine using this XPath statement in a select= attribute for <xsl:apply-templates>.

Now let's see what sorts of choices we have for each part of the location path.

The Thirteen Axes

An axis specifies a direction in the XML tree and the scope of that direction.

In XPath, there are really only two directions: before the current context and after the current context. There are thirteen variations on those two directions because we need to define the scope of our interests in either direction.

In the following sections we're going to describe each axis and which nodes it selects in an XML tree, starting from a given current context. Figure 26, *An XML Tree*, on page 99 presents the XML tree as an arrangement of nodes, numbered in document order. We'll use those numbers to understand the scope of each axis in for following descriptions.

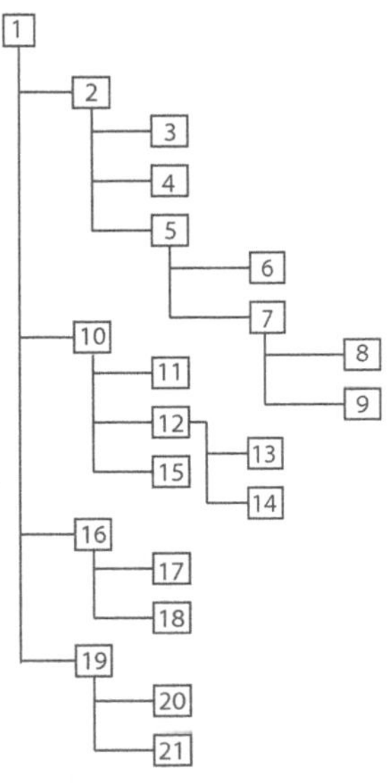

Figure 26—An XML Tree

Here, then, are the thirteen axes of XPath, with examples of their scope:

ancestor

The direction of *ancestor* is before the current node, and the scope is all of the ancestors of the current node.

In the example figure, if node 13 is the current node, *ancestor* selects nodes 12, 10, and the root element (1). If the root element is the current node, nothing is selected.

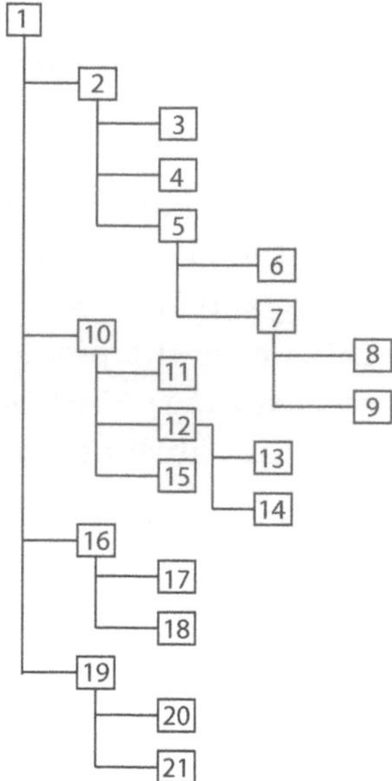

ancestor-or-self

The direction of *ancestor-or-self* is before the current node, and the scope is all of the ancestors of the current node *plus* the current node.

In the example figure, if node 13 is the current node, *ancestor-or-self* selects nodes 13, 12, 10, and 1. If the root element is the current node, the root element is selected.

attribute

The direction of *attribute* is after the current node, and the scope is all of the attributes that belong to the current node.

In the example figure, if node 2 is the current node, *attribute::** selects all the attributes of node 2. If the element has no attributes, nothing is selected.

Although the attribute axis can be represented by `attribute::`, most of the time it is represented by the attribute shortcut @.

child

The direction of *child* is after the current node, and the scope is only the immediate children of the current node. In the example figure:

- If node 2 is the current node, nodes 3, 4, and 5 are selected.
- If node 8 is the current node, nothing is selected.

descendant

The direction of *descendant* is after the current node, and the scope is all of the descendants of the current node. In the example figure:

- If the root element is the current node, nodes 2 through 21 are selected.
- If node 10 is the current node, nodes 11 through 15 are selected.
- If node 14 is the current node, nothing is selected.

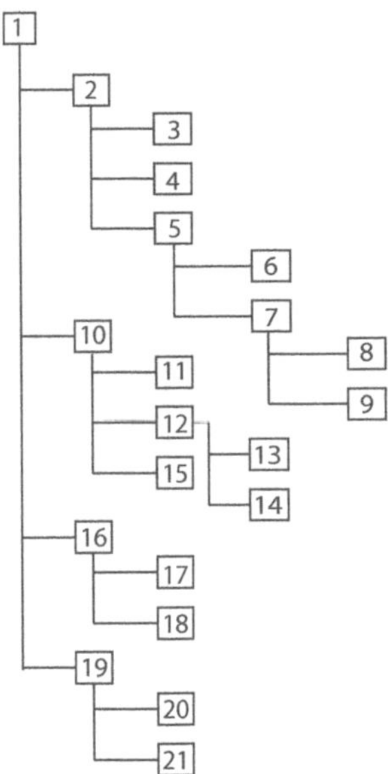

descendant-or-self

The direction of *descendant-or-self* is after the current node, and the scope is all of the descendants of the current node *plus* the current node.

In the example figure, if node 10 is the current node, nodes 10, 11, 12, 13, 14, and 15 are selected. If node 5 is the current node, nodes 5, 6, 7, 8, and 9 are selected.

following

The direction of *following* is after the complete context of the current node (that is, after the closing tag of the current node), and the scope is all of the nodes with a higher number in the document order. Note that since the scope starts *after* the closing tag of the current context, none of the children of the current node are selected.

In the example figure:

- If node 12 is the current node, nodes 15 through 21 are selected.
- If node 16 is the current node, nodes 19 through 21 are selected.
- If node 17 is the current node, nodes 18 through 21 are selected.
- If node 19 is the current node, nothing is selected.
- If node 20 is the current node, node 21 is selected.

following-sibling

The direction of *following-sibling* is after the current node, and the scope is all of the nodes that have the same parent as the current node. In the example figure, if node 3 is the current node, nodes 4 and 5 are selected.

namespace

The direction of *namespace* is after the current node, and the scope is the current node. In the example, if the current node is 10, the selected node is the namespace (or namespaces) of 10.

parent

The direction of *parent* is before the current node, and the scope is only the element that contains the current node. Only elements can be parents. In the example, if the current node is 16, the selected node is 1.

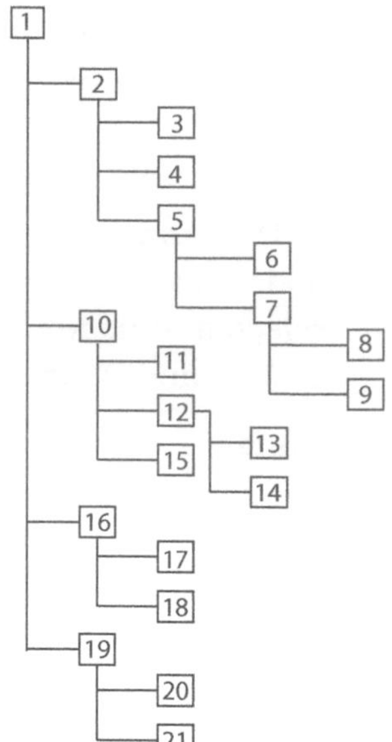

preceding

The direction of *preceding* is before the current node, and the scope is all nodes with a smaller number in the document order except for ancestors of the current node, attribute nodes, and namespace nodes.

In the example figure:

- If node 12 is the current node, nodes 1 through 9 and node 11 are selected.
- If node 16 is the current node, nodes 2 through 15 are selected.
- If node 17 is the current node, nodes 2 through 15 are selected.
- If node 2 is the current node, nothing is selected.
- If node 20 is the current node, nodes 2 through 18 are selected.

preceding-sibling

The direction of *preceding-sibling* is before the current node, and the scope is all nodes that have the same parent as the current node.

- If node 19 is the current node, nodes 2, 10, and 16 are selected.
- If node 12 is the current node, only node 11 is selected.

self

The direction of *self* is after the current node, and the scope is only the current node.

If 16 is the current node, only node 16 is selected.

Axis Shortcuts

Some of the axes have shortcuts, which you will find convenient as long as you remember what they are shortcuts for! These shortcuts can be used in most of the places where the full axis name can be used. (See Table 3, *Axis Shortcuts*, on page 103.)

Later we'll also see abbreviations (or *wildcards*) for nodes and attributes.

Axis	Shortcut	Description
self	.	represents the *self* axis; it select the current node
parent	..	represents the parent of the current node
child	(no text)	child:: can be omitted from a location path. The XSLT processor assumes that the given node test represents a child (or attribute or namespace) of the current node. For example, when we use <xsl:apply-templates select="p">, the contents of the select= attribute are equivalent to *child::p*. So we've already been using this shortcut quite a bit.
root/descen-dant	//	Gives a scope of everything within the document root. When a node test follows this (for example, //author), it selects all the nodes in the current document that match the node test. If a node precedes it (for example, chapter//, it selects everything beneath the given node, assuming that the given node is in the context of the current node. In this example, if the current node is a <part> tag, where <chapter> is an immediate child element, we could use chapter//note to select all the <note> elements inside all the child chapters.

Table 3—Axis Shortcuts

Node Tests

Now that we have the left side of our path set up, we can pay attention to *node tests*. By a node test, we mean that we describe a node or set of nodes; any node that matches our node test from the current context evaluates to true and therefore gets selected.

We talked about how nodes are named in the section on the data model (*The Data Model*, on page 96). Those names or naming conventions are used as node tests, along with wildcards and slashes to extend the paths. That's it—no big deal about it. Let's look at a few examples of node tests combined with the axes to see how they work.

First, here's some XML we want to run tests on. This is a variation of the example with node numbers that we used before, but this time we're including attributes and comments as well as elements and text:

xpath-order/nodetests-1.xml

```
<?xml version="1.0" encoding="UTF-8"?>
<?xml-stylesheet type="text/xsl" href="nodetests-1.xsl"?>
<doc id="doc-1">
  <chapter id="chapter-1">
    <p id="para-1">one</p>
    <p id="para-2">two</p>
    <p id="para-3">three
      <!-- This is an extraordinary comment! -->
      <footnote id="fn-1">four</footnote>
      <footnote id="fn-2">five
        <xref id="xref-1">six</xref>
        <xref id="xref-2">seven</xref>
        <bold id="bold-1">WOWSERS!</bold>
      </footnote>
    </p>
  </chapter>
  <chapter id="chapter-2">
    <?php echo $fox; ?>
    <p id="para-4">eight</p>
    <p id="para-5">nine
      <footnote id="fn-3">ten</footnote>
      <bold id="bold-2">OH, GOOD GRIEF!</bold>
     </p>
    <note id="note-1">eleven
      <p id="para-6">twelve
         <footnote id="fn-4">thirteen</footnote>
      </p>
    </note>
    <p id="para-7">fourteen</p>
  </chapter>
</doc>
```

Figure 27—Example XML for demonstrating node tests

Table 4, *Selection with Axes and Node Tests*, on page 105 shows some of the things we can select with node tests:

Extended Node Paths

In some cases, a single node name is not enough. Let's say we're in a chapter and we want to select the footnotes that are inside <note> elements. One way to do that would be:

```
descendant::note/p/footnote
```

Current Context	Location Path	...Selects...
<footnote>	ancestor::chapter	Only the chapter element in which the footnote appears
<chapter id="chap-1">	descendant::footnote	<footnote> elements where id="fn-1" and id="fn-2"
<doc>	descendant::@id	chap-1, para-1, para-2, para-3, fn-1, fn-2, xref-1, xref-2, chap-2, para-4, para-5, fn-3, fn-4, para-6 Without anything in the XPath expression to restrict which id= we're after, we get all the id= attribute values that are descendants of <doc>.
<chap id="chap-1">	descendant::comment()	This is an extraordinary comment!
<footnote id="fn-3">	ancestor::chapter/@id	The id= attribute that has the value chap2
<footnote id="fn-1">	following-sibling::bold	<bold> where id="bold-1"

Table 4—Selection with Axes and Node Tests

Slashes are separators that work just like they do in a file path, leading us from one element to its next relative. Remember, if you just give an element name, the assumption is that the element is a child of the current context. So the expanded version of the node path given above would be:

```
descendant::note/child::p/child::footnote
```

What this suggests is that you could put some different axis in front of each node in the path, providing it made sense in the context of the previous node in the path. With that idea, we're now really getting somewhere. The idea that we can specify a new axis *at any point in the path* gives us the possibility of navigating from one node in the XML to any other node, anywhere. This is where the real power of XPath begins to show itself.

Suppose the current context is <bold> where id="bold-2" and we want to know what the id= attribute is for the <bold> in the previous chapter. We're going to have to do something fancy to get there:

```
ancestor::chapter/preceding-sibling::chapter/descendant::bold/@id
```

Take a look back at the code on page 104 and follow the thread of what is happening in this statement. From <bold id="bold-2">, the ancestor::chapter takes us up to <chapter "chap-2">. Then preceding-sibling::chapter moves the context to <chapter "chap-1">, and from there, the descendant::bold takes us to the only <bold> element in the first chapter. (If there were more than one <bold>, this expression would select all of them.) Then we get that last @id, which finally selects the id= attribute of the <bold> tag.

Essentially, the use of the location path in an extended fashion means we can navigate to any node or set of nodes in the document, then take a step in any of the thirteen axis directions to select any other set of nodes. That's pretty powerful stuff!

Selecting Multiple Node Paths

Sometimes you'll need to select more than one set of nodes, and it would make life a lot easier if you could do it in a single selection statement. That's easy enough—you just use a *logical OR* or a *logical AND* between the path statements. For example, let's say that the chapter element has three possible child types (*p*, *note*, and *figure*), and you only want to select only two of them (*note* and *figure*). You would place both paths in the select statement, separated by a pipe (|) character. The match or select statement would look like this:

```
<xsl:apply-templates select="note | figure">
```

As we saw earlier, the pipe character represents a union of node sets. You can put location paths together in other sorts of logical relationships using XPath expressions as well, and sometimes these can become quite long and complex. For readability, it's useful to break the expression just before each pipe, as shown in the following example that matches all three of the elements in <chapter>:

```
<xsl:template match="p/text()
   | note/text()
   | figure/text()"
```

The spaces on either side of the pipe character aren't required, but they make for more readable code.

Predicates

We defined predicates earlier, but let's get a little more formal:

- Predicates appear in square brackets ([]) after the axis and node test.
- The brackets contain expressions that resolve to a boolean (true or false); or, if the predicate contains only a number, the number represents a position.

- The XSLT processor finds nodes that are in the scope of the axis and node test and evaluates them against the expression in the predicate. If the predicate evaluates to true for a given node, the node is returned in the resulting node set.

Again referring to our bibliography XML example, suppose we wanted to show only the first author listed for a book. If our current context is <book>, we can say we want *child::author[1]*. Here, the predicate [1] contains the expression *1*, which in this case means "the first instance of the node of which I am a predicate." The *child::author* part of the path brings all of the <author> tags into scope; the XSLT processor evaluates each child <author> tag against the predicate expression and returns the one instance that evaluates to *true*, which is the first one.

Predicates can contain much more than just numbers. We haven't covered expressions yet, but it wouldn't hurt to get a taste for what they can do. The following list shows some of the types of expressions you'll find in a predicate.

ancestor::ul[1]

A number in a predicate specifies an ordinal value; that is, it specifies which instance to return from an ordered set of nodes, where the node set is defined by the location path that precedes it. In this case, the node set is all <ul> elements above the current context in the hierarchy, and the instance to return is the first, that is, the closest.

Higher numbers select nodes that are further from the current context. We talked about which direction in the tree each axis selects in *The Thirteen Axes*, on page 99. If the axis selects before the node, the predicate is evaluated from the current context backward in the document order, and if the axis selects after the node, the predicate is evaluated from the current context forward. So in this example, since ancestor:: selects backward, if we were at the bottom of a nested set of <ul> lists, the predicate would select the ancestor <ul> closest to the current context.

descendant::*[footnote]

This selects any element that is a descendant of the current context and that contains a child <footnote>.

Do you see why this is this different from saying descendant::footnote? The * wildcard is the node test—it selects any element. The predicate says [footnote], but remember: if there is no preceding axis for an element, the default axis is child::. What the XPath statement says above is really:

```
descendant::*[child::footnote]
```

So it will return any element that has a footnote as a child.

//xref[contains(.,'figure')]

The expression in the predicate means the context contains the text "figure". In this case, the context is represented by the . ("self"), which is the node defined by the location path. So this predicate returns all the <xref> tags in the whole document whose text contains the string "figure".

following-sibling::*[self::p | self::note]

This selects any following sibling that is either a <p> or a <note>.

following::*[@*]

This selects any following element that contains any attribute. Note that it doesn't select the attribute itself, only the element.

ancestor::*[ancestor::*]

This selects any ancestor that has an ancestor. In other words, it selects all ancestor elements from the current context except the root element.

descendant::*[@id = 'ab1429z07']

This selects a descendant with `id="ab1429z07"`.

A great way to get comfortable with the combination of axes, node tests, and predicates is to play with them. Try it yourself: use a stylesheet that consists of an identity transform plus one other template. (You remember Chapter 5, *Filtering with the Identity Transform*, on page 57, right?) In the second template, match on an element of interest, then use an <xsl:value-of> with an XPath statement to retrieve values from elsewhere in the XML document. You might even add some text around the <xsl:value-of> tag to set off the results from the rest of the document.

Multiple Predicates

A location path can have more than one predicate. You might need to combine several criteria for selecting nodes out of the scope of the node-set. Let's take the example using a finder app on our mobile device: we want to find a Thai restaurant with highly rated bathrooms—preferably the closest one! If our XPath statement selects all restaurants, and restaurants have attributes like cuisine and number of stars for restrooms, the location path might look like: `restaurant[@cuisine='Thai' and @restroomstars > 4][1]` (where > means *greater than*).

The trick here is that the first predicate filters the node set, then the second predicate is applied to the filtered node set. In this example, the set of restaurants is restricted to Thai restaurants with highly rated restrooms, then the second predicate picks the first one of those.

If we did it the other way around, it might not work out so well. Check it out: *restaurant[1][@cuisine='Thai' and @restroomstars > 4]*. Here we're saying, give us the first restaurant we find, then select it if it's a Thai restaurant with a great restroom. Chances are, if we're on a highway, the first restaurant will be a McDonald's or a Cracker Barrel, and we won't return anything from the second predicate. Keep driving, and good luck!

Functions

We've talked around functions a little in earlier chapters, but now it's time to pin them down.

So far, we know that they are language tokens that return values, and we know that they take the form `function-name()`, where the parentheses may or may not contain arguments. Functions are frequently used in XPath statements, but they can also be used in other parts of XSLT. (We'll see more of this when we get to Chapter 9, *The Value of Values*, on page 145.) Functions are often used in expressions to give values for comparison and testing, as well as in variables for calculation, decision-making, and output.

What sort of values can we get out of functions? Here's the list:

- Boolean values (true or false)
- Numbers
- Strings
- Node sets

Chapter 9, *The Value of Values*, on page 145 gives more formal definitions of these value types.)

In the following sections, we'll have a look at a single function to get a feel for how they work, then spend time on how to deal with the parameters. Then I'm going to do a total cop-out and refer you to Appendix 2, *Function and Expression Operator Reference*, on page 245 for more information about using functions. There are a bunch of them, and we won't have time to see them all in action.

Functions at Work

Let's have a look at a function that takes three parameters and returns a string value: `substring()`. This is one of the most flexible of the string functions, so it gets a lot of exercise. Basically, you specify a string and give the positions of the first and last letter of the substring you want to return from the string.

In the example below, we're going to take the first 45 characters of a string to use as the teaser for a news article. (Hopefully the writer knows how to make a punchy lead-in sentence!) This sort of string would typically be linked to the full article elsewhere. We won't create the link in this example, but we will see how to create the teaser string.

Here's the first paragraph of the content for the article itself:

```
<p>NASA revealed that aliens invaded Anchorage, Alaska
  during the last major snowstorm. Apparently no one noticed
  because their spacesuits looked like snow gear. </p>
```

Let's take a look at the template we would use for showing only the first 45 characters:

```
Line 1 <xsl:template match="p">
2        <xsl:value-of select="substring(.,1,45)"/><xsl:text>...</xsl:text>
3      </xsl:template>
```

Looking more closely at line 2, check out how we specified the first parameter: it's just the period (.). As we learned earlier, the period is XPath shorthand for the current context. In this case, the period returns the text of the current context, which is the whole paragraph string that we want to operate on.

Following the . (period) is a comma to separate the parameters, then a 1 for the second parameter, which tells the function where to start the substring. The convention for string positions in XPath is that the first character position is numbered 1, the second 2, and so forth. So we're telling the function to start the substring with the first character.

The second comma sets off the third parameter, which tells the function which character position will be the last in the substring. We want 45 characters, so we specify 45 for this parameter. The result is a titillating lead-in for our article:

```
NASA revealed that aliens invaded Anchorage...
```

As a general pattern for the use of functions, this example demonstrates several things. First, the function is used in the context of an attribute of an XSLT instruction. Functions always do their work within XSLT attributes.

Second, a function can be used to send its value to the output. This isn't always true, though—you can also used functions as parts of expressions to evaluate conditions and make decisions about processing. That is to say, the values can be used for internal processing purposes within the XSLT as well as for creating output.

Third, parameters are always separated by commas. If you need to use a comma in a parameter, the parameter needs to be enclosed in single quotes (''). In our example, for instance, we could have just put a literal string (including a comma) in the function, with the string inside single quotes like so:

```
<xsl:template match="p">
  <xsl:value-of select="substring('NASA revealed that aliens
    invaded Anchorage, Alaska',1,45)"/><xsl:text>...</xsl:text>
</xsl:template>
```

Of course, using the . (self shortcut) for the first parameter rather than all of that text would make this template more useful for situations other than when aliens invade Anchorage...

Joe asks:

Can I use functions as parameters for other functions?

A function can indeed supply a value as the parameter of another function, like this:

```
<xsl:value-of select="translate(normalize-space(),'ABCDEFGH','12345678')"
```

Nested functions are evaluated from the inside out. In this example, the text of the current node has its extra whitespace removed with normalize-space(), the translate() function converts the alpha characters to numerals.

It's theoretically possible to nest functions to any depth. I've found that making them too deep can be a dicey proposition with some XSL processors, though. It's more reliable to place the value of a deeper function into a separate variable, then use the variable in the parameter rather than the function itself, like this:

```
<xsl:variable name="normalized">
  <xsl:value-of select="normalize-space()"/>
</xsl:variable>
  <xsl:value-of select="translate($normalized,'ABCDEFGH','12345678')"
```

We're jumping a little ahead of ourselves with variables (see *Variables*, on page 148), but you get the idea.

The main thing is to test your functional expressions thoroughly before releasing them to the public!

One important point to note: parameters for substring() can be static values or variable values that are defined elsewhere. In this example we used static values for the second and third parameters because we haven't gotten to variables yet. But even that period in the first parameter represents a dynamic value: we have no idea what the actual string will be until runtime.

And we can easily imagine wanting to change the size of the teaser based on the type of device the news is being delivered to. To do that, we would need to use a variable for the third parameter. We'll get a good look at creating that kind of control when we get to Chapter 9, *The Value of Values*, on page 145.

While this section presents a general guideline to functions and their usage, it doesn't begin to touch all the functions and how they can be employed in XSLT. Appendix 2, *Function and Expression Operator Reference*, on page 245 lists the functions available for XPath 1.0, and those will handle a lot of situations in XSLT. We'll see more uses for functions when we get into *Expressions*, on page 112 and other parts of this book. We'll even see situations where we use functions within the parameters of other functions.

As your use of XSLT matures, you will want to check out the functions available in later versions of XPath,[1,2] as well as in various XSLT extensions, such as EXSLT[3] and FunctX.[4] For a list of the extended functions available in the Saxon XSLT processor, refer to Saxon's documentation.[5] If you are adept at other programming languages, you can even create your own extended functions.[6,7] Custom extended functions are well beyond the scope of this book, but keep in mind that this is one of those areas where the "X" (eXtensible) in XSLT comes into play.

Expressions

We've seen three aspects of XPath: the data model, location paths, and functions. In our fourth and final act, we'll look at expressions, which round out XPath into a fairly robust tool for handling XML.

Plain and simple, the function of XPath expressions is to derive values that can be used for controlling our XSLT processor. The form of an expression can be as simple as a single static value or as complex as a mathematical formula. Within XPath constructions, expressions frequently take the form of relationships that are evaluated as true or false. For example, you might see an expression in the predicate of a select= attribute, like this:

```
<xsl:apply-templates select="following-sibling::phone-number[@type = 'home']"/>
```

1. http://www.w3.org/TR/xpath-functions/
2. http://www.w3.org/TR/xpath-functions-30/
3. http://www.exslt.org/func/index.html
4. http://www.xsltfunctions.com/
5. http://saxonica.com/documentation9.4-demo/html/extensions/
6. http://msdn.microsoft.com/en-us/magazine/cc302079.aspx
7. http://ode.apache.org/custom-xpath-functions.html

XPath 1.0 functions are a meager offering...

Let's face it: XSLT 1.0 and XPath 1.0 can seem like a starter set of building blocks when you're faced with creating industrial-strength output of any meaningful complexity. In those cases, it's best to stay away from the XSLT processors built into web browsers if you possibly can. Then you can take advantage of the legions of useful functions offered in XPath 2.0 and in various XSLT extensions.

One of the more popular extension projects is EXSLT,[a] a nonprofit community that provides a ton of useful functions for things like date and time handling, math functions, regular expressions, and extended string handling. But you'll find that there are numerous function libraries out there for a variety of programming languages and XSLT processors.

As in everything else, though, these additional functions come with a caveat. Most XSLT processors don't support all of the EXSLT functions, although many processors support a good subset of them. You'll have to check the specifications for the XSLT processor you use, or you'll have to point the processor to other processing tools that can handle the extended functions.

The ability to use extensions means you aren't stuck with just the XPath 1.0 functions. I find that I can get by with XSLT 1.0 for a very large percentage of the problems I encounter. But there is no question that XSLT 2.0 and XSLT extensions can bring a little sunshine into your XSLT adventures.

a. http://exslt.org/

Here we can imagine that our current context is an <address> tag that includes a lot of other tags like <address-line-1>, <city>, and several <phone-number> tags. If all we want is the home phone number, we set up the expression in the predicate ([@type = 'home']) to be true when the processor gets to the tag that looks something like <phone-number type="home">. When that expression is true, the <xsl:apply-templates> goes to work. For <phone-number> tags with other values for type=, the processor just says "meh" and keeps working.

In the following sections we'll take a look at some fundamental characteristics of expressions: how they are constructed, what language elements can be used in them, how they are evaluated, and some typical use cases. By the end of this chapter you should understand the basic structure and use of XPath expressions. And in subsequent chapters we'll see expressions put through their paces to solve a variety of problems.

The Structure of Expressions

As mentioned earlier, expressions can be very simple, or they can be fairly complicated. Here's a select= attribute with a one-character expression, the 1 inside the square brackets []:

```
<xsl:apply-templates select="following-sibling::phone-number[1]"/>
```

The expression evaluates to true when the processor reaches the first instance of the <phone-number> tag in the current context. In this case, the 1 is really a short-hand form for an expression that goes more like position() = 1, but it still qualifies as an expression.

An expression can consist of one on more parts. An expression does not necessarily consist of a relationship; it can be a simple static value, a variable, a function, or a combination of tokens, and it may include *operators*. Operators are special characters that modify or create relationships between things in an expression.

The expression position() = 1 is a relationship. It consists of the position() function, which produces different values based on the position of the specified element within its current context, and a static value, 1. The = sign is an operator. There are a bunch of operators that can be used in expression.

Appendix 2, *Function and Expression Operator Reference*, on page 245 gives a list of the operators used in XSLT and XPath expressions. If you're knowledgeable in other software languages, you'll find most of these operators familiar.

Using operators, you can construct fairly sophisticated expressions to evaluate for an endless variety of conditions. For example:

```
<xsl:apply-templates select="p[count(preceding-sibling::p) &gt;= 1]
  [not(preceding-sibling::*[not(self::p or self::title or self::i)])]"/>
```

This little snarl of logical obscurity is intended to select for <p> tags that have the following characteristics:

- The number of preceding <p> tags in the current context is greater than or equal to one. (That >= is a relationship operator meaning *greater than or equal to*.)
- *and* it is not the case that any of those preceding sibling tags are anything other than <p> OR <title> OR <i>. In this part of the expression, the *or* tokens are logical operators that work just like they did in your old algebra courses. You remember those, don't you?

In general, expressions are formed by the arrangement of one or more things that represent values, and they might be separated by operators that establish relationships between the values. Structurally, it sounds fairly simple. In practice, though, we'll see that there are many kinds of things that represent values and many kinds of things that act as operators; between the values and the operators, expressions can adapt to almost any situation we need to address.

The Contents of Expressions

What sorts of things can expressions contain? We've seen static values, functions, and relational operators so far. Expressions turn out to be pretty flexible—all sorts of thing can go into them. The trick for constructing a useful expression is finding the appropriate kinds of things to put in it to get the value we need. We can't really go through all the possibilities in this short section, but we can at least take a look at what kinds of options are available for constructing expressions.

Here's a list of XSLT constructions we might find in an expression:

- Strings
- Numbers
- Nodes or node-sets
- XPath statements (location paths) that select nodes or node-sets
- Functions
- Variables and parameters
- Operators

We're familiar with most of these. We haven't looked at variables and parameters yet, but we'll get to them in Chapter 9, *The Value of Values*, on page 145. You can think of them as placeholders for values determined at runtime.

In general, other than operators, all these items evaluate to the four basic value types in XSLT: numbers, strings, Boolean values, and nodes. Operators, of course, have a different kind of function.

The Values of Expressions

What kind of value will you get out of an expression? We've seen that expressions are used in the context of attributes, and different attributes require different types of values. In some cases you may need a simple Boolean value; in other cases, a variable that returns a complex string. Depending on how the expression is set up, you can derive these types of values:

- Numbers
- Strings
- Booleans
- Nodes or node-sets

(Again, refer to Chapter 9, *The Value of Values*, on page 145 for the definition of these value types.)

How do you know you're going to get the right sort of value out of an expression? Look at the largest containing structure in the expression and determine what sort of value it returns. For example, an expression with an = in the middle will return a Boolean value, regardless of what's on either side. An expression that is couched in the parentheses of a function will return whatever type of value that function normally returns. And an expression that starts with an XPath address will likely return a node or node-set.

If nothing else, you can always experiment!

What We Did

Well, that was pretty much a whirlwind tour of XPath. If you're feeling dizzy, exhausted, nervous, restless, and not the least bit sleepy—it's probably all the caffeine it took to get through this chapter.

In this chapter we covered all the elements and principles of XPath 1.0 – no mean feat for twenty-some-odd pages. We saw that XPath is composed of four major functional areas: the data model, location paths, functions, and expressions. Location paths in turn are divided into three parts: axes, node tests, and predicates. Node tests can contain wildcards, and predicates can contain functions, expressions, and more location paths.

And then, of course, each of those functional areas has its own list of things that can go into them.

In the next chapter, and the rest of the book, we'll find that we will not stray far from the use of XPath statements. We'll see a lot of examples while we are demonstrating other aspects of XSLT. As you recall, we were in the middle of the problem of re-ordering XML elements when we suddenly went off on this extravagant diversion. It's time to get back to the original problem now that we've taken XPath into our growing toolset. We still need to change the order of elements in our little essay on grizzly bears.

My effort was crowned with a success which appalled me no less than it seemed to surprise the Martian warriors, for it carried me fully thirty feet into the air and landed me a hundred feet from my pursuers and on the opposite side of the enclosure.

Edgar Rice Burroughs, A Princess of Mars

CHAPTER 8

Using XPath to Change the Order of Documents

Putting XPath to Work

Now we're going to apply XPath to solve the remaining problem with the Grizzly essay. Beyond that, we'll put XPath to work solving a variety of problems that require us to access content all over the place. We'll see a method called *pull processing*, which runs contrary to the normal functional model of XSLT, but is useful on occasion; we'll see grouping and sorting; and we'll talk about other reasons to retrieve content or test the structure of nodes elsewhere in the document.

Writing the List-Buster: Part 2

At the end of Chapter 6, *Changing the Structure and Order of Content*, on page 75 we wrote XSLT to handle the chapter heading and the chapter-level paragraph, but what about the next-level headings and their content? Just to refresh ourselves, Figure 28, *Output for the grizzly bear essay*, on page 118 shows the output we want.

The next-level headings (where font-size="12pt") should all come after the chapter-level paragraph, so we can add an <xsl:apply-templates> statement in the chapter-level template to process those (see Figure 29, *Content for the chapter-level template*, on page 118).

Line 6 selects the heading-level paragraphs. So, as we did with the chapter title, we need to create a template to process those paragraphs and put them into a <title> tag. We may as well wrap them in the <section1> tags while we're at it, because the <title> tags have to go inside the <section1> tags.

orderorder2/grizzly-output.xml
```
<?xml version="1.0" encoding="UTF-8"?>
<chapter>
  <title>Grizzlies and People</title>
  <p>Since the Ice Age, man has feared the great denizens of the north.
    But why is that?</p>
  <section1>
    <title>Horribleness</title>
    <p>Grizzlies are so horrible, they are named <emph>Ursus horribilis</emph>.
      'Nuff said?</p>
  </section1>
  <section1>
    <title>Largeness</title>
    <p>Male grizzlies can average 900 pounds and 9 feet tall. That's a lot of bear
      to feed, and they don't mind a little human in the diet!</p>
  </section1>
  <section1>
    <title>Aggressiveness</title>
    <p>Grizzlies are too large to escape danger by climbing trees; instead, they
      stand their ground.</p>
  </section1>
  <p>All that being said, humans are still more dangerous than grizzly bears!</p>
</chapter>
```

Figure 28—Output for the grizzly bear essay

orderorder2/listfix.xsl
```
<xsl:template match="/document">
  <chapter>
    <xsl:apply-templates select="p[@font-size='14pt']"/>
    <xsl:apply-templates select="p[@font-size='10pt'
      and not(preceding-sibling::p[@font-size='12pt'])]"/>
    <xsl:apply-templates select="p[@font-size='12pt']"/>
  </chapter>
</xsl:template>
```

Figure 29—Content for the chapter-level template

Now we get to the tricky part. We need to insert the remaining text paragraphs within the <section1> tags we just created. To do this, we need to select the <p> tags that meet these conditions:

- <p> tags that follow the current <p> tag and that have font-size="10pt".
- AND that don't follow any <p> tag with font-size="12pt" that comes after the current <p> tag. When we reach the next <p> tag with font-size="12pt", it means we've reached the end of the current section and the beginning of the next section.

Templates should emit well-formed output

Isn't it possible to create an open <section1> in the template for the heading-level paragraphs, then add the closing </section1> in the template for the last paragraph in the section?

Quick answer: no. XSLT is designed to emit well-formed XML.

Slow answer: not really. You could probably bluff your way into it by using something like <section1> in the one template and </section1> in the other template, and the character entities would get converted into angle brackets, creating tags in the output. But don't do it. The XSLT processor parses the XML output to make sure it is well-formed. To fool the processor, you would have to emit some output that looks like text (as I've shown here). There would be no way to guarantee that you're creating good XML.

Because XSLT is designed to create well-formed output, it helps to think about structuring your templates so they create chunks of XML with beginning and end tags. Doing so leads to good stylesheet design and self-contained templates that can be reused easily.

If you find that you're struggling to get the open and close tags in one template, you might need to reconsider your stylesheet design.

Save yourself a lot of trouble and stick to the normal processing model. Create well-formed output in each template!

How do we convert that logic into XSLT syntax? You can probably do the first logical part yourself at this point. What about the second part? We know we need a way to keep track of what the current <p> tag is. As the XSLT processor looks at each <p> tag for inclusion, we need a way to find out whether a preceding <p> tag with font-size="12pt" is the one we started with or one of the ones that follow what we started with. To do this, let's create a variable with the ID value of our initial <p> tag:

```
<xsl:variable name="id">
  <xsl:value-of select="generate-id(.)"/>
</xsl:variable>
```

We'll see more about variables in Chapter 9, *The Value of Values*, on page 145, but at the moment, just think of a variable as a placeholder for a value. It has a name, and we can retrieve the value in an XSLT attribute by putting a dollar sign in front of its name.

Now we can create the XSLT that looks for the conditions we've described, as shown in Figure 30, *Is the 10pt paragraph in the current section?*, on page 120

```
<xsl:variable name="id">
<xsl:apply-templates select="following-sibling::p[@font-size = '10pt' and
     preceding-sibling::p[@font-size = '12pt'][1][generate-id() = $id]]"/>
```

Figure 30—Is the 10pt paragraph in the current section?

Ouch! That's pretty hairy—take a minute to look through those lines. We've got some XPath in our back pocket now, so we should be able to figure it out.

First, look at the big picture. We're selecting all the following-sibling <p> tags, but we've added a predicate to select only the tags we want. The predicate starts out like predicates we've seen before, just selecting for a font size equal to 10 points. But to that requirement we add another: the selected tag must also have a preceding sibling that is a <p font-size="12pt">. The [1] says that this has to be the first preceding sibling that meets the font size condition, and the [@id = $id] condition says that it must also have the same generated ID value as the one we generated for the <p font-size="12pt"> that we matched on to begin with. If the processor gets to a <p> that follows the next <p font-size="12pt">, then preceding-sibling::p[@font-size = '12pt'][1] won't have the same ID value, and nothing will be returned. Sweet.

Okay—with this great huge clunker of a select= statement, we're almost home free. We just need to take the next step and add a template that matches the <p font-size="10pt"> tags. Remember that the paragraph tag immediately after the chapter title also matches this description, so we'll have to add a little something in our select statement to make sure we omit that one. Can you figure it out?

Ask yourself: what is the difference between the <p> tags?

And the reward for all our hard work (and huge, hairy predicates): the complete stylesheet, shown in Figure 31, *The complete listbuster stylesheet*, on page 121.

We run it and get a nicely restructured piece of XML. Sure, that was a lot of work for a little piece of XML, but what would you say to several hundred pages of XML in the same format? Personally, I'd be ecstatic to spend the time on this stylesheet. Beats restructuring it by hand (or with regular expressions or HTML filters) in a heartbeat!

You can see in line 40 how we crafted the match= statement to avoid picking up that one paragraph immediately after the chapter title. The part of the expression after the and tells the processor that the selected <p> tag must orderorder2/listfix2.xsl

```
<xsl:stylesheet xmlns:xsl="http://www.w3.org/1999/XSL/Transform" version="1.0">
  <xsl:output indent="yes"/>
  <xsl:template match="/document">
    <chapter>
      <xsl:apply-templates select="p[@font-size='14pt']"/>
      <xsl:apply-templates select="p[@font-size='10pt'
        and not(preceding-sibling::p[@font-size='12pt'])]"/>
      <xsl:apply-templates select="p[@font-size='12pt']"/>
    </chapter>
  </xsl:template>

  <xsl:template match="p[@font-size='14pt']">
      <title>
        <xsl:apply-templates/>
      </title>
  </xsl:template>

  <xsl:template match="p[@font-size='10pt'
    and not(preceding-sibling::p[@font-size='12pt'])]">
    <p>
      <xsl:apply-templates/>
    </p>
  </xsl:template>

  <xsl:template match="p[@font-size='12pt']">
    <xsl:variable name="id">
      <xsl:value-of select="generate-id(.)"/>
    </xsl:variable>
    <section1>
      <title>
        <xsl:apply-templates/>
      </title>
      <xsl:apply-templates select="following-sibling::p[@font-size='10pt' and
        not(preceding-sibling::p[@font-size='12pt'
        and preceding-sibling::p[generate-id() = $id]])]"/>
    </section1>
  </xsl:template>

  <xsl:template match="p[@font-size='10pt'
    and preceding-sibling::p[@font-size='12pt']]">
    <p>
      <xsl:apply-templates/>
    </p>
  </xsl:template>
</xsl:stylesheet>
```

Figure 31—The complete listbuster stylesheet

follow a <p font-size="12pt"> tag. That condition eliminates the paragraph after the <p font-size="14pt"> tag.

Job well done! It was a long journey that started way back in *Adding structure to flat lists*, on page 86 and took us through an entire chapter about XPath. We have used the attributes of a flat list of <p> tags to create an XML document with hierarchical structure that better represents the underlying structure of the content, which is just what we wanted.

Now that we have XPath in our tool chest, we can begin to address problems that are considerably more complicated. And, you know what? Given the XML that we'll find out there in the wild, we're going to need all the tricks we can find.

What Else We'll Do in This Chapter

Now that we've finished our complex restructuring job, let's take a look at some other ways we can use XSLT with XPath to restructure and re-order our content. We'll be using XPath in most of these approaches, but XPath won't be all. We're also going to have a look at some methods for grouping and sorting content—restructuring with a vengeance!

These techniques will give you enough power to address a large number of XML restructuring problems. Of course, we haven't gotten to the use of conditional processing, which will help even further—but we'll first need to learn about variables and parameters (Chapter 9, *The Value of Values*, on page 145) before we can start working with conditional structures. In the meantime, we still have some excellent restructuring strategies to cover in this chapter.

"Pull" Processing: Empirical Processing with XSLT

We're going to see a method for specifying exactly what we want and where we want it using an approach that will look remarkably like a traditional empirical language. XSLT purists would probably call this section "Doing It Wrong." But really, what's wrong with a little shortcut here and there? Maybe it's the right thing to do under certain circumstances. The great thing is that XSLT enables you to do it, and the XSLT processor won't leave snarky notes in the code reviews to tweak your conscience.

"Pull" processing is simply a way to use XPath statements to retrieve content while not actually allowing the XSLT processor to walk through the XML document. You can start it at any level of the XSLT stylesheet, but for our purposes, let's imagine that we only want to write one template that matches on the root of the document. How would we get output if we had a complex XML source document?

Well, yes, we could just write <xsl:apply-templates/> and retrieve all the text in document order. You already knew that. But suppose we want to be a little more selective about our output, and maybe even put some tags around it somewhere. Let's try putting a bunch of <xsl:apply-templates/> tags together with select= statements that contain XPaths. First, here's the sample XML document we're going to work on:

orderorder2/grain1.xml

```
<?xml version="1.0" encoding="UTF-8"?>
<?xml-stylesheet type="text/xsl" href="pullprocess.xsl"?>
<FERMENTABLES>
  <FERMENTABLE>
    <NAME>Acid Malt</NAME>
    <VERSION>1</VERSION>
    <TYPE>Grain</TYPE>
    <AMOUNT>0.000000</AMOUNT>
    <YIELD>58.7</YIELD>
    <COLOR>3.0</COLOR>
    <ADD_AFTER_BOIL>FALSE</ADD_AFTER_BOIL>
    <ORIGIN>Germany</ORIGIN>
    <SUPPLIER/>
    <NOTES>Acid malt contains acids from natural lactic acids.
      Used by German brewers to adjust malt PH
      without chemicals to adhere to German purity laws.
      Also enhances the head retention. </NOTES>
    <COARSE_FINE_DIFF>1.5</COARSE_FINE_DIFF>
    <MOISTURE>4.0</MOISTURE>
    <DIASTATIC_POWER>0.0</DIASTATIC_POWER>
    <PROTEIN>6.0</PROTEIN>
    <MAX_IN_BATCH>10.0</MAX_IN_BATCH>
    <RECOMMEND_MASH>TRUE</RECOMMEND_MASH>
    <IBU_GAL_PER_LB>0.000</IBU_GAL_PER_LB>
    <DISPLAY_AMOUNT>0.00 lb</DISPLAY_AMOUNT>
    <INVENTORY>0.00 lb</INVENTORY>
    <POTENTIAL>1.027</POTENTIAL>
    <DISPLAY_COLOR>3.0 SRM</DISPLAY_COLOR>
  </FERMENTABLE>
</FERMENTABLES>
```

This is an ingredient listed in BeerXML[1] that obviously contains a lot of technical information. Good for beer brewers, not so good for lay readers like myself. So let's concoct a stylesheet that returns just a few items of general

1. http://www.beerxml.com

interest for a beer-taster's website. Matching only on the root, we'll create a web page that contains only the ingredient name, origin, and notes.

orderorder2/pullprocess.xsl

```
<xsl:stylesheet xmlns:xsl="http://www.w3.org/1999/XSL/Transform" version="1.0">
  <xsl:template match="/">
    <html><head></head>
      <body>
        <h1><xsl:value-of select="FERMENTABLES/FERMENTABLE/NAME"/></h1>
         <p><xsl:value-of select="FERMENTABLES/FERMENTABLE/NOTES"/></p>
        <p>
          <xsl:text>Origin: </xsl:text>
          <xsl:value-of select="FERMENTABLES/FERMENTABLE/ORIGIN"/>
        </p>
      </body>
    </html>
  </xsl:template>
</xsl:stylesheet>
```

And, voilà:

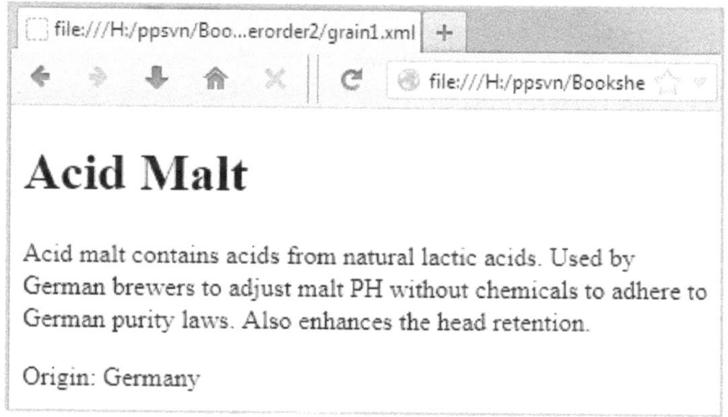

That, my friends, is pull processing. You just find a comfortable place in the XML and use XPath to bring the content to you.

And please don't tell anyone who showed it to you!

So why am I showing it to you if it's so naughty? Because in spite of what purists might think, it can actually be quite useful, in the right situation. For instance, in the example above, using the traditional approach I would have to write a template that matched the /FERMENTABLES/FERMENTABLE part of the path, then three other templates, one each for NAME, NOTES, and ORIGIN. In my pull-processing shortcut, I've only had to write one template.

Another advantage is that this approach makes it easy to swap the order of the content. Check the order of the notes and the origin in the output.

The great thing is that you don't need to be at the document root for this to work. You might have matched an element further down in the XML structure and realized that all you need at that point are two or three of its distant relatives (scattered somewhere across a labyrinthine, booby-trapped XML structure). Toss in some <xsl:apply-templates> or <xsl:value-of> instructions with appropriate XPath statements, and you're doing pull processing.

If pull processing is so useful, why is it frowned on? You can probably guess: XML is a flexible, tricky sort of thing, and you may have no way to anticipate what the structure might be. For instance, I haven't actually seen a DTD or schema for BeerXML, so I don't know whether ORIGIN or NOTES are required fields, and I don't know whether there might be more than one origin. Think what would happen, for instance, if we ran into this:

```
<xsl:variable name="id">
    <ORIGINS status="disputed">
      <ORIGIN>Germany</ORIGIN>
      <ORIGIN>Netherlands</ORIGIN>
    </ORIGIN>
```

Suddenly our pull processing doesn't work so well. In a case like this, we're better off sticking with the fall-through template approach that allows XSLT to keep up with the complexities of XML.

Still, if we know the structure well enough, pull processing can be a useful shortcut for retrieving—and re-ordering—small amounts of data.

XPaths to Anywhere

So far we've re-ordered content with a top-down approach, but on a regular basis, we're going to need to deal with content that's a lot more dispersed. Let's imagine a set of pharmaceutical data that has been sorted into various sections. (Real pharmaceutical XML is usually more complex than we can deal with in our examples here.) In one section is a list of standard descriptions for standard types of side effects, and in another section is a list of medications offered by a company. It might look a bit like this:

orderorder2/pharmEffects.xml

```
<?xml version="1.0" encoding="UTF-8"?>
<?xml-stylesheet type="text/xsl" href="pharmEffects.xsl"?>
<substanceEffects>
  <sideEffects>
    <negative>
      <effect reference="A">dizziness</effect>
      <effect reference="B">drowsiness</effect>
      <effect reference="D">dyspepsia</effect>
    </negative>
```

```
    <positive>
      <effect reference="E">awesome strength</effect>
      <effect reference="H">reduced risk of heart attack</effect>
    </positive>
    <curious>
      <effect reference="I">desire to wear colorful spandex</effect>
    </curious>
  </sideEffects>
  <substances>
    <substance status="experimental">
      <invented_name>Spydybyty</invented_name>
      <sideEffects>
        <effect ref="A"/>
        <effect ref="E"/>
        <effect ref="I"/>
      </sideEffects>
      <description>This refined, radioactive spider venom
      is similar to a form accidentally discovered in 1962.
      </description>
    </substance>
     <substance status="common">
      <invented_name>Acetylsalicylic acid</invented_name>
      <sideEffects>
        <effect ref="B"/>
        <effect ref="D"/>
        <effect ref="H"/>
      </sideEffects>
      <description>Acetylsalicylic acid, while used
      in natural forms since antiquity, was first
      manufactured in 1899. It is better known as
      aspirin.
      </description>
    </substance>
  </substances>
</substanceEffects>
```

Our mission is to turn this gobbledygook into something a bit more readable, like this:

Pharmaceutical Substances and Their Effects

Spydybyty

This refined, radioactive spider venom is similar to a form accidentally discovered in 1962.

Side Effects

- dizziness
- awesome strength
- desire to wear colorful spandex

I know you can do the first parts of this, so why not give it a try. When it's time to do the list of effects, we'll see a technique that we haven't explored.

When we get to a tag like <effect ref="A"> in the <substances> section, we need to find an <effect> in the <sideEffects> section with references= equal to the ref= attribute we started with. So one thing we need to learn is how to keep track of a value that we pick up in one place and compare it to a value in another place.

Here's the template that performs this piece of the work:

orderorder2/pharmEffects.xsl

```
<xsl:template match="effect">
  <xsl:variable name="ref_code">
    <xsl:value-of select="@ref"/>
  </xsl:variable>
  <li>
  <xsl:value-of
   select="/substanceEffects/
   sideEffects//effect[@reference = $ref_code]"/>
  </li>
</xsl:template>
```

Figure 32—Retrieving the effects yext for each substance

In this example our XPath statement starts all the way back at the root with that introductory slash (/), then works its way back down the hierarchy. The double-slash (//) in the path is a neat piece of shorthand to ignore the fact that the <effect> tags are in three different container elements. We want to look in all of those containers, so we use // to say "any path from the <sideEffects> tag to any <effects> tag." (Note that we had to include the <sideEffects> element in the path. If we had eliminated it, the statement would also have picked up those <effect> tags in the <substances> section.

Although this approach works, backing all the way up to the root and then working back down can take a lot of processing overhead. Another way we could have done the same thing is by using a relative path. In this case, the path would have had to refer up to a common ancestor then work its way down, like this:

```
<xsl:value-of
 select="ancestor::substanceEffects/sideEffects//effect[@reference = $ref_code]"/>
```

Between you and me, there's not much difference in this case, but in larger chunks of XML the difference may be considerable. Be kind to your processors!

Joe asks:

How Do I Handle Those Incredibly Long XSLT Expressions?

XSLT expressions can be as complex as the patterns of XML you encounter, and they can become incredibly long at times. In those cases, you'll want to add line breaks to the expressions where possible to make them more readable. Some valid places to break XSLT expressions are:

- Before or after the quote marks enclosing the expression
- Between expression operators. I like to put the expression operator at the beginning of the second line so I can see the type of relationship more easily, but a lot of people do it the other way around.
- Between predicate square brackets
- Within function parentheses
- Between attributes
- Before or after the slashes in an XPath path. I like to bring the slash down to the next line so I can see that it's part of a path.

For example, this expression...

```
<xsl:template
  match="/docroot
  /a
  | docroot/b
  [contains(.,
  'yes'
  )]
  [@id
  = 2]"
/>
```

...is valid and functionally the same as...

```
<xsl:template match="docroot/a | docroot/b[contains(.,'yes')][@id = 2]"/>
```

For myself, I like to place the breaks so there are parallel groupings from line to line —large predicates, halves of relational statements, and so forth. It helps with scanning through the code. XSLT is infamous for being verbose. Managing all that verbage can become a significant issue when troubleshooting your code.

If you compare the predicate in line 8 (Figure 32, *Retrieving the effects yext for each substance*, on page 127) with the predicate in line 35 in the code Figure 31, *The complete listbuster stylesheet*, on page 121, you'll detect a pattern. This is a strategy we'll often use in conjunction with XPath statements: we put the value of some attribute of an element into a variable where it will stay put, then we use XPath to find some other element with a similar or identical attribute value. In the first example we used an ID value that we generated with XSLT. In the second example we used a reference value that was intentionally set up for this purpose.

I don't know whether this strategy has a name, but it should. "Snare and compare?" Corny, I know, but let's go with it. We will see this strategy again in our XSLT travels.

Grouping

Grouping and sorting are two fundamental activities in database handling, and likewise in the world of XML processing. In this section we'll see how to handle grouping with XSLT, then we'll follow up with sorting in the next section.

By grouping, we mean that we are going to gather similar sorts of things together. As part of this gathering, we may find it helpful or convenient to place certain repeated parts of the data into an overall heading for the group, then list the group members without the repetitive parts of the data.

With the work that we've already done with XPath, we'll find that grouping is not really a big deal. Not unlike rearranging XML content piece by piece, as we saw in *XPaths to Anywhere*, on page 125, the secret of grouping is to place the <xsl:apply-templates> tags judiciously, choose our XPaths carefully, and decide what and what not to process.

In a basic form of grouping, let's say we have some XML about bicycles that looks like this, only with, say, several hundred models:

```
<bikes>
  <bike>
    <brand>Raleigh</brand>
    <model>Revenio 3.0</model>
    <price>1199</price>
    <group>105</group>
    <shop>REI</shop>
  </bike>
   ...
  <bike>
    <brand>KHS</brand>
    <model>Flite 750</model>
    <price>1999</price>
    <group>sram rival</group>
    <shop>TLC Bikes</shop>
  </bike>
</bikes>
```

Figure 33—Example XML for bike models and shops

We'd like to get all that data into a more manageable form—say, group the bikes by store, if we're serving up a friendly website that lists bike models by bike shop. There are at least two ways to do this: the sneaky way and the classically correct (hard) way. We'll see both methods.

Grouping with Modes: Finding First Instances

First, let's think about what we're trying to do. We want to construct a list of stores, and each store will have a secondary list of the bike models it has available. It's a long list, and we don't necessarily know the name of each store we're likely to encounter, so our stylesheet has to take into account that we need a list of models for any store we happen to encounter. We can't tell it exactly what to look for.

In the sneaky solution, we use XPath to match on each store, but we add a predicate to make sure that there is no previous entry for the same store, so we get only the first entry for each store. Then we apply templates to all the following entries and take the ones that match the current store.

We're going to have to add one more XSLT tool to the utility belt to make this one work. But first let's have a look at the stylesheet in Figure 34, *Listing bike models by bike shop*, on page 131.

Modes: Switching Tracks in the Processing Flow

No doubt you noticed that `mode=` attribute we've thrown into the mix. A template is simply a way of adding a name to `<xsl:template>` and `<xsl:apply-templates>` as a way to allow a separate "branch" of processing.

Sometimes we need to process one or more elements more than one time, in different ways. For instance, we might process all the tags in a book three times—once for the table of contents, once for the body, and once for the index. If we just used a `match=` or `select=` statement for the tags we needed to process a second time, those statements would probably look identical to the ones we used to process the tags the first time. As some of my friends like to say, "that dog don't hunt." And besides, XSLT parsers get cranky about duplicate template matches.

We solve the problem by using modes. Modes can be named anything you like (without spaces), the more descriptive of their purpose the better. Templates for processing the table of contents might have a `mode="toc"`, and so forth.

We can think of a mode as a secondary railroad track, where the use of `mode=` throws the processor into a parallel set of processing, except in our case, the orderorder2/bike-grouping.xsl

```
<xsl:stylesheet xmlns:xsl="http://www.w3.org/1999/XSL/Transform" version="1.0">
  <xsl:output indent="yes"/>
  <xsl:template match="/bikes">
    <store-models>
      <xsl:apply-templates
        select="bike[not(preceding-sibling::bike/shop = shop)]"/>
    </store-models>
  </xsl:template>

  <xsl:template match="bike">
    <xsl:variable name="this-shop">
      <xsl:value-of select="shop"/>
    </xsl:variable>
    <shop>
      <shop-name>
        <xsl:value-of select="shop"/>
      </shop-name>
      <xsl:apply-templates select="." mode="bikelist"/>
      <xsl:apply-templates
        select="following-sibling::bike[shop = $this-shop]" mode="bikelist"/>
    </shop>
  </xsl:template>

  <xsl:template match="bike" mode="bikelist">
    <bike>
      <brand>
        <xsl:value-of select="brand"/>
      </brand>
      <model>
        <xsl:value-of select="model"/>
      </model>
      <price>
        <xsl:value-of select="price"/>
      </price>
    </bike>
  </xsl:template>
</xsl:stylesheet>
```

Figure 34—Listing bike models by bike shop

train (the XSLT process) may split in half and go down both tracks at the same time. Figure 35, *Conceptual diagram of processing with modes*, on page 132 gives a diagram that demonstrates this idea.

The secondary track has a name that we use to keep track of what gets processed—there may be many more templates with the same mode.

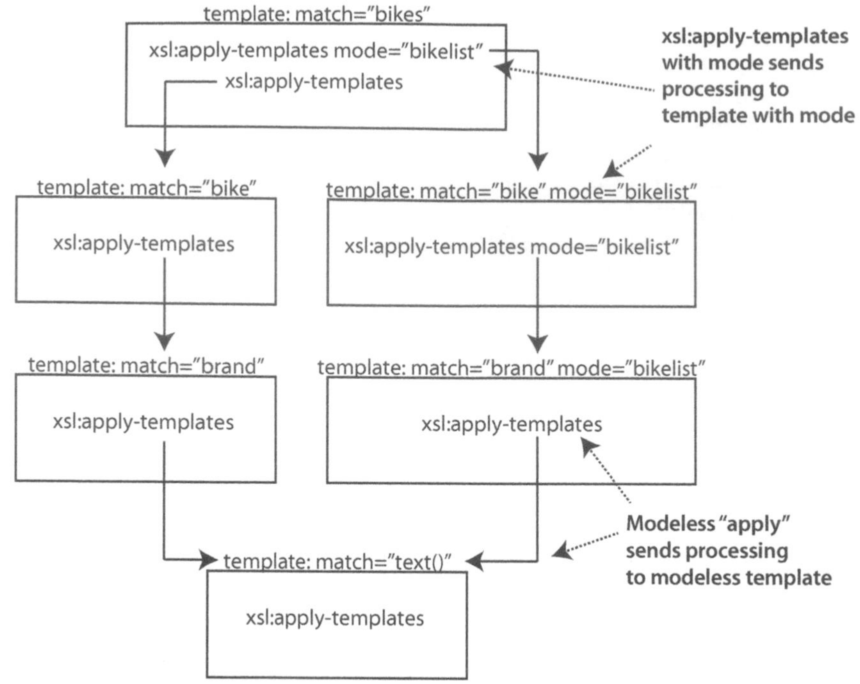

Figure 35—Conceptual diagram of processing with modes

Also, we have to add mode= to the <xsl:apply-templates> tag to make sure we send the processing off to the template using the appropriate mode. The <xsl:apply-templates> is where we throw the switch on the track. If we later forget to use mode= in <xsl:apply-templates> while we're in a given mode, the track immediately switches back to the original track without a mode.

Let's get back to our original grouping problem and see how it works with the use of modes.

In the XSLT script in Figure 34, *Listing bike models by bike shop*, on page 131, we first match on the root element and set up the wrapper XML tag for our output, <store-models>. Then comes the first part of our strategy: in line 6, we select the first instance of <bike> by checking whether there is any preceding <bike> that has the same value in the <shop> element as the current instance. If there is no preceding occurrence, this is the first bike for that bike shop. Selecting only the first instance of <bike> for each shop, we go off to the template for <bike> and do more processing.

In the template for <bike>, we make some tags for the shop and shop name. Since we have the information for the first bike within the current <bike> tag, we use an <xsl:apply-templates>(line 18)—with the mode="bikelist" that we talked about—to process the tags for this bike.

Note that the value of the select= statement is a period (.), which selects the current element, which is <bike>. To keep the templates compact, we want to select the <bike> tag here so we can use the same template we use when selecting the following <bike> tags. In other words, we want the entry for the first bike, which we've already selected, to look like the entries for the rest of the bikes we're about the select.

Now we need to process all the other <bike> tags for the same shop. Ah—here's where our XPath friend, following-sibling, comes in handy. In line 20 we use the old "snare and compare" method to process through the remaining bike tags with the name of our current bike shop in hand. (I told you we'd see it again.) Where a following <bike> tag has a <shop> tag with the same value as our first <bike> tag, we again apply the template for <bike> in the mode="bikelist" mode.

Finally, the last template on line 24 fills in the details for each bike. And that's it! With three carefully arranged templates, we've sifted through the XML to give us bike grouping by shop, sort of like this:

```
<store-models>
  <shop>
    <shop-name>REI</shop-name>
    <bike>
      <brand>Raleigh</brand>
      <model>Revenio 3.0</model>
      <price>1199</price>
    </bike>
    <bike>
      <brand>Diamondback</brand>
      <model>Podium 4</model>
      <price>1499</price>
    </bike>
    ...
  </shop>
  ...
</store-models>
```

This approach to grouping—finding the first item in a group then iterating over the remaining items—works okay, but it can lead to some lengthy XPath statements as the XML structure becomes more complex. For instance, what do we do if <bike> is not always at the same level in the structure? This iterative method is okay for simple hierarchies, but to deal with more complex XML, we're going to need a more industrial-strength method.

Grouping with Keys: the Muenchian Method

To manage the grouping in a more abstract and flexible fashion, we use a tool called a *key*. The use of keys involves two parts: the <xsl:key> tag, which defines what we're looking for, and the key() function, which we place where we need to use the key we've defined. The "what we're looking for" part is an XPath expression that defines a node-set.

Introduction to Keys

So, very quickly, here are the technical details on the <xsl:key> and the key() function. Don't get too bogged down in the details, though—it's best to see these guys in action to understand how they work.

<xsl:key>

<xsl:key> tags appear at the same level as the <xsl:template> tag in the stylesheet. By convention, they are usually placed before any templates at the top of the stylesheet so they are easy to keep track of. By being placed at the top level in the stylesheet, they can be used in any template. (In other words, they have *global scope*—although we haven't gotten to the concept of scope quite yet.)

Following are the pertinent attributes for <xsl:key>:

Attribute	Required?	Function
name	Yes	Gives the name of the key, which will be called by the key() function. The name must not contain spaces, but it may contain a namespace prefix.
match	Yes	Provides the XPath pattern that will be matched when the key is used.
use	Yes	Gives an expression for the value to be matched in the nodes retrieved by the match= attribute. The expression can match values in the attributes, text, or children of the matched node. Note that the expression is evaluated in the context of the path given by the match= attribute. For example, using our bike shop example in Figure 33, *Example XML for bike models and shops*, on page 129, if we say <xsl:key name="bike-brand" match="bike" use="brand"/>, it's valid because <brand> is a child of <bike>.

key({string},{object})

The key() function uses the definition of the key.

Parameter	Required?	Function
string	Yes	Gives the name of the <xsl:key> to be used.
object	Yes	Specifies what value will be supplied to the use= expression in the key.

For key() to work properly, it needs to be placed where the path of the match= attribute is valid. In our bike example, if we define the key <xsl:key name="bike-brand" match="bike" use="brand"/>, we need to use key('bike-brand','Specialized') in a context where that match="bike" makes sense—in our case, when we have matched the <bikes> tag. We'll see that arrangement in action in our next example.

In their simplest use, the <xsl:key> tag and key() functions work to select specific items from a list. For example, let's say that in our list of bicycles we want only the list of bikes made by Specialized. Here's a stylesheet to do the trick:

orderorder2/bikes-by-Specialized.xsl

```
<?xml version="1.0" encoding="UTF-8"?>
<xsl:stylesheet version="1.0"
  xmlns:xsl="http://www.w3.org/1999/XSL/Transform">

<xsl:key name="bike-brand" match="bike" use="brand"/>

<xsl:template match="/bikes">
  <html>
    <body>
      <xsl:apply-templates select="key('bike-brand', 'Specialized')"/>
    </body>
  </html>
</xsl:template>

<xsl:template match="bike">
  [template contents]
</xsl:template>
</xsl:stylesheet>
```

The result is a list that matches <bike> where <brand> has the value *Specialized*.

As you can see, we've placed the key() function in the template that matches <bikes> so the match="bike" attribute makes sense. And since we've specified use="brand" in the key itself, and the key() function specifies we want the value Specialized, the combination works to retrieve all instances of <bike> where <brand> is Specialized.

The Muenchian Method and <xsl:for-each>

Keys are helpful when we need to match the same element many times with one or more values, even if we aren't necessarily grouping things. But it does suggest that keys could be used for grouping. The catch is that the simple usage shown in *Introduction to Keys*, on page 134 doesn't create a heading for the items to be listed under, and it doesn't select all the brands that might appear in <brand>. To go this extra step, we're going to apply an extra twist—and interestingly enough, it also uses the "snare-and-compare" method. This approach is commonly called the *Muenchian method*, named after Steve Muench, an early XSLT developer and proponent who developed it.

To demonstrate the Muenchian method in its classical form, we're going to need to learn a new XSLT tool, the <xsl:for-each>instruction. We've been using <xsl:apply-templates> to accomplish some of the work it does, but <xsl:for-each> will make the form of the solution much easier in the long run. And more tools are almost always better.

<xsl:for-each>

The <xsl:for-each> instruction is an *iterator*: it directs the XSLT processor to execute its contents as many times as necessary to satisfy its conditions. The conditions it specifies are defined by an XPath expression in the select= attribute. The condition is satisfied when the processor has found all of the instances of the XPath expression it can find, or when it determines that no nodes match the XPath expression.

<xsl:for-each> is a bit like the <xsl:apply-templates> in that it tells the processor to select some node and act on it, and it's a bit like the <xsl:template> tag in that it contains additional instructions for the processor to execute within the context of the selcted tag. Which brings up another interesting point: <xsl:apply-templates> and <xsl:for-each> are the only two tags that can be used to change the current context of the XSLT processor within the XML content. The select= attribute in both instructions is the ticket for the XSLT processor to move down the road.

Although <xsl:for-each> temporarily changes the execution context of the processor, execution returns to the template in which it appears once all its conditions are satisfied. If the template contains other instructions after the <xsl:for-each>, those are executed next.

Another point worth mentioning is that if you define a variable within the <xsl:for-each> instruction that variable is defined the same way each time the contents of the <xsl:for-each> instruction are executed. That means that the results of a previous execution of <xsl:for-each> can't be used to change the contents of the variable. If you run into that sort of issue, you probably want to use *iteration*, a technique we will see in Chapter 10, *Large-Scale Stylesheet Strategies*, on page 183

select= is the only required attribute for <xsl:for-each>.

We'll see <xsl:for-each> in a bit of sample code shortly.

Joe asks:

Is Using <xsl:for-each> Good Form?

Frequently, XSLT programmers insist that <xsl:for-each> should not be used: anything it can do can be done with <xsl:apply-templates> and a matching template. And by using a separate template, you enable reuse of the code within the template.

This is probably true, but <xsl:for-each> has its uses. If the code it executes is small or unique, putting it in a separate template really doesn't help much. And if you have a bunch of variables already set up in the current template, and you need to use them, porting those variables over to another template can be a pain.

My take on all this is: if it's not something you're likely to reuse, <xsl:for-each> is a peach. Go for it!

So, going back to our previous example, where we listed only the bikes of a particular brand, we still have a problem: how would we group all of the bikes by all of the brands in our XML example (Figure 33, *Example XML for bike models and shops*, on page 129)? Let's take a look.

First, let's set up a key, as shown in line 3 in Figure 36, *The Muenchian grouping method*, on page 138.

Then we create a single template that makes use of the key, starting in line 5. And that's it. If nothing else, it's much more terse than what we did before.

Let's have a look at what's going on here. First, you'll see that we've set up the key exactly as we did when we were just picking out a single entry. This time, however, we're going to generalize our use of the key to select multiple entries.

In line 7, we've placed a <xsl:for-each> that uses the key. The <xsl:for-each> will iterate through the path specified by the select= statement.

In this case, though, we've limited the selection to one item. The select= statement says we're going to look through all the <bike> elements, then the predicate checks whether the ID generated for this instance is the same as the ID generated for the first instance in the key (similar to the "snare and orderorder2/bike-grouping-muenchian.xsl

```
1  <xsl:stylesheet xmlns:xsl="http://www.w3.org/1999/XSL/Transform" version="1.0">
2    <xsl:output indent="yes"/>
3    <xsl:key name="bike-brand" match="bike" use="brand"/>
4
5    <xsl:template match="/bikes">
6      <store-models>
7        <xsl:for-each
8          select="bike[generate-id() = generate-id(key('bike-brand', brand)[1])]">
9          <h1>
10           <xsl:value-of select="brand"/>
11         </h1>
12         <ul>
13           <xsl:for-each select="key('bike-brand',brand)">
14             <li><xsl:value-of select="model"/>, <xsl:value-of select="shop"/></li>
15           </xsl:for-each>
16         </ul>
17       </xsl:for-each>
18     </store-models>
19   </xsl:template>
20 </xsl:stylesheet>
```

Figure 36—The Muenchian grouping method

compare" method we've used elsewhere). If the two generated IDs are equal, this instance is the first in the list. (Jeni Tennison suggests another method for handling the predicate,[2] but either should do the trick.)

Having selected the first instance, we insert a few tags for the output to create our brand heading. Now we need to list all the instances of bikes of that brand. Here again we use <xsl:for-each> with the key to iterate through the node-set (in line 13). Since we've already established the name of the brand when we went through the first <xsl:for-each>, the second <xsl:for-each> iterates through the all of the <bike> nodes containing that brand. The results will be a list of all the bikes of that brand, showing only the two values we're outputting in line 14.

Hey, that wasn't so bad! You probably recognize some of the similarities with the method we covered earlier. The difference is that with the key, we can do it a lot more efficiently.

As you play with keys, you'll see that you can adjust the match= and use= expressions to cover a wide range of relationships in the document. Remember, XPath is your friend. The key (so to speak) is that the use= expression has to

2. http://www.jenitennison.com/xslt/grouping/muenchian.html

be valid within the context of the node-set returned by the match= statement, and the key() function has to be used where the match= statement makes sense. Remember those two points, and you're well on your way to becoming a key master.

Excellent! Grouping is one of the more complicated techniques we'll learn in this book, so we've done well. We can now select items and group them by various sorts of affinities within their content. But there's one more technique we need to add to our quiver to give us fundamental control over our lists. We now need to sort what we've retrieved so our audience isn't presented with a random batch of whatever happens to get stuffed into the source document.

Sort of a Short Sortie on Sorting

I have to confess: I enjoy baseball statistics. I'm not nearly the statistics junky that some people are, but I like to go to stats websites and browse through those monstrous wide tables of player statistics. One of the things I like best about those sites is the little widget at the top of each column to sort the players by each statistical category. Does a high number of triples correspond to a high number of stolen bases? Does a high ratio of homers per at-bat correspond to a high number of plate appearances? A sad case, no doubt about it.

You'll inevitably need to supply someone with a sorted list at some point. Try looking through an unsorted list of a few hundred items to find five or six specific entries. Wouldn't it be nice if someone had just sorted the furshlugginer[3] thing?

We don't want to be responsible for creating furshlugginer sorts of things, so let's sort out this sorting business.

The primary actor in most sorting methods is, as you might guess, the <xsl:sort> instruction. Let's get its vital statistics, then we'll put it through its paces with a continuation of our bike shop example.

<xsl:sort>

The <xsl:sort> instruction specifies the order in which data will be output. It must be used as the first element within an <xsl:apply-templates> or <xsl:for-each> instruction. This instruction is always used as an empty tag. The default order, if no attributes are given, is for data to be sorted in ascending order as text.

---

3. http://en.wiktionary.org/wiki/furshlugginer

Attribute	Required?	Function
select	No	Specifies the node that will be the basis for sorting the node-set selected by the <xsl:apply-templates> or <xsl:for-each> tag ("the selected node"). This implies that the node specified in this attribute must be a descendant of the selected node, or it must be the selected node itself. If this attribute isn't used, the data is sorted on the selected node.
order	No	The value *ascending* or *descending* specify whether the sort order will be ascending or descending. The default order is ascending.
data-type	No	Specifies how the data will be treated for sorting purposes. Valid values are *text*, *number*, and *qname*. The default value is *text*. When *number* is specified, values are sorted by their numeric value rather than by their first characters. For example, in the group 45, 90, 135 (because 1 comes before 4), the alphabetical ordering arranges them as 135, 45, 90, while the numeric ordering herds them back into a sensible 45, 90, 135.
case-order	No	The value upper-first or lower-first specify whether uppercase or lowercase letters will be first. This attribute only has an effect when data-type="text" The default value is language-dependent and also has a dependency on the XSLT processor.
lang	No	Specifies the language to be used as the basis for sorting. Valid values are the language codes as defined by the IEFT Network Working Group.[4] If you're up on your XML and HTML, it's the same language codes you use in those.

There's the dull stuff out of the way—now let's watch it work.

Looking back at our bike shop grouping exercise (Figure 36, *The Muenchian grouping method*, on page 138), we can see there are a couple of opportunities for sorting. Let's pop an <xsl:sort> under each <xsl:for-each> and see what we get. Here's the code with our addition:

4. Tags for Identifying Languages, http://www.ietf.org/rfc/rfc4646.txt

orderorder2/bike-grouping-muenchian-sorted.xsl

```
<xsl:stylesheet xmlns:xsl="http://www.w3.org/1999/XSL/Transform" version="1.0">
  <xsl:output indent="yes"/>
  <xsl:key name="bike-brand" match="bike" use="brand"/>

  <xsl:template match="/bikes">
    <store-models>
      <xsl:for-each
        select="bike[generate-id() = generate-id(key('bike-brand', brand)[1])]">
        <xsl:sort/>
        <h1>
          <xsl:value-of select="brand"/>
        </h1>
        <ul>
          <xsl:for-each select="key('bike-brand',brand)">
            <xsl:sort select="model"/>
            <li><xsl:value-of select="model"/>, <xsl:value-of select="shop"/></li>
          </xsl:for-each>
        </ul>
      </xsl:for-each>
    </store-models>
  </xsl:template>
</xsl:stylesheet>
```

Figure 37—Sorting the bicycle output

As you can see, we didn't bother with any of the attributes for the brand in the first <xsl:sort>. Good old alpha sorting, nothing fancy. In the second sort, we said that we wanted to sort by brand. Figure 38, *Unsorted bike list beside sorted list*, on page 142 shows the results, side-by-side with the unsorted version.

Finally, let's put the icing on the cake for our grouping/sorting extravaganza. Can we sort on two or more fields at the same time? And how do those numbers sort out? For this exercise to look good, we'll need a little more data, and we'll want to pull in the prices of our bikes. We'll add another <xsl:sort> under the second one in the code Figure 37, *Sorting the bicycle output*, on page 141, this time with `select="price"` and `data-type="number"`. Now our code looks like Figure 39, *List sorted by two fields*, on page 143 (see line 16).

And the results are spiffin' (Figure 40, *Sorting on two fields*, on page 143).

As you can see in the beefed-up section on Specialized bikes, the models are sorted in alphabetical order, but where the models have the same name, the results are further sorted by the numeric value of the prices. The numeric sort is because we added that `data-type="number"` to the <xsl:sort> instruction.

```
<?xml version="1.0" encoding="utf-8"?>
<store-models>
    <h1>Raleigh</h1>
    <ul>
        <li>Revenio 3.0, REI</li>
        <li>Revenio 4.0, REI</li>
    </ul>
    <h1>Fuji</h1>
    <ul>
        <li>Roubaix SL, Performance</li>
        <li>Roubaix 1.1, Performance</li>
    </ul>
    <h1>Felt</h1>
    <ul>
        <li>F75, Flythe</li>
    </ul>
    <h1>Trek</h1>
    <ul>
        <li>madone 2.1, Flythe</li>
        <li>madone 2.3, Flythe</li>
    </ul>
    <h1>Diamondback</h1>
    <ul>
        <li>Podium 4, REI</li>
    </ul>
    <h1>Cannondale</h1>
    <ul>
        <li>CAAD10-3, REI/Bicyle Chain</li>
    </ul>
    <h1>Cervelo</h1>
    <ul>
        <li>P1 Ultegra, Inside Out</li>
    </ul>
    <h1>Specialized</h1>
    <ul>
        <li>Allez Race 105, Bicycle Chain</li>
        <li>Allez Comp105, Bicycle Chain</li>
    </ul>
    <h1>Scott</h1>
    <ul>
        <li>Speedster 10, REI</li>
    </ul>
    <h1>KHS</h1>
    <ul>
        <li>Flite 750, TLC Bikes</li>
    </ul>
</store-models>
```

```
<?xml version="1.0" encoding="utf-8"?>
<store-models>
    <h1>Cannondale</h1>
    <ul>
        <li>CAAD10-3, REI/Bicyle Chain</li>
    </ul>
    <h1>Cervelo</h1>
    <ul>
        <li>P1 Ultegra, Inside Out</li>
    </ul>
    <h1>Diamondback</h1>
    <ul>
        <li>Podium 4, REI</li>
    </ul>
    <h1>Felt</h1>
    <ul>
        <li>F75, Flythe</li>
    </ul>
    <h1>Fuji</h1>
    <ul>
        <li>Roubaix 1.1, Performance</li>
        <li>Roubaix SL, Performance</li>
    </ul>
    <h1>KHS</h1>
    <ul>
        <li>Flite 750, TLC Bikes</li>
    </ul>
    <h1>Raleigh</h1>
    <ul>
        <li>Revenio 3.0, REI</li>
        <li>Revenio 4.0, REI</li>
    </ul>
    <h1>Scott</h1>
    <ul>
        <li>Speedster 10, REI</li>
    </ul>
    <h1>Specialized</h1>
    <ul>
        <li>Allez Comp105, Bicycle Chain</li>
        <li>Allez Race 105, Bicycle Chain</li>
    </ul>
    <h1>Trek</h1>
    <ul>
        <li>madone 2.1, Flythe</li>
        <li>madone 2.3, Flythe</li>
    </ul>
</store-models>
```

Figure 38—Unsorted bike list beside sorted list

All in all, an excellent approach for comparison shopping to keep you away from those spreadsheet apps!

What We Did

We've sliced and diced our content so many ways, it's starting to look like last week's leftovers. We've rearranged flat lists, we've learned a couple of methods for grouping content, we've learned keys for selecting content, and we've learned how to sort our results into satisfying patterns.

We've spent three chapters learning how to manipulate the order of content, and it's time to give ourselves a nice pat on the back. This type of content manipulation is at the heart of XSLT, and we've dealt with a big chunk of it. Sure, there are a lot more complicated problems than what we've shown here, orderorder2/bike-grouping-muenchian-sorted2.xsl

```
<xsl:stylesheet xmlns:xsl="http://www.w3.org/1999/XSL/Transform" version="1.0">
  <xsl:output indent="yes"/>
  <xsl:key name="bike-brand" match="bike" use="brand"/>

  <xsl:template match="/bikes">
    <store-models>
      <xsl:for-each
        select="bike[generate-id() = generate-id(key('bike-brand', brand)[1])]">
        <xsl:sort/>
        <h1>
          <xsl:value-of select="brand"/>
        </h1>
        <ul>
          <xsl:for-each select="key('bike-brand',brand)">
            <xsl:sort select="model"/>
            <xsl:sort select="price" data-type="number"/>
            <li><xsl:value-of select="model"/>, <xsl:value-of select="shop"/>,
              <xsl:value-of select="price"/></li>
          </xsl:for-each>
        </ul>
      </xsl:for-each>
    </store-models>
  </xsl:template>
</xsl:stylesheet>
```

Figure 39—List sorted by two fields

```
<h1>Specialized</h1>
<ul>
   <li>Allez Comp105, Bicycle Chain, 1749</li>
   <li>Allez Race 105, Bicycle Chain, 1700</li>
   <li>Rockhopper 29, Specialized, 700</li>
   <li>Rockhopper 29, Art's, 879.99</li>
   <li>Rockhopper 29, controlbike.com, 880</li>
   <li>Rockhopper 29, Likes Bikes, 1090</li>
   <li>Secteur Double, Specialized, 850</li>
</ul>
```

Figure 40—Sorting on two fields

but the methods for handling most of those problems are variations on what we've learned here.

So why not take a break and digest what you've learned. Because when we get to the next chapter on using and handling values, we're going to take XSLT to a whole different level.

Concentrating my mind upon the massive lock I hurled the nine thought waves against it. In breathless expectancy I waited, when finally the great door moved softly toward me and slid quietly to one side.

> *Edgar Rice Burroughs,* A Princess of Mars

CHAPTER 9

The Value of Values

We've been dancing around a certain subject in these early chapters, and now it's time to get face to face with it: *values*, how they are handled in XSLT, and the kinds of things we can do with them.

Every programming language has to be able to count things, manipulate text, deal with dates, identify objects—and values are how we do that. We've already seen values at work in a number of ways—we've seen variables used in the <xsl:variable> instruction, we've seen numbers being used in XPath expressions, and we've used the text() function to get the text value of elements. We've dealt with these methods of handling values as part of other methods and solutions, but if we're going to have a thorough understanding of the XSLT toolset, we need to cover all the bases.

That being said, this wouldn't be the solution-oriented guide of choice if we just listed the value-handling mechanisms and let it go at that. So we're going to take it a little further. We're going to learn about a technique called *recursion*. We'll also learn two forms of conditional control (<xsl:if> and <xsl:choose>), and we'll see a re-usable, named template that we call directly with the <xsl:call-template> instruction. We'll use these conditional controls and named templates as part of the technique of recursion.

As we learn these techniques, we'll see that the grease that keeps the gears going 'round will be values and the XSLT mechanisms that manage them. So let's dig in.

Value Types

In *The Contents of Expressions*, on page 115, we mentioned that there were four basic types of values in XSLT: numbers, strings, Boolean values, and nodes. Let's get a little more specific than that, because there are nuances hidden in these categories.

Numbers

Numbers are what you think they are—good old base 10 values represented by the Arabic numeric characters 0 through 9. In XSLT 1.0, numbers are usually recognized as numbers rather than as strings. (This isn't always the case in XSLT 2.0.)

Still, in some cases where there may be issues with the data typing of a result, you can be sure that the result is treated as a number by using the number() function. Even if the argument of number() isn't really a number, we can usually convert it to a number with the number() function.

Strings

We've seen strings aplenty in our earlier examples, so there's not much to talk about here.

One thing we haven't talked about, though, is how to treat numbers like strings. That's because you don't really have to. If you apply a string-related function (like substring-before()) with a number as one or more of the arguments, XSLT understands. The number gets treated like a common string. For example, if I have an XML tag <bignum>1234567890<bignum/> and want to get artsy and replace the 3 with an E, I would match on <bignum> and use something like:

```
<xsl:value-of select="substring-before(.,3)"/>
<xsl:text>E</xsl:text>
<xsl:value-of select="substring-after(.,3)"/>
```

Out pops the highly useful string 12E4567890, and we're in some kind of business.

Boolean Values

If you've studied logic or computer programming, you know that "Boolean values" means "true" and "false." But what does that mean in XSLT terms?

As we'll learn in the sections on <xsl:if> and <xsl:choose>, we sometimes need to check conditions with a test= attribute. Or we may need to check a condition within an XPath expression. We may need to know, simply, whether a condition is logically true or false. But how do we check for trueness or falseness? What kind of value is "true," and what kind is "false?"

The funny thing about Boolean values is that the value is assigned to an object. We don't see the value of the Boolean explicitly. Instead, we have to test the object to know what Boolean value it has.

In *The Contents of Expressions*, on page 115 we talked about relational operators that are used to create expressions that yield Boolean values. We can also test whether an object is true or false by using the boolean() function. For example, if we said <xsl:value-of select="boolean(4 = 5)">, we would get the string "false". But "false" is just a string representing the Boolean value, not the value itself.

To make the example a little muddier, what would happen if we said <xsl:value-of select="boolean('false')">. We would get the result "true"! That's because the string "false," taken by itself, is not a zero-length string. So 'false' is true. (And people wonder why XSLT gets such a bad rap.)

Besides using the boolean() function to test the truth-value of an object, we can also use the true() and false() functions to explicitly specify a Boolean value. Basically, the value of true() is a Boolean true value, and the value of false() is a Boolean false value.

Here's a short guide to how different types of XML objects are evaluated as true or false.

- A positive zero, negative zero, or NaN ("Not a Number") is false; any other number is true.
- Any string longer than zero characters is true.
- Any node-set that is not empty is true.
- A Boolean true value is true, and a Boolean false value is false. (Goes without saying, I know, but there, I said it.)

Nodes

Nodes are the usual suspects—elements, attributes, text nodes, the root, comments, programming instructions, and namespaces. Nodes can be considered individually or as a group. Thinking about nodes as values, we usually think of a node-set, that is, a group of nodes.

A node-set is usually created by the use of an XPath expression. We've seen XPath expressions in action before, and we've made use of the node-sets that get returned, so we don't need to explore that relationship much more. But what if we need to refer to the node-set many times? Do we need to write the XPath expression every time?

It turns out we can store a node-set in a variable, then use the variable for testing for nodes as well as for retrieving nodes. We'll see more about this usage of node-sets when we get to the next section.

Variables

It turns out that we use variables all over the place in our stylesheets, so we should give them a little more attention. By the end of this chapter, we're going to need them.

The Dossier on Variables

Let's begin with a quick run-down on the formalities, then talk a bit about what variables are used for. Then we'll put them to work in a couple of interesting ways.

<xsl:variable>

The `<xsl:variable>` instruction defines a named symbol for holding and using values. Once a value is defined for a variable within its given scope, that value is static until the variable's scope is released.

Within the scope of the variable, the value can be retrieved by using a dollar sign ($) immediately followed by the variable name. The variable is usually retrieved in the context of an XSLT attribute.

Here are the attributes that can be used with `<xsl:variable>`:

Attribute	Required?	Function
name=	Yes	Assigns a name to the variable. This name will be used, preceded by a dollar sign ($), to retrieve the value stored in the variable.
select=	No	This attribute takes an expression that specifies the value to be assigned to the variable. If this attribute is not used to assign a value, the `<xsl:variable>` tag must enclose additional content to specify the value of the variable. But if this attribute is used, the `<xsl:variable>` tag must be empty.

That's only a part of the story. The use of variables entails a few other interesting tidbits:

- Variables can contain any of the data types defined in *Value Types*, on page 145. The data type of the value will condition how we retrieve and use the value. For example, if the variable contains a string and we try to use it as we would use a node-set, we'll probably get an error message.

- If we define a variable but don't have anything after it in the template, the XSLT processor may post a message to the effect that the variable isn't actually doing anything. It won't stop the processing, but we might want to check whether something is missing.
- We can define variables within variables to any level, but I'm not sure there's a point. Anything defined inside a variable can also be defined outside the variable.
- A variable can only be used within its *scope*. The scope is global if the variable is defined as a top-level element in a stylesheet, and the scope is local if it is defined within a template. A global variable can be used anywhere in the stylesheet, while a local variable can only be used in the template where it is defined. (We'll cover a way to get around some of that limitation with <xsl:param> later in this chapter.)
- If the variable is globally defined, its placement in the stylesheet does not matter. If it is defined in a template, the variable can only be used after where it is defined in the template.
- The <xsl:for-each> tag imposes its own scope. You cannot pass the value of a variable defined inside <xsl:for-each> to anything outside the <xsl:for-each>.

  If you think you need to capture values from a repetitive process, a variable inside <xsl:for-each> may not be the answer to your problem. Maybe you could put the <xsl:for-each> inside the variable, in which case the variable would contain all of the data output by the entire <xsl:for-each> operation.

  You might also consider using <xsl:apply-templates> with the same select= statement as the <xsl:for-each> (remembering to create the appropriate template to go with it). If you do this, you may need to pass the variable to the template with a parameter (as described later in *Parameters and xsl:call-template*, on page 160 Or you might need a recursive process, which we will describe in *Putting It All Together with Recursion*, on page 175 later in this chapter.

And that's the book on variables—a shifty sort of character with questionable values. Amd we'll question those values a lot once we get to the test= attribute in <xsl:when> and <xsl:if>. But let's take a look at examples of <xsl:variable> in its various guises before we take on conditional processing.

Variables in Action

One use for a variable is to give it the value of something that we can't know until we are processing the XML source, then to take some action based on the variable. For example, suppose our XML consists of a mixture of elements that need to be numbered, and both the numbering and the indent level will reflect the depth of the element within a hierarchy of these mixed elements. Every level needs to be indented another half an inch, and every level gets a period and its own number added to the number of its parent. That may sound a little abstract, so here's an example:

```
<task id="1">Build a robot.
  <step>Draw a plan.</step>
  <task>Implement the plan.
    <steps>
      <step>Build the hardware.</step>
      <step>Write the software.</step>
      <step>Test the robot.
          <steps>
            <step>Tell it to go.</step>
            <step>Tell it to stop.</step>
          </steps>
      </step>
    </steps>
  </task>
  <task>Take over the world
    <task>Repeat task <ref href="1"/> 6 billion times.</task>
  </task>
</task>
```

Figure 41—A Mixture of Task and Steps

As you can see, this XML is a little gnarly. For us to get the level of the element (either <task> or <step>), we're going to have to count ancestors. Our variable to hold the value of the level is going to look like this:

```
<xsl:variable name="tag-level">
  <xsl:value-of
  select="count(ancestor-or-self::*[name() = 'task' or name() = 'step']"/>
</xsl:variable>
```

Could we have put that count() function into the select= statement of the <xsl:variable>? Yes, and it would have made no difference, it would work either way. Sometimes you will need to put the expression for the value into the contents of the <xsl:variable> tag, because it can become very complicated, and I generally like doing things only one way as much as possible. But let's not rule out the possibility of the other mechanism. And remember, when creating node-sets, the select= attribute is a necessity.

Now when we want to use the level number we just ask nicely by placing the $tag-level variable in the appropriate place. For example, to get the half-inch spacing we're looking for, we might create the following attribute:

```
<xsl:attribute name="margin-left">
  <xsl:value-of select="concat( ($tag-level * 0.5) ,'in' "/>
</xsl:attribute>
```

Here we multiply the tag level times 0.5 to get the amount of indentation, then we concatenate the string with the unit of measurement in (inches) to create the value for the margin-left= attribute.

What about the numbering we talked about for the elements? We want the first-level elements to be numbered 1, 2, 3, the second-level elements to be numbered 1.1, 1.2, 1.3 and 2.1, 2.2, 2.3, and so forth, as many levels down as we need. We could probably work that all out with our tag-level variable and the count() function, but that approach would quickly bog down in repetition and long XPath expressions. We would have to count elements at our current level, then count the number of elements preceding and including the parent element, taking into account that we don't want to count the <steps> tag at all—very messy.

We can avoid that mess very easily with a neat tag for numbering called, oddly enough, <xsl:number> (not to be confused with the number() function, which does something completely different). It's a powerful way to generate number streams in a document. But we're not going to get to it just yet.

Variables Controlling Conditional Structures

XSLT includes two instructions for making decisions about processing: <xsl:if> and <xsl:choose> with its child elements <xsl:when> and <xsl:otherwise>. The heart of these instructions is the test= attribute, which specifies the condition(s) under which to execute the contents of the tags. Once again, let's get a quick formal rundown on these tags, then let's put them to work in some examples.

<xsl:if>

This tag is used to wrap around content that may or may not be executed. The content of the test= attribute, evaluated in the current context, determines whether the contents will be executed.

Content of the <xsl:if> can be text, tags, and XSLT instructions in any combination.

Attribute	Required?	Function
test=	Yes	Contains an expression that evaluates to a boolean value. If the boolean value is true(), the contents of the <xsl:if> tag are executed. Otherwise, the contents of the <xsl:if> tag are ignored.

<xsl:choose>

This tag can only contain two types of instructions: <xsl:when> and <xsl:otherwise>. It also does not have any significant attributes. The purpose of <xsl:choose> is to hold one or more <xsl:when> tags and, optionally, a single <xsl:otherwise>.

<xsl:when>

The purpose of <xsl:when> is to allow for the choice of a single option out of multiple options instead of just one. Otherwise, this tag works like the <xsl:if> tag. The test= attribute fulfills exactly the same function, and the contents of the <xsl:when> are executed only when the test= attribute is true. The major difference between this tag and <xsl:if> is that this tag exists only inside <xsl:choose>.

Each <xsl:when> contains a test= attribute that may or may not evaluate to true(). If more than one <xsl:when> tag exists in the <xsl:choose>, the first one that evaluates to true() has its contents executed, and the remainder of the tags are ignored. If none of the <xsl:when> tags contains a condition that is true, and there is an <xsl:otherwise>, the contents of the <xsl:otherwise> will be executed.

If none of the <xsl:when> tags are true and there is no <xsl:otherwise>, nothing in the <xsl:choose> tag is executed, and the processor goes along to the next instruction as if nothing had happened.

<xsl:otherwise>

The <xsl:otherwise> tag does not get much choice in the conditional processing party. It can only appear once in the <xsl:choose> tag, and only after all of the <xsl:when> tags. It only has its contents executed if none of the <xsl:when> tags find anything of interest.

It also has no attributes. However, like the <xsl:if> and <xsl:when> tags, it can contain any sort of content for execution. The <xsl:otherwise> tag is useful for providing fallback behavior when you aren't sure the conditions in the <xsl:when> tags are going to catch every case.

But we're really here to talk about variables, so let's get a sense of what these guys can do for us by putting them to work on the XML sample give in Figure 41, *A Mixture of Task and Steps*, on page 150.

First let's set ourselves a reasonable task. For each tag, we want to output the same number of asterisks as there are levels, plus the text, as we see in some forms of wiki markup. If that's all we need to do, we don't even need a separate template for the different elements in the XML. See what you can do with the problem first—define a variable that contains the value of the element's level, then use that variable in an <xsl:choose> instruction.

I know, you can't stand the tension. Here's what I've got:

```
<xsl:template match="*">
  <xsl:variable name="tag-level">
    <xsl:value-of
       select="count(ancestor::*[name() = 'task' or name() = 'step']) + 1"/>
  </xsl:variable>
  <xsl:choose>
    <xsl:when test="$tag-level = 1">*</xsl:when>
    <xsl:when test="$tag-level = 2">**</xsl:when>
    <xsl:when test="$tag-level = 3">***</xsl:when>
    <xsl:when test="$tag-level = 4">****</xsl:when>
  </xsl:choose>
  <xsl:text>  </xsl:text>
  <xsl:value-of select="text()">
</xsl:template>
```

In this example we only want the characters to appear for the <task> or <step> tags, so we don't put in an <xsl:otherwise> instruction to catch any outliers. We add a couple of spaces with the <xsl:text> instruction, then we output the text of the tag. The main point is that we've used our tag-level variable to good effect, selecting the correct number of asterisks to go with our text.

We might also create a variable with a text string in it. One good use for a text string is when our XSLT needs to supply hard-coded text. The problem is, you never know what language that text might need to appear in—the XML being processed might contain any sort of language, not just English. If you need to supply a "NOTE" or "WARNING" label to go with that text, you might need to make arrangements for multilingual processing. One way to do that is to create a set of tags with a language= attribute, so the tags contained the same word, but in different languages, as in Figure 42, *XML source to be processed with a text variable*, on page 154

With this markup tucked away somewhere, we can set up a variable to bring in the correct form of the label. Let's say that the language we'll be processing

```
<terms>
  <term id="note" language="de">Hinweis</term>
  <term word="note" language="en">Note</term>
  <term word="note" language="es">Nota</term>
  <term word="note" language="fi">Huomaa</term>
  <term word="note" language="fr">Remarque</term>
</terms>
```

Figure 42—XML source to be processed with a text variable

is declared in an attribute in the root node of our XML document, for example, <document language="fi">. Now we can set up the variable to bring in our correct note label when we match on a <note> tag, as in the following template:

```
<xsl:template match="note">
  <xsl:variable name="current-language">
    <xsl:value-of select="/document/@language"/>
  </xsl:variable>

  <xsl:variable name="note-text">
    <xsl:value-of select="//terms/term[@language = $current-language]"/>
  </xsl:variable>

  <xsl:value-of select="$note-text"/>
  <xsl:text>: </xsl:text>
  <xsl:apply-templates/>
</xsl:template>
```

In this arrangement, the use of the note-text variable gives us a level of abstraction from the actual wording. All we need to do is send a little Finnish XML through the processor, and, sure enough, out comes our "Huomaa."

In this example we've used the variable for language within the definition of the variable for note-text. We'll find this type of chaining of variables to be quite useful for handling complex situations. Breaking the problem down into bits and handling it with a long series of variables can be useful and necessary; however, we'll also need to check the variables at every step to make sure we're getting the expected values. This sort of situation will be dealt with in Chapter 11, *Troubleshooting*, on page 217.

We've now seen variables at work with numbers and text strings. The purposes they're put to and the expressions by which we create their values are as endless as our needs and imaginations. We'll find that we can also use variables with node-sets in a variety of ways. The following two sections cover two of the more common uses of node-sets in variables.

Testing for Nodes by Using a Variable

As we've seen, conditional processing instructions allow us to test variables by means of expressions that evaluate to true or false. One use we can make of this testing is to make choices based on the presence or absence of elements, attributes, or attribute values. For example, we might not want to create an element in the output until we know that the source includes an element or group of elements with a given attribute and attribute value. If this is a test that we need to perform many times, it would be helpful to capture the set of elements to be tested in a variable one time, then perform testing on that variable many times.

Let's say we need to feed some XML to a pharmaceutical label processing system, but there may be issues with confidentiality, relevance, or sheer data quantity in our source. Figure 43, *XML Source for Labeling Pharmaceuticals*, on page 156 shows an example of the type of XML we might need to handle. It contains a section under the <structure> element that indicates the structure by which the content is related, then it contains another area consisting of one or more (possibly dozens or hundreds) of <language> tags that provide the language-specific contents for the labels, but in a flat structure for ease of translation. The job is to feed the flattened content into the empty structure using the right language.

When we transfer the file over to the processor, we may want to omit one or more elements within each <language> element. In this case, we only want to copy over the elements that have an id= value that corresponds to a ref_id= in the <structure> part of the XML. We may not know ahead of time which items will be missing from the structure, so we can create a variable to capture the structure, then test that variable each time we process an <instance>. Figure 44, *The template for the instance tag*, on page 157 shows how the template for <instance> would look.

When the language is English, the output would then look like this:

```
<instance id="en-01">Rosuvastatin</instance>
<instance id="en-02">film-coated tablets</instance>
<instance id="en-03">10mg</instance>
<instance id="en-06">11 December 2014</instance>
<instance id="en-07">OUTER CARTON BOTTLE AND LABEL</instance>
```

The <instance id="en-16"> is omitted because it did not have a corresponding refid= in the structure section.

You'll notice a couple of interesting new facts about line 2 in Figure 44, *The template for the instance tag*, on page 157. For one thing, it's not in a template.

values/labeling.xml

```
<?xml version="1.0" encoding="UTF-8"?>
<?xml-stylesheet type="text/xsl" href="labeling.xsl"?>
<labels>
  <structure id="label_1" name="bottle">
    <label>
      <substance>
        <name ref_id="01"/>
        <form ref_id="02"/>
        <dose ref_id="03"/>
      </substance>
      <packaging>
        <date ref_id="06"/>
        <type ref_id="07"/>
      </packaging>
    </label>
  </structure>

  <language lang="en">
    <instance id="en-01">Rosuvastatin</instance>
    <instance id="en-02">film-coated tablets</instance>
    <instance id="en-03">10mg</instance>
    <instance id="en-06">11 December 2014</instance>
    <instance id="en-07">OUTER CARTON BOTTLE AND LABEL</instance>
    <instance id="en-16">Film-coated tablet.</instance>
  </language>

  <language lang="fr">
    <instance id="fr-01">Rosuvastatin</instance>
    <instance id="fr-02">comprimés pelliculés</instance>
    <instance id="fr-03">10mg</instance>
    <instance id="fr-06">11 Décembre 2014</instance>
    <instance id="fr-07">EMBALLAGE EXTERIEUR (ETUI FLACON)
      ET ETIQUETTE FLACON</instance>
    <instance id="fr-16">Comprimé pelliculé.</instance>
  </language>

  <language lang="de">
    <instance id="de-01">Rosuvastatin</instance>
    <instance id="de-02">Filmtabletten</instance>
    <instance id="de-03">10mg</instance>
    <instance id="de-06">11. Dezember 2014</instance>
    <instance id="de-07">FALTSCHACHTEL FLASCHE UND
      FLASCHENETIKETT</instance>
    <template id="de16">Filmtablette.</template>
  </language>
</labels>
```

Figure 43—XML Source for Labeling Pharmaceuticals

values/test-node-in-variable.xsl

```
1  <xsl:stylesheet xmlns:xsl="http://www.w3.org/1999/XSL/Transform" version="1.0">
2    <xsl:variable name="structure" select="/labels/structure"/>
3
4    <xsl:template match="/ | * | @*">
5      <xsl:copy>
6        <xsl:apply-templates select=" * | @*"/>
7      </xsl:copy>
8    </xsl:template>
9
10   <xsl:template match="instance">
11     <xsl:variable name="instance_id" select="@id"/>
12     <xsl:if test="$structure//*[@ref_id = $instance_id]">
13       <xsl:copy>
14         <xsl:apply-templates/>
15       </xsl:copy>
16     </xsl:if>
17   </xsl:template>
18 </xsl:stylesheet>
```

Figure 44—The template for the <instance> tag

Is that even legal? Yes—in fact, in this case, it's also desirable. We want to be able to use the variable in any template, so by defining it outside of a template, the variable now has *global scope*. When we define a variable inside a template, it can only be used inside that template, which means it has *local scope*.

To define a global variable, we have to remember that we are not yet inside the root of the document, so any XPath expression first has to match on the root, as we've done here.

Next, in line 4, we see our old friend the identity transform. We're going to copy everything from the source—except the <instance> tags we filter out in the next template.

And finally, the part that we started out to do in the first place: in the template for <instance>, we get the test in line 12. Here we compare the id= attribute of the current <instance> with all the ref_id= attributes stored in the node-set in our structure variable. To retrieve the value of the variable, we have used the variable name preceded by $. Then we add a slash (or in this case a double slash so we can cut to the chase) to start working our way down from the root of the node-set to the nodes we're interested in. Since several types of elements may have a ref_id=, we use a wildcard (*) for the element of interest, then we put our comparison expression in the predicate. If an <instance> doesn't have an element with a ref_id= that corresponds to its id=, we don't copy it.

Joe asks:

Why the select= attribute in the variable for the node-set?

One interesting aspect of line 2 is that we've used the select= attribute to select the node-set for us. Why? It's complicated. The short story is that if we used <xsl:value-of>, it would only give us the text values, and if we used <xsl:copy-of> or <xsl:apply-templates>, it would give us an aggravating type of data called a *result tree fragment*. A result tree fragment is kind of like a node-set, except that it can't be accessed by XPath expressions, which makes it fairly useless in XSLT 1.0. It was so useless that by XSLT 2.0 it disappeared, so there are only node-sets.

Result tree fragments can be accessed by XSLT extensions, but there's no guarantee that a browser is going to support the extension.

If you're programming XSLT for browsers and stuck with XSLT 1.0, it's best just to pretend that result tree fragments don't exist. And they won't exist, unless you happen to create them. Use <xsl:variable> with select= to create node-sets, and you'll be fine.

In addition to testing for nodes in a variable with a node-set, we can also retrieve nodes and values, as we'll see in the next section.

Retrieving Nodes from a Node-Set Stored in a Variable

When we use a node-set many times, we can retrieve nodes from a variable much the same way we test them. To check it out, we'll re-use the example XML we set up in Figure 43, *XML Source for Labeling Pharmaceuticals*, on page 156.

This time we want to populate the set of nodes in the <structure> section with the corresponding text in each <language> section, so it looks like Figure 45, *The XML Structure Populated with English Content*, on page 159 (for English).

We could do this a couple of different ways. In one case, we could start by processing all the elements in the <structure> section, repeating the processing once for each <language> section. Or we could put the elements in the <structure> section into a variable, then process each <language> tag, using the elements from the <structure> tag where we need them.

The advantage of the second method is that by creating the node-set variable, we can reduce the number of times the XSLT processor has to evaluate an values/labeling-output.xml

```
<labels>
  <label language="en">
    <substance>
      <name>Rosuvastatin</name>
      <form>film-coated tablets</form>
      <dose>10mg</dose>
    </substance>
    <packaging>
      <date>11 December 2014</date>
      <type>OUTER CARTON BOTTLE AND LABEL</type>
    </packaging>
  </label>
 ...
</labels>
```

Figure 45—The XML Structure Populated with English Content

XPath expression to retrieve content for each of the elements in <structure>. But it's probably easier to see it than to read about it, so:

values/labeling.xsl

```
<xsl:stylesheet xmlns:xsl="http://www.w3.org/1999/XSL/Transform" version="1.0">
  <xsl:variable name="structure" select="/labels/structure"/>
  <xsl:template match="/labels">
    <labels>
      <xsl:apply-templates select="language"/>
    </labels>
  </xsl:template>

  <xsl:template match="language">
    <label language="{@lang}">
      <substance>
        <xsl:apply-templates
          select="*[contains(@id,'01')
          or contains(@id,'02')
          or contains(@id,'03')]"/>
      </substance>
      <packaging>
        <xsl:apply-templates select="*[contains(@id,'06')
          or contains(@id,'07')]"/>
      </packaging>
    </label>
  </xsl:template>

  <xsl:template match="instance">
    <xsl:variable name="ref_id">
      <xsl:value-of select="substring-after(@id,'-')"/>
    </xsl:variable>
```

```
28      <xsl:variable name="element_name">
29        <xsl:value-of select="name($structure//*[@ref_id = $ref_id])"/>
30      </xsl:variable>
31
32      <xsl:element name="{$element_name}">
33        <xsl:apply-templates/>
34      </xsl:element>
35    </xsl:template>
36
37  </xsl:stylesheet>
```

The lines to pay attention to are 2 and 29. In 2 we define the structure variable that selects the <structure> element in the XML. When we select this element, we get that element and all its contents (elements, attributes, text, the works) in the variable.

When we get to line 29, we need to make use of our node-set. We want to create an element for each <instance> tag that corresponds to the id= value of the <instance>. We put the $structure variable into the name() function, and we add a //* with a predicate to the end of $structure to find the element that has the same id= as the <instance> tag. The name() function returns the name of that tag. Since we've placed the element name in the variable at line 28, we use that variable in the attribute value template at line 32. (Remember attribute value templates in *Adding Elements and Attributes Dynamically*, on page 52?)

The result is a handsome lineup of XML like the partial example shown in Figure 45, *The XML Structure Populated with English Content*, on page 159.

Node-sets in variables can take a little fidgeting to get used to them, but it sure beats writing out long XPath expressions when you need to use the same one over and over.

Parameters and <xsl:call-template>

We've talked a little about how variables have scope. Variables defined within a template are only valid for use within that template, which is kind of a pain if you've set up a complicated bunch of XSLT for a variable and you'd like to use it elsewhere.

In this section, we're going to see how to use the values from variables (and other sources) in templates other than where they are defined. There are still some limitations on where the values can be used, but it adds flexibility and re-usability to our templates.

The mechanism we'll use is called a *parameter*. Parameters are a bit like variables in that they contain values (all sorts), but they are a bit different in that they can be used for passing values between templates.

Speaking of flexibility and re-use, we'll also learn a new way of invoking templates in order to re-use our XSLT functionality. The new invocation method is the <xsl:call-templates> instruction. With it, we will explicitly call a template to be used within another template.

Eventually, we'll use parameters and called templates for the final goal of this chapter, which is to perform recursive processing.

Parameters

Parameters, as we said, are similar to variables. You could define them and use them exactly the same way, if you'd like:

```
<xsl:variable name="language" select="/labels/language/@lang"/>
```

or

```
<xsl:param name="language" select="/labels/language/@lang"/>
```

And you would invoke them both the same way:

```
<p>The language we will be learning today is <xsl:value-of select="$language"/></p>
```

Their definition and usage are so similar, giving them both the same name in the same scope would make our XSLT invalid. Don't do it!

If they're so similar, what's the point of <xsl:param>? As we mentioned, parameters do something that variables can't do, which is to pass their values between templates. When a new template is invoked from the current template, values can be passed from the current template to the next template by means of parameters. To do this, though, we need to use two different instructions. One is the <xsl:with-param> instruction in the *invoking* template, the other is the <xsl:param> instruction in the *invoked* template.

Here's an example of how it works. Suppose we've worked out an indent level for a mixed list, and all the items within the list are going to need the information about that indent. We may have no idea what sorts of things are in our list, although we have templates for anything that might be possible. We need to pass along our hard-won indent information to any template that might need it. As we see in the following code, we can place that information in an <xsl:with-param> tag. The <xsl:with-param> goes within an <xsl:apply-templates> or <xsl:call-template> instruction and sends the value on its way.

```
<xsl:template match="list">
  <xsl:variable name="indent">
    <xsl:value-of select="concat(count(ancestor::list) * 0.5,'in')"
  </xsl:variable>

  <xsl:apply-templates>
    <xsl:with-param name="margin-indent" select="$indent"/>
  </xsl:apply-templates>
</xsl:template>
```

But for this to work, there has to be a receiver for the parameter in the template or templates that are invoked. Within our list we might have <p>, <li>, <note> or <info> tags. For the template for the <p> tag, we would then see something like this:

```
<xsl:template match="p">
  <xsl:param name="margin-indent"/>

  <li margin-left="{$margin-indent}">
    <xsl:apply-templates/>>
  </li>
</xsl:template>
```

The example above demonstrates a few rules about paramaters. The first is that <xsl:param> has to be the first instruction following the <xsl:template> tag, or it will be invalid. The second is that name= in the <xsl:param> must be the same as the name= in the <xsl:with-param> tag in the template that invoked this one. A third rule is that the <xsl:param> tag does not have to specify a value, itself. You can assume that a value will be passed to it. However, if you want to specify a back-up, default value for the <xsl:param> tag, just in case the <xsl:with-param> was a dud, you can specify the value with the select= attribute. If a value does get passed to <xsl:param>, the default value will be ignored.

Parameters, like variables, also work on a global scope. You can specify <xsl:param> at the top level of a stylesheet, just the same as you can <xsl:variable>. Of course, that begs the question: if the purpose of <xsl:param> is to receive a value, what could possibly pass it a value at the global scope? Variables and parameters at the global scope are evaluated before templates, so a template could not be the source of a value for <xsl:param>.

Could something from outside the stylesheet pass a value into the stylesheet by way of a global parameter? Yep, you've got it. As we'll see in Chapter 10, *Large-Scale Stylesheet Strategies*, on page 183, the invoking mechanism for an XSLT stylesheet can pass in an external value. This type of control is great for re-using stylesheets for different purposes. For example, we could pass the language in for each time we processed our pharmaceutical labeling stylesheet, and we would only output the labels for the language we wanted. But we're getting a little ahead of ourselves.

Now that we've seen parameters at work, let's take a look at <xsl:call-templates>. We may or may not use parameters with named templates, but for an effective recursion processing strategy, we'll use both.

Introducing the <xsl:call-template> Instruction

The <xsl:call-template> instruction is similar to using <xsl:apply-templates>, but with a twist. One clue to their differences is in the plural "templates" part of <xsl:apply-templates> and the singular "template" part of <xsl:call-template>. When we use <xsl:apply-templates>, it will invoke any number of other templates, based on whatever XML tags are within the current context. For the <xsl:call-template> instruction, only one template is invoked—the one that is named. Where <xsl:apply-templates> matches elements within the current context of the XML, <xsl:call-templates> has no interest in current context. It doesn't match on anything, and it doesn't change the current context. Instead, it uses the *name* of a template, and the template it calls uses the name= attribute rather than the match= attribute. (A template can have both match= and name= so it could be invoked by either <xsl:apply-templates> or <xsl:call-template>.)

Calling a named template is a great way to re-use logic that will be meaningful within more than one template. For example, you might need to evaluate every element to determine whether it needs to have an id= attribute generated for it, or whether it already has one. The logic for doing this is straightforward. Here's an example of a template with some fairly reusable logic in it.

```
<xsl:template match="p">
  <para>
    <xsl:attribute name="id">
    <xsl:choose>
      <xsl:when test="@id">
       <xsl:value-of select="@id"/>
      </xsl:when>
      <xsl:otherwise>
        <xsl:value-of select="generate-id()"
      </xsl:otherwise>
    </xsl:choose>
    </xsl:attribute>
    ...
   </para>
</xsl:template>
```

You wouldn't want to have to put all that into each and every template in your stylesheet. Instead, it would be nice to place it in some reusable area somewhere and just call it as needed:

```
<xsl:template match="p">
  <para>
    <xsl:call-template name="id-maker"/>
    ...
  </para>
  </xsl:template>

  <xsl:template name="id-maker">
    <xsl:attribute name="id">
    <xsl:choose>
     <xsl:when test="@id">
      <xsl:value-of select="@id"/>
     </xsl:when>
     <xsl:otherwise>
       <xsl:value-of select="generate-id()"
     </xsl:otherwise>
   </xsl:choose>
   </xsl:attribute>
</xsl:template>
```

Now any template in the stylesheet, not just the one that matches on <p>, can make use of the code for creating id= attributes.

If you use <xsl:call-template> to call a template by a certain name, the XSLT processor expects a template with that name to exist, or it will post an error. Another thing to remember is to make sure the results of the called template make sense within the context of the <xsl:call-template> instruction.

For instance, in the code above, if we had put <xsl:call-template> after some other code rather than an element, the XSLT processor would post an error to the effect that an attribute can't be created once an element has been formed. Think about the content that's returned from the called template in the context where it is called.

Using Named Templates and Parameters Together

One interesting aspect of a named template is that the current context in the XML is the same for the named template as for the template where <xsl:call-template> calls it. That's the reason we could get away with using the @id token to retrieve the value of the id= attribute when we were in the id-maker template in the example above.

But what about variables? Suppose we wanted all the ID values to be prefaced with a variable that we had defined in the calling template (and that we were actually going to use in the calling template). Rather than defining the variable twice, we could pass it in to the named template with a parameter, the same as we did with <xsl:apply-templates>.

For example, we might take the first two letters of the element name and concatenate it with the level at which the element occurs in the XML hierarchy. We need to use the level number elsewhere in the template to calculate the indent amount, so we first create the variable for the level inside the calling template, then we pass both the abbreviated element name and the element level to the called template for its own use. Since this approach does not use any new techniques for us, why not take a little break to work out how that would look.

When using parameters with called templates, watch out for a couple of things. Make sure the parameters being passed in to the called template make sense for how the parameter is used in the template. If the template is doing numeric calculations on a parameter for a margin width, and you're capturing the margin width from an attribute that looks like `width="3.5in"`, you'll need to strip the `in` part of the string off the value before passing it to the named template.

Also, try to generalize the named template as much as possible to make sense for how it will be reused in different parts of your stylesheet. A template that parses text for shortening might also be used to parse text for keywords—think about a processing method that will work for both, and define the parameters generically enough not to push yourself into a conceptual corner. Named templates can be used successfully for several purposes and called from different types of contexts if they are carefully thought out.

Generated Values

We've talked a good bit about variables and parameters, which are containers for values that we generate or derive by various means during runtime. But in general, we've created or derived those values without giving too much attention to the methods we've used for getting them. Our primary methods have been either to find the value in the XML itself, or to count some aspect of the XML with the `count()` function. That's all well and good, but there are occasions when we could use a little more help than that.

XSLT provides several tools for generating values of different types, which we'll see here. These may be values that we place into variables or parameters, or they may be values that we send directly to our output.

Instructions and functions for generating values include:

- count()
- position()
- last()
- number()
- format-number()
- generate-id()
- <xsl:number>

We're not going to spend a lot of time creating elaborate structures with these guys. Other than the <xsl:number> instruction, they're fairly straightforward. Let's go through the vital statistics, saving <xsl:number> for a separate section so we can spend a little extra time on it.

count()

We've seen count() work before. It takes a single argument, which is a node or node-set, usually defined by an XPath expression. The nice thing about count() is that the XPath expression allows us to count just about anything anywhere. We just need to remember our XPath chops, and off we go.

One temptation with count() is to use it for numbering sequences in an output. It would probably be okay for simple arrangements, but we'll find <xsl:number> offers a lot more functionality than count() for numbering things.

position()

position() is another handy tool for generating numbers, but it can be deceptive. It takes no arguments, and it returns a number equal to the position of its current context within the sequence of nodes the current context belongs to. In a sense, it sounds like we should be able to use this for creating numbers for a numbered list, but beware: the kinds of things that are in the current context's sequence may be more than you expect. There may be spaces between the nodes you want to number, and spaces create text() nodes. Many is the XSLT coder who has been dismayed to find his numbered steps coming out with the sequence 2, 4, 6, 8, not realizing there were invisible nodes for whitespace (line returns) in the content.

The value associated with the first position in the sequence is 1, not 0, so plan accordingly.

The position() function is an ideal counter if you need to know the true position of the current context in its sequence, regardless of what else is being counted, or if you know that the current sequence holds no extra whitespace text nodes.

last()

The last() function holds the same caveats as the position() function: it takes its value from the sequence of peers containing the current context. Only in this case, it doesn't return the value of the current context, it returns the value of the position of the last item in the sequence. This makes it great for things like long lists, where you need to inform the reader, "You are now viewing item 3 of 750,487." And again, be sure you understand what is counted: your reader might be disgruntled to find out that 750,000 of those items were just line returns.

number()

The number() function is a little different from the previous three functions because it doesn't take its value from a node-set. Instead, it takes a single argument, which can be any of the four data types, and returns a value depending on the input. The argument can also take optional whitespace and a minus sign (-) before the rest of the argument.

For the four data types that may be input, the results from the number() function are:

Number Returns the number that was input

Boolean Returns a 1 for true() and a 0 for false()

String Returns a number if the string can be converted to a number according to the rules of the IEEE 754 specification.[1] Basically, if it's digit-like and doesn't have weird characters in the string, it will give you the number you expect. For any other string, it will return the string NaN (Not a Number). So you can't input "one" and get 1 back out.

Node-set If we put a node-set in number(), the node-set is first converted to a string, if possible, then the string is evaluated the same as described above for a string. Otherwise we'll get the deadly NaN.

generate-id()

We've seen generate-id() at work—it generates a unique string based on the position of the context node within the current document. We frequently use this function to provide a value for an id= attribute, typically for the purpose of acting as a reference point for some additional XSLT processing.

One interesting aspect of generate-id() is that no matter how many times you invoke it, from whatever part of the stylesheet or by whatever XPath

1. en.wikipedia.org/wiki/IEEE_754-1985

expression it takes, it will always generate the same value for a given node. For example, if we're in the root node and do generate-id() for that context, we might get a value like d10001. Then, if we're almost finished processing all the XML, and we use an XPath expression to point from the last node back to the root, the generate-id() value for the root will again be d10001.

We can take advantage of this fact to create references between nodes, such as textual cross-references, wherever we need to. Here's an example where we create an ID for a chapter, then later reference the chapter by pointing to the <chapter> and getting the value of its ID, in both places using the generate-id() function.

```
1  <xsl:template match="book">
2    <body>
3      <xsl:apply-templates select="chapter"/>
4      <h2>List of Chapters</h2>
5      <xsl:apply-templates select="//chapter" mode="LOC"/>
6    </body>
7  </xsl:template>
8  <xsl:template match="chapter">
9    <element name="h1">
10     <xsl:attribute name="id">
11       <xsl:value-of select="generate-id()"/>
12     </xsl:attribute>
13     <xsl:apply-templates select="title"/>
14   </element>
15   <xsl:apply-templates select="*[not(name() = 'title')]"/>
16 </xsl:template>
17 <xsl:template match="chapter" mode="LOC">
18   <p>
19     <a href="{generate-id()}">
20       <xsl:apply-templates select="title"/>
21     </a>
22   </p>
23 </xsl:template>
```

In the template matching <book>, we apply templates once to process all the chapters, probably to render the text of the book. Then we come to an <h2> tag that sets up a section for the list of chapters, followed by another <xsl:apply-templates> for chapters, except this time in a different mode. The two different template that match on <chapter> process the <chapter> tags at different times, but both of them put the generate-id() function to use. The one in line 11 created the ID for the <h1> element for that chapter, and the one in 19 places the value in the href= attribute to link back to the corresponding chapter in the rendered text.

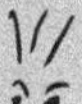

Joe asks:

How consistent is the value of the generated ID from one execution of the stylesheet to another?

The XSLT specification does not require an XSLT processor to generate the same value for a given node every time it processes the XML document—it only has to give a unique value within the scope of each processing pass. Even if the XML and stylesheet do not change between processing passes, we can't assume the value for a given node will be the same each time it is processed.

Usually it does stay the same, but since it's not required, I wouldn't bet my paycheck on it.

Why mention it? Because sometimes it's tempting to see that same generate-id() value in the output numerous times, and to make things easy, just refer to that ID value literally in the code. Don't do it. It may work 1000 times, but eventually it will come back to bite you.

<xsl:number>

I saved the best for last: `<xsl:number>` is a powerful, multifaceted tool for counting nodes. It derives its value from the position of the current node for the template in which it is active. It also has several attributes that work together to provide some pretty sophisticated output for numbering. Have you ever seen a document that uses MilSpec (U.S. military standard) numbering? The numbers look like a thesis outline gone berserk: consider appendix paragraph A.4.2.1.3.e. Ouch! But no sweat: that's a piece of cake for `<xsl:number>`.

Programmers sometimes make odd assumptions about this tag, so it does bear a little extra scrutiny. Once again, let's take a look at its vitals, then proceed to some examples. The attributes we want to pay careful attention to are `count=`, `from=`, and `level=`. These three work together to determine what value is returned. The rest mostly have to do with formatting.

<xsl:number> Attributes

Following are the most important attributes that can be used with `<xsl:number>`. (To save space I've omitted attributes relating to different languages, but you can learn about them at http://www.w3schools.com/xsl/el_number.asp.) Don't despair if these descriptions don't click immediately—we'll see examples in short order.

Note that none of these attributes are required. If no attributes are present, <xsl:number> bases the count on the preceding sibling nodes of the current context, and it gives a single-level number in Arabic format.

count=
: This attribute takes an XPath expression to specify what nodes will be counted. If it is omitted, the current node is counted along with any other node of the same node type. For example, if level="single" and our node is the seventh <date> element within a larger set of siblings of mixed elements, it will generate a value of 7.

from= The from= attribute takes another XPath expression. It specifies the *ancestor node* that constrains the scope of the counting. For example, if we only want to count within the parent of the current node, we give the name of the parent; if we want to count within the grandparent of the current node, we give the name of the grandparent.

It's as if this value has a phantom ancestor:: axis added to the expression we give–we don't need to give it ourselves, and it will be rejected if we do. And we'll want to be careful: the counting scope is defined at the first match found in the chain of ancestors going up from the current node. If the element occurs at multiple levels, the scope is defined at the first match in the ancestor chain up from the current context.

level= This attribute specifies what levels of the XML hierarchy will be considered in returning the number or set of numbers. It can take one of three values:

single (default value) This setting limits the count to a single level in the XML hierarchy, and it returns only a single number. Counting is limited to the children of the current node's parents.

Although the from= attribute can legally be used with level="single", the XSLT 1.0 specification is not clear what should happen in this case. Implementations in different XSLT processors may differ. In tests with Saxon, it appears to have no effect.

any This value also returns only a single number, but it counts the nodes that match what's in the count= atribute no matter what level they're at. If from= is present, counting only occurs within the descendants of the nearest ancestor node that matches from=.

multiple With level="multiple", we get into Milspec territory. With this value, multiple numbers may be returned, with one number for each level of the XML hierarchy that is being counted. Again, from= determines the scope of what is counted, and count= determines what is counted.

As an example, suppose we have the following book outline:

```
<book>
  <chapter>Spiders</chapter>
  <chapter>Flies
    <section>Fruit Flies</section>
    <section>Butterflies</section>
    <section>Time Flies...
      <subsection>...like an arrow.</subsection>
      <subsection>...like a banana.</subsection>
      <subsection>...like a fly.</subsection>
      <subsection>...like a dragon flies.</subsection>
    </section>
  </chapter>
  <chapter>Dragonflies</chapter>
</book>
```

We can make a handy template to number all the parts as we might find them in a table of contents:

```
<xsl:template match="chapter | section | subsection">
  <xsl:number count="chapter | section | subsection" level="multiple"/>
  <xsl:text> </xsl:text>
  <xsl:apply-templates/>
</xsl:template>
```

Our output will look like:

```
1. Spiders
2. Flies
2.1 Fruit Flies
2.2 Butterflies
2.3 Time Flies...
2.3.1 ...like an arrow.
2.3.2 ...like a banana.
2.3.3 ...like a fly.
2.3.4 ...like a dragon flies.
3. Dragonflies
```

XSLT creates numbers only for the number of levels it has encountered within a given context. That way you get the number 1. for a top-level element instead of 1.0.0. If you actually want those extra zeroes as placeholders, you'll need to figure out how many levels you need, then add them yourself.

format= This attribute determines how the value will be formatted for output. It takes a string of tokens that represent the format of the number. The tokens can be as follows:

- 1—gives traditional Arabic numerals for output.
- A—gives uppercase alphabet characters for the output. At value 27, the output goes to AA.
- a—gives lowercase alphabet characters for the output.
- I—gives uppercase Roman numerals for the output.
- i—gives lowercase Roman numerals for the output.
- Other characters—The interpretation of other characters is processor-dependent. In general, though, you can add punctuation characters after the value to give it the punctuation you want. Prefixes are also possible. For these types of additional text, though, I would place the text outside the <xsl:number> tag. Just let the tag do what it does best: count stuff.

value= This variable allows you to specify a value to be output instead of having the value based on the position of the context node.

grouping-separator= This attribute allows you to specify a separator character to use between the numbers in a multi-level number. The default, as we have seen, is a period.

Examples with <xsl:number>

Okay, that was a lot of crazy talk. Wouldn't an example be easier? Sure—formal definitions can cover a lot of ground, but they do tend to be a little abstract. So let's see what it all means in the real world. First we need a chunk of XML that wants numbering:

values/number-instruction-1.xml

```
<?xml version='1.0' encoding='UTF-8'?>
<?xml-stylesheet type="text/xsl" href="number-instruction-1.xsl"?>

<section>
  <title>Examples of XSLT Templates</title>
  <p>What are some of the more common forms of XSLT templates?</p>
  <section>
    <title>Simple templates to change tags</title>
    <example>
      <codeline><xsl:template match="/labels"></codeline>
      <codeline>  <category></codeline>
```

```
12        <codeline>    <xsl:apply-templates select="language"/></codeline>
13        <codeline>  </category></codeline>
14        <codeline></xsl:template></codeline>
15      </example>
16      <example>
17        <codeline><xsl:template match="/labels"></codeline>
18        <codeline>  <element name="category"></codeline>
19        <codeline>    <xsl:apply-templates select="language"/></codeline>
20        <codeline>  </element></codeline>
21        <codeline></xsl:template></codeline>
22      </example>
23    </section>
24    <section>
25      <title>Base template for identity transform</title>
26      <example>
27        <codeline><xsl:template match="/ | * | @*"></codeline>
28        <codeline>  <xsl:copy></codeline>
29        <codeline>    <xsl:apply-templates select=" * | @*"/></codeline>
30        <codeline>  </xsl:copy></codeline>
31        <codeline></xsl:template></codeline>
32        <codeline></codeline>
33      </example>
34    </section>
35  </section>
```

For the first example, let's do something easy. We just want to number the lines of code, so our template for the <codeline> tag should include an item like this:

```
<xsl:number count="."/>
```

Simple enough. Since our context is <codeline>, we're going to count other tags with the same name. And since we haven't specified the from= or level= attributes, we're going to get a single level that starts from the parent. Just what we wanted.

Now let's crank it up a notch. We want the code numbering to be continuous within a given section, so having from= be the default of parent:: won't get the job done. How about this?

```
<xsl:number count="." from="section"/>
```

This version takes its scope from the <section> tag in line 7 of our example XML, so all the <codeline> tags in the examples in lines 9 and 16 will be numbered continuously, even though they are in two different <example> tags. When we get to the <codeline> tags in the <example> in line 26, the numbering starts over.

What about that fancy MilSpec numbering? This is a good opportunity for <xsl:number> to really shine. Let's say we want numbering on both levels of <section>, alphabetic counting on the <example> tags, and numeric counting again on the <codeline> tags. We know we're going to use level="multiple", and from= has got to be from the root ("/") to get the top-level <section> tag, right? So now give a little thought to what you would put for the count= and format= attributes before you peek at the code example below.

Here's my take on the templates for a stylesheet that does nothing but output the numbers for <section>, <example>, and <codeline>:

values/number-instruction-1.xsl

```
<xsl:stylesheet xmlns:xsl="http://www.w3.org/1999/XSL/Transform" version="1.0" >
  <xsl:template match=" / | * ">
    <xsl:apply-templates select=" * "/>
  </xsl:template>
  <xsl:template match="section | example | codeline">
    <xsl:text>
    </xsl:text><xsl:number level="multiple" from="/"
      count="section | example | codeline" format="1.1.a.1."/>
    <xsl:apply-templates select=" * "/>
  </xsl:template>
</xsl:stylesheet>
```

The output appears as we would like:

```
1.
1.1.
1.1.a.
1.1.a.1.
1.1.a.2.
1.1.a.3.
1.1.a.4.
1.1.a.5.
1.1.b.
1.1.b.1.
1.1.b.2.
1.1.b.3.
1.1.b.4.
1.1.b.5.
1.2.
1.2.a.
1.2.a.1.
1.2.a.2.
1.2.a.3.
1.2.a.4.
1.2.a.5.
1.2.a.6.
```

And that's the power of <xsl:number>!

As an afterthought, let's think how we would handle it if the requirement were to have, say, the same numbering scheme we have in the example above, but instead of the codelines having their numbers restarted with each new <example> tag, we want them numbered continuously throughout the document. This sort of thing occasionally happens with figures and tables in some documents, where the chapter number is followed by the figure number, but the figure numbering is continuous throughout the book rather than being reset at each chapter.

With this sort of Franken-number, we're best off combining two <xsl:number> tags, each following the rules for its own numbering stream. I'll leave that exercise for you to have fun with—you've probably gotten the hang of it by now.

Putting It All Together with Recursion

Recursion is about doing something until you get it right.

There's no big secret to the definition of recursion: it's simply the act of doing something over and over, usually acting on the same piece of content, or on some variation of a piece of content.

For instance, we might want to take a string of words and place each word in its own tag. That's a perfect situation for using recursion. We just define a template to lop off the first word, place it in a tag, then call the same template again with the original string, minus its first word. Lather, rinse, repeat.

We know that a template with a <match> statement will repeat any time the processor finds a node that matches its target, but it will only execute one time per match. By using a named template, we can call the template from *inside itself* using its own template name. Given that possibility, here's the simplest recursive template you could imagine:

```
<xsl:template name="recursor">
  <xsl:call-template name="recursor"/>
</xsl:template>
```

Of course, you'll notice at once that this little monument to bad coding contains two fatal flaws. For one thing, it doesn't do anything other than call itself. For another thing, it creates an endless loop. You might think that it will never end, but it will—when the memory stack overflows and the XSLT processor dies of dizziness. The lesson to take from this: always set a condition that will ensure that the recursion ends.

The word "condition" should give a clue as to how recursive templates are normally set up. Typically, the inclusion of a <xsl:choose> or <xsl:if> statement allows you to specify conditions that will alter the sequence of processing once a given end-condition tests true or false.

Let's have a look at the problem we talked about earlier, wrapping each word in a text string with a tag. Thinking it through, our template needs to have one thing going into it and another thing coming out of it. Going into the template, we need the text string. Coming out of it, we need the tagged text.

As we saw earlier, one way to pass a value into a named template is with an <xsl:param> instruction. So initially, let's say we are in a template for a <commandlist> tag, and the contents of the tag are several command names in a space-separated list. The template we'll use to kick off our named, recursive template would look like this:

```
<xsl:template match="commandlist">
   <xsl:call-template name="word-tagger">
     <xsl:with-param name="string" select="normalize-space(.)"/>
   </xsl:call-template>
 </xsl:template>
```

The <xsl:with-param> tag creates the string parameters and takes the value of the current context, the <commandlist> tag. Note the use of the normalize-space() function. We don't know what kind of whitespace we might have in our string; the great thing about normalize-space() is that it chops off all leading and trailing whitespace, it removes linebreaks, and it reduces all incidents of multiple spaces to a single space. We're using it to condition our text going in so we know there is only one space between each word, and nothing else.

Any time we pass a parameter with <xsl:with-param>, we also need to define a receiver in another template. So let's set up the word-tagger template with a parameter:

```
<xsl:template name="word-tagger">
  <xsl:param name="string"/>
</xsl:template>
```

Again, this template doesn't do anything (yet), but at least it doesn't crash the memory stack every time we run it.

Notice that we've kept the names of the template and parameter fairly generic. Our template might not always be used for tagging commands in a list. We might want to generalize it later to create any type of tag we need (based on a name we pass in from our originating template, possibly by way of a second parameter). So let's keep the names as general as possible, to reflect its potential for re-use.

For the moment, let's just tag every word with a <command> tag.

To do that, we're going to get just the first word in the string. That's easy enough—we'll use the substring-before() function. The complete section of code looks like this:

```
<command>
  <xsl:value-of select="substring-before($string,' ')"/>
</command>
```

We don't have our recursion yet, and we don't have our condition for stopping, either. If we put this line into the template above, it will execute perfectly, but only once. So what's next?

We know we're going to need a call back to our same template, so we could go ahead and add that to the template. But we'll also need to pass in the string for it to operate on. If we pass it the original string parameter, it will just snag the same first word again, and around and around we'll go. Instead, we'll need to pass it a version of the original string with the first word lopped off. Again, we'll use a substring function to preserve the part of the string we want. With all that in mind, our call to the template should look like this:

```
<xsl:call-template name="word-tagger">
  <xsl:with-param name="string" select="substring-after($string,' ')"/>
</xsl:call-template>
```

The second time the template is called, it is calling itself (recursion!), but this time with a shorter string. The next word is snagged and tagged, and the template is called a third time with yet a shorter string. This goes on and on and on...

What happens if we run out of string? Our control mechanism doesn't have a stopping point, even if the string it keeps passing around is empty. So we need to figure out what the end condition will be, then devise a way to test for it.

In our case, we know that when we get to the last word there shouldn't be any spaces left in the string. So before we execute the <xsl:call-template>, we can test for the presence of a space in the string. If there is a space, we'll keep executing, otherwise we stop. We could do our testing a couple of ways, but let's keep it simple and just wrap an <xsl:if> around the <xsl:call-template>. We'll test to see if there is a space in the string—if not, we've reached the last word.

(Have we tagged it yet?) With that extra piece of code, we should have our complete string tagger in place:

```
<xsl:template name="word-tagger">
  <xsl:param name="string"/>
  <command>
    <xsl:value-of select="substring-before($string,' ')"/>
  </command>

  <xsl:if test="contains($string,' ')">
    <xsl:call-template name="word-tagger">
      <xsl:with-param name="string" select="substring-after($string,' ')"/>
    </xsl:call-template>
  </xsl:if>
</xsl:template>
```

Figure 46—The Word Tagger Template

And that, my friends, is recursion in action.

Recursion is a great way to handle situations where there is a need for repetition that can't be handled by simply letting templates match on elements. Several examples come to mind. We've seen the notion of recursing through words—we could also use this method to match on words and do word substitutions. We might also need to intercept special characters in the text.

Recursion through XML elements in a list is another possible use. For the most part, repeating an action in a list of tags can be done with matching templates, but we may find special cases where matching is a little more difficult than we'd like. Suppose, for instance, we only want to process the first ten tags in a parent tag. Those tags may or may not be the same type of tag. One way to do it would be to call a template and pass in a number representing the ending count for the elements we want to process, and another number starting at 1 that we will use as a counter. We'll add 1 to the count each time the template calls itself. Within the template, we match on the element at that position by means of a predicate containing the counter We include a test for when our counter reaches the number where we want to stop, and that's the end of it.

Let's take a look at that idea in actual code (see Figure 47, *Processing the first ten tags*, on page 179).

A couple of things to think about here: The test in the <xsl:if> is set up to allow the processing to continue until counter is equal to end-count, then to call the template one more time before it stops. Can you think of a way so that it stops

```
<xsl:template name="partial-list-processor">
  <xsl:param name="end-count"/>
  <xsl:param name="counter"/>

  <xsl:if test="$counter &lt;= $end-count">
    <xsl:apply-templates match="*[$counter]"/>

    <xsl:call-template name="partial-list-processor">
      <xsl:with-param name="end-count" select="$end-count"/>
      <xsl:with-param name="counter" select="$counter + 1"/>
    </xsl:call-template>
  </xsl:if>
</xsl:template>
```

Figure 47—Processing the first ten tags

when they are equal to each other, so the template isn't called an extra time? (Consider using the <xsl:choose> tag rather than <xsl:if>.)

Also, notice that the <xsl:call-template> tag contains an <xsl:with-param> tag for the end-count parameter. If we defined it once, and we're not changing it, shouldn't it just stay the same value? No—because when we use the <xsl:call-template> tag, we are losing the scope of the parameter, even if it is calling its containing template. We need to pass in the value just the same as if we were calling the template from some other template.

Parsing Strings with Recursion

Recursion is an excellent tool for parsing through strings of text to replace words or letters. The secret is to pass the string in to a "right-side string" parameter, then slowly parse off the first word (as we did in the word-tagger template in Figure 46, *The Word Tagger Template*, on page 178), and concatenate that value in a parameter that accumulates the processed "left-side string" value. Add a condition that tests for a particular word, and you can substitute a new string for that word in the process.

To make the recursive template general enough to be handle a variety of situations, we'll create original and replacement parameters to allow us to pass in the word we want to change and the word we want to change it to. Our calling template places the subject string into the right-side-string parameter to start the process, then the recursion takes over to parse through the whole string (see Figure 48, *Recursive template for word substitution*, on page 180).

In line 8 we test for a condition that means we need to continue. If this is not true, we end the process with our <xsl:otherwise> at line 39. If it is true, we

```
1  <xsl:template name="word-substituter">
2    <xsl:param name="original"/>
3    <xsl:param name="replacement"/>
4    <xsl:param name="left-side-string"/>
5    <xsl:param name="right-side-string"/>
6
7    <xsl:choose>
8      <xsl:when test="contains($right-side-string,' ')">
9        <xsl:variable name="first-word">
10         <xsl:value-of select="substring-before($right-side-string,' ')"
11       </xsl:variable>
12
13       <xsl:variable name="remaining-string">
14         <xsl:value-of select="substring-after($right-side-string,' ')"
15       </xsl:variable>
16
17       <xsl:choose>
18         <xsl:when test="$first-word = $original">
19           <xsl:call-template name="word-substituter">
20             <xsl:with-param name="original" select="$original"/>
21             <xsl:with-param name="replacement" select="$replacement"/>
22             <xsl:with-param name="left-side-string"
23               select="concat($left-side-string,$replacement,' ')"/>
24             <xsl:with-param name="right-side-string" select="$remaining-string"/>
25           </xsl:call-template>
26         </xsl:when>
27
28         <xsl:otherwise>
29           <xsl:call-template name="word-substituter">
30             <xsl:with-param name="original" select="$original"/>
31             <xsl:with-param name="replacement" select="$replacement"/>
32             <xsl:with-param name="left-side-string"
33               select="concat($left-side-string,$first-word,' ')"/>
34             <xsl:with-param name="right-side-string" select="$remaining-string"/>
35           </xsl:call-template>
36         </xsl:otherwise>
37       </xsl:choose>
38     </xsl:when>
39     <xsl:otherwise>
40       <xsl:value-of select="concat($left-side-string,$right-side-string)"/>
41     </xsl:otherwise>
42   </xsl:choose>
43 </xsl:template>
```

Figure 48—Recursive template for word substitution

create a couple of variables with our familiar substring functions, then we set up a second <xsl:choose> to test whether the first word matches the word we want to replace (line 18).

If it's the word of interest, we put together the existing left-side string (which will be null when we start), the replacement string, and a space to replace the one we used for our substring identification (line 23), which we pass as a value to the left-side string for the next iteration of the template. If the first word is not the word of interest, we do almost the same thing, except we add the original word back to the left-side string, leaving things just as we found them. In both cases, the remaining-string value gets passed back to the template as the right-side string. The template moves through the string, space by space, inch by inch, until there are no spaces left.

Recursion with Numbers

Recursion can be used for doing math as well as handling strings and tags—see if you can do a Fibonacci series (F_n) = $F_{n-1} + F_{n-2}$ to 10 iterations. Just be sure to give the template a clear way to end the processing, or it will speed along like a runaway train until the Java stack blows up.

Recursion is a useful tool in situations where it is difficult or impossible to create a template to allow the processor to do repeated processing for you. It has its limitations, as we've seen—it needs a clear ending, and you may find that with very long content, even with a well-defined end condition, the number of repetitions is still too much for the memory. In a situation like this, you might need to find a way to divide the content into more manageable chunks. Or you might consider alternatives to recursive processing.

In some cases, the content may just be too much for XSLT to handle on a computer with finite memory (which is most of them in the universe, so far). In that case, there is the alternative to hand off the processing to another program—a desperate, last-ditch strategy that we try to avoid when possible. And if you do need it, you will need to use an XSLT extension. The core XSLT funtionality does not support external program calls.

What We Did

We've covered a lot in this chapter! The management of values in XSLT programming is a broad topic. We had a look at the types of values availabe, each with its idiosyncrasies. We checked out variables, taking a look at how they can be manipulated, and how in turn they can be used in conditional structures and boolean tests, among other things. We even wrestled with nodes in variables for a while. When it came to parameters, we also introduced the <xsl:call-template> tag and had a look at how named templates work. Then we looked at a variety of functions that are used to generate values, including the <xsl:number> instruction.

Finally, we put several parts of our new knowledge to work with a processing strategy called recursion. Here we used parameters, functions for manipulating string values, and numeric counters to control a little code machine for repeating instructions until it reached a specified end condition.

Recursion is one of the more complex XSLT processing structures we have seen so far. With this technique in hand, we are well on our way to understanding XSLT templates and how to use them. This is a great time to stop for a moment and look back over all the scenery we've covered. We aren't done yet, but by this point you should be able to see real progress—our starting point is just a little stream of smoke down in the valley below, and maybe a couple of rooftops in the trees.

Find a rock or a stump to sit on, take a breather, and relax a while. We still need to cover some of the strategies for handling stylesheets at a higher level than just the templates. Once we get over that peak, though, the view should be well worth the effort.

"Jeddak of Helium," returned Tars Tarkas, "it has remained for a man of another world to teach the green warriors of Barsoom the meaning of friendship; to him we owe the fact that the hordes of Thark can understand you; that they can appreciate and reciprocate the sentiments so graciously expressed."

> *Edgar Rice Burroughs,* A Princess of Mars

CHAPTER 10

Large-Scale Stylesheet Strategies

Looking Beyond the Template to Stylesheet Structure

Rested up? All right, let's get back on the trail. So far we've talked mostly about the mechanics of templates: template matching, called templates, things that go on inside templates, values that get passed between templates, along with various kinds of problems we can solve with template-based processing. But stylesheets consist of more than just templates.

We've already seen instructions that work at the top level of the stylesheet with <xsl:template>, namely <xsl:key>, <xsl:variable>, and <xsl:param>. There are a variety of other instructions that work at the top level of the stylesheet, and they bring a lot of global functionality with them. In this chapter, we'll look at the major controls and what they can do for us.

Among other things, we'll see that we can control global formatting of our output in various ways. We'll also see strategies for grouping attributes into named sets so we can reuse them, much the same way rules are set up in HTML's CSS syntax. We'll go even further by using the <xsl:include> tag to place templates and attribute sets in separate files, and we'll get an understanding of how this approach can enable us to reuse stylesheets for different situations.

While we're breaking out of the confines of the <xsl:template> tag, we'll also break out of the confines of our XML source file. The document() function provides a way to bring in information from an additional source file. Using data from more than one document tremendously enhances our abilities to process complex XML or to produce complex results.

Now that we've mastered some of the basics, let's get a bigger picture of stylesheets and what we can do to increase their power and flexibility.

Global Controls in the Stylesheet

First, let's mention two attributes on the <xsl:stylesheet> tag itself. These two control namespace prefixes in the output:

extension-element-prefixes=
: Use this attribute to specify what namespaces are associated with XSLT extensions.

exclude-result-prefixes=
: Use this attribute to exclude namespace prefixes from the output.

Neither of these are heavily used, although if you see that certain tags in your output are getting annoying namespaces attached to them, specify the namespace in exclude-result-prefixes=. (It takes a space-separated list of namespace prefixes.) The annoyance vanishes.

Moving along from the attributes on the <xsl:stylesheet> tag, here's the list of instructions that can be used at the top level of a stylesheet. Some of these we already know; others we will be getting to shortly.

<xsl:output>
: Controls various aspects of the output format, including things like character encoding, XML doctype statements, indentation, and output method (for example, HTML- or XML-type output).

<xsl:preserve-space>
: Specifies the names of elements in the source XML whose whitespace in the output will be left exactly as it is in the source. It takes a space-separated list.

<xsl:strip-space>
: Specifies the names of elements in the source that will have all extraneous whitespace removed in the output. It takes a space-separated list.

<xsl:decimal-format>
: Defines how numbers will be converted to strings when using format-number(). Refer to Appendix 1, *XSLT 1.0 Element Reference*, on page 237 for the arguments and syntax of this element.

<xsl:attribute-set>
: Contains a set of <xsl:attribute> tags. The name of the attribute set can be used to associate the attributes with elements that are created in the templates.

<xsl:include>
Provides a method for inserting templates from another stylesheet file into the location of this instruction in the current stylesheet.

<xsl:namespace-alias>
Allows us to map a namespace from the stylesheet into a different namespace in the output document.

<xsl:key>
Look back at Chapter 8, *Using XPath to Change the Order of Documents*, on page 117 for the definition and examples of this instruction.

<xsl:variable>
We've seen <xsl:variable> in Chapter 9, *The Value of Values*, on page 145, but we saw it used inside templates. It does the same thing outside templates, but, as with parameters, the variable is available to all templates when it is defined outside of a template.

<xsl:param>
We described this instruction in Chapter 9, *The Value of Values*, on page 145.

<xsl:template>
This is the workhorse of the stylesheet. You know a good bit about this instruction already.

<xsl:transform>
This is a synonym for <xsl:stylesheet>, and it's generally not used. It's safe to ignore this one. It's included here only for the sake of completion.

We'll have a look at a few of these in depth. The output controls will be particularly important because output requirements vary considerably from output type to output type.

Passing Data into the Stylesheet with Parameters

In some cases, we may want to provide the stylesheet with additional information each time the process is kicked off. If we can get a parameter value from the command line (or however you kick off the XSLT process) to the stylesheet, we can use the value of that parameter to supply text or control processing characteristics, as needed.

Looking back at *Using the Command Line*, on page 41, let's have another look at a Java command line for Saxon:

```
java -jar C:Saxon/Saxon6-5-5/saxon.jar -o output.xml accounts.xml streamline.xsl
```

We can add parameters to this command line to be passed in to the stylesheet. The passing of a parameter from command line to stylesheet works much like the passing of parameters from one template to another. There has to be a passing structure, and there has to be a receiving structure.

To add the parameter to the Saxon command line, simply add the name of the parameter plus the value to be passed in, separated by an equal sign. (In Windows you may need to add quotes around the parameter value.)

Let's say we want to provide information about the reading platform the output is targeted for—for example, mobile or browser. For this run of the document, we want to target it for mobile devices with a target parameter. The command line from about now looks like this:

```
java -jar C:Saxon/Saxon6-5-5/saxon.jar -o output.xml accounts.xml streamline.xsl target="mobile"
```

For the second part of the parameter equation, we need to set up our stylesheet to accept this parameter value. We set up the <xsl:param> tag at the top level of the stylesheet with the given parameter name:

```
<xsl:stylesheet>
  <xsl:param name="target"/>
  ...
  [body of stylesheet]
  ...
</xsl:stylesheet>
```

We can pass in as many parameters as we like, keeping them separated by spaces on the command line.

Once the value is passed in, we can use it for conditional processing to make choices about how content is presented.

If we'd like, we can add a default value for the parameter by placing it in the <xsl:param> tag, the same way we can for parameters in templates:

```
<xsl:stylesheet>
  <xsl:param name="target" select="'browser'"/>
  ...
  [body of stylesheet]
  ...
</xsl:stylesheet>
```

If a value is passed in from the command line, we use that value, otherwise we use the default. If no default is specified and no value is passed in from the command line, the parameter does not have a value. In general, it's best to provide some kind of backup plan in case the command line doesn't come through. That way our stylesheet processing does not run into odd little surprises when we use the parameter.

External parameters are one form of control we have over our stylesheet at runtime. It enables us to use the stylesheet for multiple purposes, giving it a layer of flexibility. Rather than having a host of variant stylesheets for different purposes, we may be able to reuse our work within a single stylesheet.

And this is just a taste. We'll see other enablers of flexibility and reuse in other instructions covered in this chapter. As we open up the stylesheet to other influences, we'll find that XSLT has a number of ways to stay connected to the processing environment around it.

Output Controls

The majority of the output controls are fairly self-explanatory, but we'll take a deeper dive into the <xsl:output> tag and the exclude-result-prefixes= attribute to explore some of the more useful properties. In particular, the <xsl:output> instruction has a large number of attributes that get a lot of use.

<xsl:output> can appear anywhere at the top level in a stylesheet, and it can appear multiple times. During runtime, all the <xsl:output> tags are merged into the equivalent of a single statement. For this reason, the attributes and attribute values should not be repeated. It's best to create the <xsl:output> statement just once at the top of the stylesheet, before the templates, and have done with it.

Here are the <xsl:output> attributes:

cdata-section-elements=

Contains a space-separated list of elements whose contents are to be treated according to the XML definition of CDATA. This allows you to include things like < and & without having to represent them by XML character entities.

doctype-public=

When the output is XML, a DOCTYPE declaration may be needed. This attribute specifies the public identifier in the XML DOCTYPE declaration.

doctype-system=

Specifies the system identifier in the DOCTYPE declaration.

encoding=

Specifies what type of character encoding to use for the output. If the attribute is not present, the default encoding is UTF-8. If you have characters that are coming out weird, check the encoding. XSLT processors are only required to respect the values UTF-8 and UTF-16 for this attribute, but read the fine print for the processor you are using. Saxon, for instance, supports ASCII, US-ASCII, iso-8859-1, UTF-8, UTF-16, KOI8R, and cp1251.

indent=

Specifies whether to indent the output. It takes the values yes or no. For XML output, the default value is no, but for HTML, the default value is yes. (Go figure.) This attribute is valid only for well-formed XML output. The use of indenting is supposed to be whitespace-friendly, but be careful using it, especially if you have elements that contain both text and elements at the same level (that is, the dreaded "mixed content"). It may have an effect on the whitespace in the XML output.

media-type=

Specifies the *Internet media type.*[1] The default value is text/xml. This setting has no impact on the output itself, but it may be used by the XSLT processor to identify to other programs what type of content they are receiving.

method=

Specifies the output format. Valid values are xml, html, and text, with the default value being xml (unless the first node output is <html>, in which case it's html). The use of text means that you can't use XSLT instructions (like <xsl:element> that output well-formed XML tags. Using the html value, the HTML output will be indented. The selected output method also determines the validity of some of the other output controls.

omit-xml-declaration=

With the XML output method, set this attribute to yes to omit the XML declaration from the beginning of the output. The default value of this attribute is no.

standalone=

Used with the XML output method, this attribute inserts a standalone= attribute in the XML declaration at the top of the output file. Set the value to yes or no; this value then appears in the attribute in the XML declaration in the output.

---

1. http://en.wikipedia.org/wiki/Internet_media_type

version=

Specifies the version of HTML or XML to be output. For the XML output method, the XML version appears in the XML declaration in the output. For HTML, the effect on the output varies by the version number.

Now that we've seen the gory details of <xsl:output>, it's time to put it to work. You know by now that this book isn't about just regurgitating the specifications. We're here to solve problems. Let's ask, then: what kind of problems does <xsl:output> solve?

To answer that question, let's key off the three values we can set for the method= attribute: text, html, and xml. What sorts of controls do we typically need for creating these three types of output? The answers, especially for HTML, turns out not to be as straightforward as we might like. In the following sections, we'll have a look at all three output types and discuss some problems and approaches for each one.

Text Output

Creating text output should be relatively straightforward, right? Let's take a file we've seen before and see what the output looks like using the text method.

Let's say that I royally messed up the naming convention of the graphics files in my book (yes, I've been known to makes mistakes). I'd like to change the names of the graphics, but I've been dumping all sorts of graphics folders into a single directory, and I don't want to change them all. I'd like to list only the graphics in my book, with their complete paths (or at least the relative part I've included in the file reference attributes). I want a text file with one path per line so I can then feed the file to a batch program to change all the filenames. My image paths are in tags throughout the document, looking like this:

```
<imagedata fileref="images/standalone/Saxon_installation_directory.jpg"
   border="yes"/>
```

We need to parse through a big XML file to operate only on <imagedata> tags. This type of problem is perfect for the identity template with an extra template for <imagedata>. I won't repeat the main template for the identity template, but here is a template for the <imagedata> tag to output the content of the fileref= attribute (containing the file path) as a line of text:

```
<xsl:template match="imagedata">
   <xsl:value-of select="@fileref"/>
 </xsl:template>
```

Seems simple enough. Let's give it a whirl against the book's XML file. Initially, the output looks like the following line, only extended out to 782 character places.

```
<?xml version="1.0" encoding="UTF-8"?>images/Introduction/caution-1.pngimages/...
```

We've got a couple of problems here. First, there's that XML declaration at the top, and that won't do. I've forgotten to add the <xsl:output> tag with method="text". So let's see if that will help matters.

```
images/Introduction/caution-1.pngimages/howitlooks/bib1.pngimages/howitlooks/...
```

Better, but the paths are still all mushed together. Let's add a linebreak with the <xsl:text> tag, like so:

```
<xsl:template match="imagedata">
    <xsl:value-of select="@fileref"/><xsl:text>
    </xsl:text>
</xsl:template>
```

```
images/Introduction/caution-1.png
    images/howitlooks/bib1.png
    images/howitlooks/conceptual-process-diagram.pdf
    images/howitlooks/bib1-tree.png
    ...
```

Another improvement, but this time we've got four additional spaces at the beginning of the line because we didn't move the ending tag of <xsl:text> to the first character position in the text. Removing the extra spaces, we now get the text we're after:

```
images/Introduction/caution-1.png
images/howitlooks/bib1.png
images/howitlooks/conceptual-process-diagram.pdf
images/howitlooks/bib1-tree.png
...
```

Once you turn on method="text", the output becomes very literal. You'll have to work with spacing, removing whitespace as needed, and placing values exactly where you want in the output file. But in general, the results are fairly predictable.

HTML, on the other hand...

HTML Output

HTML output requires a little more fiddling. It's not just a matter of tagging the text to all come out as valid HTML; we also need to worry about namespaces. Spacing and indentation may not be a problem if we're just going to feed the output into a browser, but if we have to troubleshoot the output, we're going to want to pretty it up.

Let's go back to an example we saw back in Chapter 1, *Introducing XSLT*, on page 1. We had some XML that looked like the following (linebreaks added to fit it on the page).

stylesheets/caution1.xml

```
<?xml version='1.0' encoding='UTF-8'?>
<?xml-stylesheet type="text/xsl" href="caution1.xsl"?>
<note type="caution">
  <p>The potential for intergalactic broadcast range while
    using the AZGuard Protaxis unit has not yet been fully
    determined.</p>

  <p>Please avoid transmitting information that could place
    the human race at risk.</p>
</note>
```

And for the output, we originally had this:

stylesheets/caution1.html

```
<?xml version="1.0" encoding="UTF-8"?>
   <html xmlns="http://www.w3.org/1999/xhtml">
   <head><title>Caution!</title></head>
   <body><h2>WAIT JUST A SECOND THERE!!!</h2>
   <p><b>USE EXTREME CAUTION:</b></p>
   <p>The potential for intergalactic broadcast range while
    using the AZGuard Protaxis unit has not yet been fully
    determined.</p>
        <p>Please avoid transmitting information that could place
    the human race at risk.</p></body></html>
```

In the course of this book, we've gotten a little wiser. There is a lot of room for improvement in this output. For one thing, what is that XML declaration doing there at the top? And the namespace in the <html> tag, what's with that? We might not want to bother with the formalities of XHTML output when plain vanilla HTML will do just fine. And without the line returns I've added by hand, the text shoots out the side of the text editor like a comet leaving the solar system. It makes for difficult troubleshooting.

Instead of the awkward arrangement shown above, we'd like something that starts out like the following:

```
<!DOCTYPE HTML PUBLIC "-//W3C//DTD HTML 4.01 Transitional//EN">
<html>
<head>
        <title>Caution!</title>
</head>
```

To get this, we're going to need to do a few things: add the !DOCTYPE declaration, remove the namespace attribute, and add indentation. Take a look at the original XSLT stylesheet we used for this transformation in Figure 6, *XSLT stylesheet for the caution HTML*, on page 7, then give some thought to what we'll need to do to accomplish our goals. The <xsl:output> tag should handle most of this.

A few tastefully arranged attributes should do the trick, as shown in the following code.

stylesheets/caution2.xsl

```
Line 1 <?xml version="1.0" encoding="utf-8"?>
-      <xsl:stylesheet xmlns:xsl="http://www.w3.org/1999/XSL/Transform"
-        version="1.0">
-        <xsl:output method="html" doctype-public="-//W3C//DTD HTML 4.01 Transitional//EN"
5          indent="yes"/>
-      <xsl:template match="note[@type='caution']">
-        <html>
-          <head><title>Caution!</title></head>
-          <body>
10           <h2>WAIT JUST A SECOND THERE!!!</h2>
-            <p>
-              <xsl:text>USE EXTREME CAUTION: </xsl:text>
-              <xsl:apply-templates select="p[1]"/>
-            </p>
15         <xsl:apply-templates select="p[not(position() = 1)]"/>
-          </body>
-      <xsl:text>
-      </xsl:text>
-        </html>
20     </xsl:template>
-
-      <xsl:template match="p[not(position() = 1)]">
-        <p><xsl:apply-templates/></p>
-      </xsl:template>
25
-      </xsl:stylesheet>
```

Based on the output instruction we provided in line 5, the output appears as in Figure 49, *HTML output with !DOCTYPE declaration*, on page 193, untouched by human hands (which is almost always a good thing in programming).

Notice that the XSLT processor inserted a line for the content-type metadata, using a value of text/html. With method="html", the media type is supplied with the default value of the media-type= attribute on <xsl:output>. If you need it to be something different, you'll need to supply the new value explicitly with media-type=.

stylesheets/caution2.html

```
<!DOCTYPE html
  PUBLIC "-//W3C//DTD HTML 4.01 Transitional//EN">
<html>
   <head>
      <meta http-equiv="Content-Type" content="text/html; charset=UTF-8">
      <title>Caution!</title>
   </head>
   <body>
      <h2>WAIT JUST A SECOND THERE!!!</h2>
      <p>USE EXTREME CAUTION: The potential for intergalactic broadcast range while
         using the AZGuard Protaxis unit has not yet been fully
         determined.
      </p>
      <p>Please avoid transmitting information that could place
         the human race at risk.
      </p>
   </body>
</html>
```

Figure 49—HTML output with !DOCTYPE declaration

HTML isn't difficult once you get those settings right. You'll doubtlessly find nuances that will need to be fiddled with, but the settings used in the example above should get you started.

XML Output

Two of the challenges with creating XML output are getting the namespaces right and controlling the whitespace in the output. As an example, let's have a look at something called XSL-FO. XSL-FO is a sort of hodge-podge of XSLT and a markup language called Formatting Objects (FO). (Actually, you can create FO without XSL, but I wouldn't like to try.) FO is basically another form of XML, and it's used to create PDFs by feeding the FO into XSL-FO processors such as Apache FOP,[2] RenderX XEP,[3] or Antenna House XSL-FO Formatter.[4]

Tags in XSL-FO are usually written with the fo: namespace, so that will be one of our output requirements. Also, since we're going to create output for a software book like the one you're reading, we want to preserve whitespace in some of the tags so code examples appear in the PDF with controlled indentation. We won't see a complete XSL-FO stylesheet in the next example

2. http://xmlgraphics.apache.org/fop/
3. http://www.renderx.com
4. http://www.antennahouse.com/

(that could go on for pages!), but we'll have a look at the top of the stylesheet and a few templates.

stylesheets/book-parts.xsl

```
<?xml version="1.0" encoding="utf-8"?>
<xsl:stylesheet xmlns:xsl="http://www.w3.org/1999/XSL/Transform"
  xmlns:fo="http://www.w3.org/1999/XSL/Format" version="1.0">

 <xsl:preserve-space elements="code"/>

  <xsl:template match="p">
    <fo:block>
      <xsl:choose>
        <xsl:when test="parent::li | parent::poem">
          <xsl:attribute name="text-align">left</xsl:attribute>
        </xsl:when>
        <xsl:when test="parent::colophon">center</xsl:when>
        <xsl:otherwise>
          <xsl:attribute name="text-align">justify</xsl:attribute>
          <xsl:attribute name="text-indent">1.5em</xsl:attribute>
        </xsl:otherwise>
      </xsl:choose>
       <xsl:apply-templates/>
    </fo:block>
  </xsl:template>

  <xsl:template match="code">
    <fo:block white-space-treatment="preserve"
      linefeed-treatment="preserve">
      <xsl:apply-templates/>
    </fo:block>
  </xsl:template>
</xsl:stylesheet>
```

This code does not represent a complete XSL-FO stylesheet by any means—a huge amount of setup normally present for the root document and page masters aren't shown here. The templates for the <p> and <code> tags would normally work within the context of other, surrounding tags, but we're looking at them by themselves for the purpose of our example.

In the <xsl:stylesheet> tag we've added the namespace for the FO tags: `xmlns:fo="http://www.w3.org/1999/XSL/Format"`. This means we can attach the `fo:` namespace to the tags we want to output, and the namespace will appear as we want it in our output document. Without the namespace declaration, the XSLT processor would see the `fo:` namespace designation in our XSLT and just stop.

In the code itself, we've included a few fo: tags that will be included in the output. As you can see, we're also adding some attributes to one of those tags based on some conditional processing.

But something is missing. What do you think? It looks like we're adding some whitespace handling on that second <fo:block> tag, but will that do the trick?

Right—we still need to put some whitespace handling into the XSLT code itself. The instructions we're including for the fo: tags will have an effect on the content when it's processed by an FO formatter downstream, but that's not the part of the process we're dealing with at the moment. We need to add instructions to the XSLT to handle the whitespace in the <code> tag properly. As we saw earlier, we can do this by adding the <xsl:preserve-space> tag above our templates:

```
<xsl:preserve-space="code"/>
```

Now we have controls in place for the namespace we want to output and for whitespace control over a specific element. These are two of the more common controls you'll need for handling XML. We can also add indentation PUBLIC and SYSTEM identifiers if our output requires a DOCTYPE statement, as we've seen for HTML. All that seems easy enough—so what could possibly go wrong?

Creating an XSLT Stylesheet with XSLT

Let's consider one more scenario that you may encounter before we finish. The problem is simply stated: how do you create an XSLT stylesheet using XSLT? (And for that matter, why would you want to?) The issue is this: if you need to output tags that are in the xsl: namespace, how does the XSLT processor distinguish those from the XSLT tags that are doing the actual work? If we don't do something, the working tags and the output tags will be tripping all over each other.

So have a look at the code in Figure 50, *Using xsl:namespace-alias for XSLT output*, on page 196. Do you see what's happening here?

We've created a dummy namespace, myxsl: to use for the tags that we want in the output. Of course, the namespace of those tags, myxsl:, is not what we actually want in the output, so we've added the <xsl:namespace-alias> tag before the template to specify what the namespace should be translated to in the output. In this case, myxsl: will turn into xsl:.

stylesheets/xsl-stylesheet.xsl

```
<?xml version="1.0" encoding="utf-8"?>
<xsl:stylesheet xmlns:xsl="http://www.w3.org/1999/XSL/Transform"
     xmlns:fo="http://www.w3.org/1999/XSL/Format"
     xmlns:myxsl="file://myxsl.prefix" version="1.0">
  <xsl:import href="book.xsl"/>
  <xsl:include href="caution1.xsl"/>
  <xsl:namespace-alias stylesheet-prefix="myxsl" result-prefix="xsl"/>

  <xsl:template match="p">
    <myxsl:template match="{name()}">
      <myxsl:element name="{name()}">
        <xsl:if test="@id">
          <myxsl:attribute name="id">
            <xsl:value-of select="@id"/>
          </myxsl:attribute>
        </xsl:if>
        <xsl:apply-templates/>
      </myxsl:element>
    </myxsl:template>
  </xsl:template>
</xsl:stylesheet>
```

Figure 50—Using <xsl:namespace-alias> for XSLT output

To make this work, we also had to specify the dummy namespace in the <xsl:stylesheet> tag with a dummy namespace URI (xmlns:myxsl="file://myxsl.prefix"). Yeah, it's a little sleazy, but it gets the job done.

<xsl:namespace-alias> is used in edge cases when we encounter ambiguity between different namespaces. You can use it for XML namespaces as well as XSLT namespaces. There's no need to go into the deep nitty gritty here—you'll find a variety of discussions on the topic using any Internet search engine. But it's a good one to keep in mind when the going gets weird—as it often does in XSLT.

Attribute Sets

One of the major characteristics of good software is that it doesn't repeat itself. Given the amount of repetition we find in XML documents, XSLT often has to format numerous different types of data the same way. Templates for <note>,<caution> and <warning> tags might have minor differences in the output they create, but for the most part they might share the same fonts, spacing above, spacing below, indentation, and so forth. Rather than repeat ourselves each time we need a particular group of output attributes, it would be nice to put them together into a named set and just call them by name.

Attribute sets fulfill this need. They are similar to named templates, but are invoked a little differently. And like named templates, they work with paired mechanisms: the part that calls the attribute set, and the attribute set itself.

The attribute set consists of the <xsl:attribute-set> tag, which has a name= attribute, just like the <xsl:call-template> instruction.

The only legal instruction in an <xsl:attribute-set> tag is <xsl:attribute>, which also takes a name= attribute. The name of the attribute must be legal within the context of where it will appear in the output (a topic we'll get to shortly). And the contents of the xsl:attribute= tag contain the value (or set of expressions and logic that yield a value) that we want to appear in the attribute. It looks pretty simple. Here's an example:

```
<xsl:attribute-set name="notelike-blocks">
  <xsl:attribute name="text-indent">18pt</xsl:attribute>
  <xsl:attribute name="font-family">serif</xsl:attribute>
  <xsl:attribute name="space-before">6pt</xsl:attribute>
  <xsl:attribute name="space-after">6pt</xsl:attribute>
</xsl:attribute-set>
```

We'll leave the attribute set for a moment so we can talk about where the attribute set is used in the output.

When we are defining our output, in the templates, we want the attributes in the attribute set to appear with the appropriate element in the output. In the case of XSL-FO output, for instance, the attributes in our notelike-blocks attribute set would appear as attributes on an <fo:block> tag. So we specify the call to the attribute set in the same location where the final attributes need to appear, that is, as an attribute itself, like this:

```
<fo:block xsl:use-attribute-sets="notelike-block">
   Someone's glorious prose proceeds...
 </fo:block>
```

This example shows a couple of interesting points. First, there is that xsl: namespace declaration on the use-attribute-set attribute. This attribute isn't an XSL-FO attribute; it's an XSLT control, so we have to use the xsl: namespace to distinguish it from true XSL-FO attributes. And since it has an effect on output, it can only be added to XML tags that are destined for the output stream.

The second point of interest is encapsulated in that little *s* at the end of the attribute name. The plural indicates that we can enter the names of multiple attribute sets within the same xsl:use-attribute-set= attribute. This arrangement allows us some flexibility in setting up attribute sets for different purposes.

Continuing our example of notes, cautions, and warnings, suppose we want to make each type of admonishment a different font color. We could put the attribute for each color in its own attribute set to use for each type of admonition. We would still have an attribute set to be used for all the admonishment types, but only for the attributes shared by the admonishments. Now our stylesheet would contain the following attribute sets and (for the example, just one) template, as follows:

```
<xsl:attribute-set name="notelike-blocks">
  <xsl:attribute name="text-indent">18pt</xsl:attribute>
  <xsl:attribute name="font-family">serif</xsl:attribute>
  <xsl:attribute name="space-before">6pt</xsl:attribute>
  <xsl:attribute name="space-after">6pt</xsl:attribute>
</xsl:attribute-set>

<xsl:attribute-set name="note-color">
  <xsl:attribute name="color">blue</xsl:attribute>
</xsl:attribute-set>

<xsl:attribute-set name="warning-color">
  <xsl:attribute name="color">orange</xsl:attribute>
</xsl:attribute-set>

<xsl:attribute-set name="caution-color">
  <xsl:attribute name="color">red</xsl:attribute>
</xsl:attribute-set>

<xsl:template match="note">
  <fo:block xsl:use-attribute-sets="notelike-block note-color">
    Someone's glorious prose proceeds...
  </fo:block>
</xsl:template>
```

The advantage here, in terms of reusable attribute sets, is that some other template can now make use of the note-color attribute set even if it doesn't need the notelike-blocks attribute set.

If the ability to call multiple attribute sets from an output element isn't flexible enough, the designers of XSLT added another present: the ability for attribute sets to call other attribute sets. Okay—that's interesting, but what does that give us that we don't get by calling multiple attribute sets?

If we have a lot of different elements that call the same group of attribute sets, we can make some careful planning choices and call only one attribute set, which includes only our specific attribute (like font color in the example), then does the extra work of calling the shared attribute set for us. So now we would see:

```
<xsl:attribute-set name="notelike-blocks">
  <xsl:attribute name="text-indent">18pt</xsl:attribute>
  <xsl:attribute name="font-family">serif</xsl:attribute>
  <xsl:attribute name="space-before">6pt</xsl:attribute>
  <xsl:attribute name="space-after">6pt</xsl:attribute>
</xsl:attribute-set>

<xsl:attribute-set name="note" xsl:use-attribute-sets="notelike-blocks">
  <xsl:attribute name="color">blue</xsl:attribute>
</xsl:attribute-set>
<xsl:attribute-set name="warning" xsl:use-attribute-sets="notelike-blocks">
  <xsl:attribute name="color">orange</xsl:attribute>
</xsl:attribute-set>
<xsl:attribute-set name="caution" xsl:use-attribute-sets="notelike-blocks">
  <xsl:attribute name="color">red</xsl:attribute>
</xsl:attribute-set>

<xsl:template match="note">
  <fo:block xsl:use-attribute-sets="note">
    Someone's glorious prose proceeds...
  </fo:block>
</xsl:template>
```

By setting up the attribute sets like this, we don't have to remember all the different attribute set names that need to go with a specific output element. Just one will do.

We'll also see that this type of arrangement is useful when we start including external stylesheet files to override templates and attributes sets, but we're getting slightly ahead of ourselves here.

Attribute sets are indispensable when dealing with massive stylesheets that output data with complex, repeated groups of attributes. If you encounter this type of situation, I strongly recommend that you analyze the types of output you expect and collaborate closely with any others participating in the development work. Attribute sets represent a type of shared XSLT resource, and you want to be sure that everyone agrees on how they are structured. Otherwise, the results could get ugly.

But now that we've brought up the notion of shared XSLT resources and the possibility of including external stylesheet files, we may as well dive into it. Hold onto your babushka...our stylesheets are getting ready to explode.

Using External Stylesheets

XSLT 1.0 supports two instructions for including stylesheets from other files. The two differ from each other only in terms of their precedence with respect to the stylesheet that calls them. The instructions are <xsl:include> and <xsl:import>. In this section, we'll take a look at what they do and, more importantly, how they can be used to our advantage.

First the similarities. <xsl:include> and <xsl:import> are both top-level tags, so they appear outside of templates. Both instructions include an href= attribute to point to the file containing the external stylesheet. In both cases, only one stylesheet file can be referenced per instruction, but we can include as many of the instructions as we like, which means we can reference any number of external stylesheets.

Now come the differences. For one thing, <xsl:import> always has to come immediately after the <xsl:stylesheet> opening tag—it must be the first element in the stylesheet, unless it's preceded by another <xsl:import>. Conversely, <xsl:include> can appear anywhere in the stylesheet, as long as it's at the top level in the stylesheet hierarchy.

Another difference between the two instructions is in how they affect the precedence of the templates and definitions (variables and parameters) that are called in.

In both cases, the instructions use an href= attribute to call in the external stylesheet.

External Stylesheets and Precedence

The reason <xsl:include> can appear anywhere is that during runtime, all the templates in the referenced stylesheet are merged with the templates from the current stylesheet. They are treated as if they were all from the same stylesheet.

The templates from included stylesheets all have the same *precedence* as the templates in the current stylesheet. What do we mean by precedence? Basically, precedence means that if templates from two stylesheets match the same XPath result exactly, the one with higher precedence gets to do the processing. Normally, all templates start out with the same precedence. However, you can declare a value for the precedence of a template by using the priority= attribute on the <xsl:template> tag, like this:

```
<xsl:template match="p" priority="42">
```

The value of priority= is relative. By default, templates have a value of 0.5, and you can assign negative values as well as positive values.

With <xsl:import>, however, all the templates and definitions in the referenced stylesheet are given special status: they are always treated as having lower precedence than the templates in the original stylesheet. Not only that, but templates in a file imported by the first <xsl:import> tag have *lower* precedence than templates imported by a second <xsl:import> tag. By arranging the <xsl:import> tags carefully, you can craft which templates will be used and which ignored if they happen to wind up matching the same XML node or node-set.

If we decide that external templates need to have higher precedence than the templates in our main stylesheet, we'll need to use higher values in the priority= attributes for those templates, and we'll use <xsl:include> rather than <xsl:import>.

Precedence allows us to manage multiple stylesheets where there may be overlap between templates. In general, it's a good idea to keep templates from matching the same thing, but when we're bringing in other stylesheets, it's not always easy to keep track of who is doing what to whom. If we need to bring in other stylesheets, we can add priority= to the templates in our reference stylesheet to ensure that there is no collision between stylesheets, or we can always place the external templates at a lower priority by using <xsl:import>.

Using Lower-Precedence Templates

Manipulating precedence may allow us to mix and match templates from external stylesheets, but doing so changes the overrides on a global basis. If we want to use an overridden template in only a single location, we can use the <xsl:apply-imports> instruction.

We place the <xsl:apply-imports> tag inside a template that matches the same thing as the overridden template. Once we do that, the contents of the overridden template are executed in the position of the <xsl:apply-imports> within the current template.

That definition sounds a bit abstract, so we'd better have an example. Suppose in our main stylesheet we have a template matching <note> that places a <span> with a font color of red. Our stylesheet imports another set of templates, one of which matches <note> as well, only this one places another <span> around the text, this time with bold type. The imported stylesheet contains minimum standard formats, and the main stylesheet is being used to add formats for a particular situation (for instance, to a customer-facing website).

Here is the template from our imported stylesheet:

```
<xsl:template match="note">
  <span style="font-weight:bold;">
    <xsl:apply-templates/>
  </span>
</xsl:template>
```

Because our standard stylesheet is adding the red font-color to the imported bold type, we place the <xsl:apply-imports> where the span with the red font color surrounds the content of the template from the external stylesheet. In the example below, the external stylesheet containing the template for bold type is called basic.xsl.

```
<xsl:stylesheet>
  <xsl:import href="basic.xsl" />
  <xsl:template match="note">
    <span style="font-color:red;">
      <xsl:apply-imports/>
    </span>
  </xsl:template>
</xsl:stylesheet>
```

When the main stylesheet is run, the template brings in the contents of the matching template in basic.xsl, with the effect of creating a template that would look like this:

```
<xsl:template match="note">
  <span style="font-color:red">
  <span style="font-weight:bold">
    <xsl:apply-templates/>
  </span>
  </span>
</xsl:template>
```

As you might guess, the possibilities for screwing this up are enormous. In general, I have not found a lot of use for this instruction, but you may find it to be the bomb for what you need. Use it wisely.

Swapping External Stylesheets to Handle Different Conditions

When people see the possibilities of <xsl:import> and <xsl:include>, the temptation is to look for ways to include one set of template in one condition and another set of templates (matching the same nodes) in another condition. For example, for a mobile-based website we might only want to process the first two paragraphs of a news article, then add a link to the rest of the article, but in the full web version we want to process the entire article as we find it.

On the face of it, conditional templates seem like a good idea, but the XSLT implementation doesn't work that way. Remember, the <xsl:import> and <xsl:include> instructions occur outside of templates, at the top level of stylesheets. The only tools for conditional processing are inside the templates, things like <xsl:if> and <xsl:choose>. Once an XSLT process is started, the XSLT stylesheet and its includes and imports are all resolved before processing begins. So in that sense, it's not possible to conditionally include or exclude templates.

Think a little bit about the example, though. In both situations, we know what the condition is (mobile versus full web browser) before we start processing. That being the case, we can start the process by first calling a stylesheet that contains the templates that are specific to the condition we're processing for (let's say, a mobile web view). Then that stylesheet can use <xsl:import> or <xsl:include> to bring in the templates for the common, general tags.

For instance, we might know that <it> is going to give us an italic font style no matter what device we're processing for, and chances are that <p> is always going to be <p>. So we put the templates for those tags in our general stylesheet, and we call the general stylesheet into both our mobile.xsl stylesheet file and our full-browser.xsl file. When we get ready to process, we point the command line to mobile.xsl or full-browser.xsl, as appropriate.

The following example shows two stylesheets used as entry points, one for a mobile website, the other for a full browser-based site. Both of them include a third file that handles common, low-level formats.

Stylesheet 1 for mobile processing:

```
<xsl:stylesheet>
  <xsl:include href="common.xsl"/>

  <!-- Templates specific to mobile processing follow. -->
<xsl:stylesheet>
```

Stylesheet 2 for full-browser processing:

```
<xsl:stylesheet>
  <xsl:include href="common.xsl"/>

  <!-- Templates specific to full-browser processing follow. -->
<xsl:stylesheet>
```

As you can see, they're both set up the same way, just with different names and templates specific to their intent.

Of course, this arrangement assumes that we have the ability to determine our conditions before we create the command line for processing.

Conditional inclusion of templates at runtime

But what if we don't know the conditions we're processing for until runtime? Is there anything we can do conditionally to include or exclude templates at that point?

Sure, and we've already seen the answer. It doesn't necessarily have to do with imports and inclusions—we just use template modes (covered in *The xsl:apply-templates Instruction*, on page 26). We can create templates with conditions that invoke matches on identical elements, but with different modes, as in this example:

```
<xsl:template match="section">
  <xsl:choose>
    <xsl:when test="$output-type = 'html'">
      <xsl:apply-templates mode="html"/>>
    </xsl:when>
    <xsl:otherwise>
      <xsl:apply-templates mode="pdf"/>
    </xsl:otherwise>
  </xsl:choose>
</xsl:template>

<xsl:template match="p" mode="html">
  <p>
    <xsl:apply-templates/>
  </p>
</xsl:template>

 <xsl:template match="p" mode="pdf">
  <fo:block>
    <xsl:apply-templates/>
  </fo:block>
</xsl:template>
```

Here we have a parameter called output-type that we have defined elsewhere. We may have passed in the value from outside the stylesheet using a command line parameter. We use this parameter in a test to determine whether to use the html mode or the pdf mode for processing the rest of the elements. This example shows only the templates for the <p> element, but we would likely have numerous other templates for other elements.

If we have lots of templates and like to keep things neatly organized, we can put all the templates in a given mode into their own files and include them with <xsl:include>. Since they are differentiated by modes, we also don't have to worry about precedence when templates match on the same elements (like the two templates that match on <p> in the example above). The modes help keep them sorted.

All in all, the use of external stylesheets is almost unavoidable as our stylesheets grow and our different output types multiply. The insular world of the single stylesheet won't last very long once our projects start hitting the real world.

External Libraries

As we develop larger numbers of XSLT stylesheets, we'll see repetitions in the templates we develop for different deliverables. Templates that get repeated a lot are worth setting aside into their own files, even if a file contains only one or two templates that always get reused together. These stylesheet files can serve as libraries for multiple projects. They may even reside in their own directories, or even on separate servers where they need to be included with URLs.

External files can contain attribute sets, parameters, and variables as well as matching templates and named templates. There is nothing that says a stylesheet has to contain a template at all! The only rules are that XSLT stylesheets have to begin and end with the <xsl:stylesheet> tag, and the contents need to be well-formed XML using XSLT instructions. Libraries of attribute sets and parameters can be a great help in organizing large projects with multiple deliverables, or even multiple unrelated projects.

For maintainability and ease of access, it's best to follow a few simple housekeeping rules about external stylesheets:

- Keep similar things together within a stylesheet file. Try not to mix templates and attribute sets, for instance.
- Give the stylesheet files names that clearly represent their contents. For instance, a stylesheet full of attribute sets for formatting notes and warnings might be called admonition-att-sets.xsl.
- If the stylesheets apply only to certain types of output, include the output type in the filename. Also consider putting all the stylesheet files for a particular output type together in the same directory.

Good housekeeping habits with external stylesheets will go a long way toward making you look smarter—and there's never anything wrong with that!

Adding Instructions in the Output

If we're not able to generate all of the functionality we need, one strategy is to add processing instructions to the output. Essentially, we're passing off the problem to a process downstream from our XSLT processing. And this strategy is not just for last-resort situations: we may not always have the information to do the processing completely, so we hand it off to a downstream process that will add its own little piece of intelligence.

The <xsl:processing-instruction> tag creates an XML processing instruction that can be embedded in the output wherever needed. This XSLT instruction provides a single control, the name= attribute. The contents of the instruction provide the rest of the contents.

We saw an example of an XML processing instruction early in this book, the instruction we used to direct an XML file to a stylesheet to process it. (See Figure 1, *Sample XML for conversion to HTML*, on page 3.) The second line is a processing instruction:

```
<?xml-stylesheet type="text/xsl" href="caution1.xsl"?>
```

To add this processing instruction to the XML output, we'd place the following instruction in the appropriate location—probably in the template that matches on the root:

```
<xsl:processing-instruction name="xml-stylesheet">
  type="text/xsl" href="caution1.xsl"
</xsl:processing-instruction>
```

The effect of a processing instruction is dependent on the downstream processor. For our example processing instruction, the downstream processor happens to be a web browser, which uses the instructions to invoke an XSLT processor and locate the specified XSLT stylesheet. It might also be some code to validate the output against a DTD, to perform some post-processing to determine page layout, or calculations to help determine a processing schedule.

Using processing instructions gives XSLT a little bit of an extra helping hand, but what if we need that help during the processing of the files and not afterwards? The standard XSLT 1.0 toolset doesn't offer much to work with for that type of problem. Fortunately, XSLT extensions can help.

Calls to External Programs with XSLT Extensions

As long as we're opening up our stylesheets, why not open them up to other types of programs? XSLT is not necessarily the best choice for mathematical processing, for example—what if we need to call a helper program to calculate some data for our output? Or process times and dates? Complex string and table manipulations?

We mentioned at the end of *Parsing Strings with Recursion*, on page 179 that we can't call external programs using the XSLT standard instruction set. However, different XSLT processors do offer extensions to the XSLT element set to handle external program calls.

Each set of XSLT extensions is defined in its own namespace. To use the extensions, we have to declare its namespace in the <xsl:stylesheet> tag.

The extensions supported by Saxon and Xalan are not limited to those in the saxon: and xalan: namespaces. If we're lucky, we may find XSLT extension functions and elements already written to do the work for us. And if not, we'll need to find out which languages are supported for external programs by your XSLT processor, then use an extension element to call a program that you've written.

If you're feeling especially constructive, you can write your own XSLT extensions (with your own namespace), then just use your extensions elements or functions the way you'd like. Java is the language of choice for writing XSLT extensions. That's getting way beyond the scope of this book, but if you're interested, you can find guides for writing Saxon extensions[5] and Xalan extensions[6] online.

Joe asks: What if I use an extension but it's not supported on some other processor than might be used?

An extension element might not always wind up in friendly hands, but you don't necessarily what your XSLT script to barf every time it runs on a non-compatible processor. To make the use of extensions a little more reliable, the XSLT 1.0 standard includes the <xsl:fallback> tag. The contents of this element get executed only if the containing XSLT extension element isn't recognized.

For example, suppose we want to use an extension element we've developed, <xsl:unless>. Since we have a high likelihood of discovering XSLT processors that don't support this extension, we're going to want to supply a fallback option for the general run of processors, as shown here:

```
<xsl:template match="chapter">
  <xsl:unless test="title">
    <xsl:text>Chapter Title Missing</xsl:text>
    <xsl:fallback>
      <xsl:if test="not(title)">
        <xsl:text>Chapter Title Missing</xsl:text>
      </xsl:if>
    </xsl:fallback>
  </xsl:unless>
</xsl:template>
```

5. http://saxon.sourceforge.net/saxon6.5.5/extensibility.html
6. http://xml.apache.org/xalan-j/extensions.html

Before using XSLTs extensions, it's always good to test them on the XSLT processor you intend to use in production.

We can't spend a lot of time on extensions in this book, but if you feel like your XSLT toolset is too confining, check out some of the following resources:

EXSLT . . . . http://exslt.org/
To quote their website, "EXSLT is a community initiative to provide extensions to XSLT." Here you can find extensions for date and time functions, math functions, the ability to use regular expressions, extended string functions, and other niceties that you might be familiar with from other software languages.

EXSLT is supported across a number of XSLT processors, but implementations will vary from processor to processor—you'll need to check the documentation for your particular XSLT processor to see what's supported.

Saxon http://saxon.sourceforge.net/saxon7.9.1/extensions.html
If you're using Saxon, you'll have access to the saxon extension functions. The list of extended functions is modest but potentially useful; check out the list at the website given here.

Xalan-Java . . . . http://xml.apache.org/xalan-j/extensionslib.html
The library for extensions supported by Xalan is more extensive than that supported by Saxon, but like Saxon, don't expect these to work with any other type of processor. If you're using the C+ version of Xalan, you'll need to check out a different list (URL shown below) than for Xalan-Java.

Xalan-C . . . . http://xml.apache.org/xalan-c/extensionslib.html
The extension set for Xalan-C+.

External Data Files—Input and Output

So far in this chapter we have expanded the scope of our stylesheets in a number of ways. We've imported stylesheets, included stylesheets, and mentioned the possibility of using extensioned functions and calls to external programs to expand the functionality of XSLT itself.

But what about the source files and the output? Currently, the only thing we know how to do is to take a single XML file as input and create a single output file—text, HTML, XML, or other character-based files. But there are times when we'll wish we had more than that for our processing. We might need to refer to data in other XML files to provide additional input or to use for tests in our conditional processing. We may also need to parse pure text files rather than XML files as additional input. And while we're in the middle of processing a large XML file, it might be easier to create several output files at the same time rather than processing the same file several times to get multiple outputs. At the moment, we don't know how to do any of this.

Let's fix that.

Getting Additional Input from XML files

For getting additional input from external files, XSLT 1.0 comes equipped with the document() function. This function takes a URI as its argument. (There can be a second, optional argument, but it's seldom used.) A typical usage would be like this:

```
<xsl:copy-of select="document('reference.xml')"/>
```

In this case, the output would be a copy of the entire XML contents of the reference.xml file.

The path in the argument can be relative or absolute, but it has to be presented as a string (in single quotes). In XSLT 1.0, the only type of document that can be retrieved this way is an XML document. When the document() function is invoked, the XSLT processor attempts to parse the contents of the document as XML. If the document fails to parse, the XSLT processor may post an error. (But don't fret—we'll see a way to get the contents of non-XML files in just a short while.)

Joe asks:

Can I process text-only files if I don't need to process an XML file?

XSLT processors require the input file to be well-formed XML. However, you can easily process plain text files by providing a dummy XML file for the input. You then match on its root to start the stylesheet, and from that point you can include the plain text files and perform additional processing without ever touching the dummy input file.

I frequently use this for small utility processing when switching to another piece of software is more trouble than it's worth.

One point worth mentioning: even though it's a dummy file, the XLST processor will still parse it. If you use a dummy file, make sure the XML is valid—and brief!

Retrieving Parts of Other Files with XPath and document()

Suppose we don't need the entire contents of the external XML file, just a few node-sets. It turns out that the document() function can be included as the first part of an XPath statement, coming just before the root of the XML file. For example, if we wanted to retrieve only the first <h1> tag from an XHTML document named highlights.xhtml, we could create a statement like the following:

```
<xsl:value-of select="document('highlights.xhtml')/xhtml/body/h1[1]"/>
```

Starting with XPath's *root* symbol (/) after the document function, we can use normal XPath notation to retrieve node-sets from the external document. Once we get into the XML document, all the rules for XPath work the same as they would on our normal source document.

Storing the Results of the document() in a Variable

One frequent usage pattern of the document() is to store its results in a variable. The reason for doing this is to reduce the number of times the XSLT processor has to open and close the external file to read its contents. By storing the results in a variable one time at the beginning of a stylesheet, we can use the variable as many times as we want without touching the external file again.

The results of the document() function are typically a node-set. In the case of the document() function's results, the node-set might be the entire XML document, or it might be a single node, depending on how we have defined the XPath statement following the document() function. As with all variables that contain node-sets, we can apply XPath expressions to the variable to obtain specific results. (See *Retrieving Nodes from a Node-Set Stored in a Variable*, on page 158 for a refresher on handling variables that contain node-sets.)

Retrieving the Contents of a Non-XML File

The document() function won't retrieve the contents of a non-XML file because XSLT 1.0 requires the XSLT processor to parse the file as XML before it retrieves the results. If the file isn't XML, an XSLT 1.0 processor will probably post an error and stop processing. XSLT 2.0 addressed the problem with its unparsed-text() function, but we'd like to stick to XSLT 1.0 in this book. Of course, the world is filled with files that aren't formatted as XML, and many of those files contain information we'd like to use.

There's a nice trick for getting non-XML content from external files into our stylesheet, but it's not an XSLT function. Even though this book is about XSLT, we'll cover it anyway, because curious minds want to know.

Remember, XSLT is a form of XML, right? So we can include an XML system statement in our stylesheet, and within the XML system statement we can create an unparsed XML entity that takes its value from an external file. Having defined the XML entity, we can then use it wherever we want in our stylesheet. Excellent!

Following is an example that pulls the contents of a file called someplain.txt into an XML entity called plaintext. We then create a global variable that uses the value of the entity. The global variable then allows us to use the contents of the file anywhere within our stylesheet.

```
<!DOCTYPE stylesheet [
<!ENTITY plaintext SYSTEM "someplain.txt">
]>
<xsl:stylesheet xmlns:xsl="http://www.w3.org/1999/XSL/Transform"
  xmlns="http://www.w3.org/1999/xhtml" version="1.0">

  <xsl:variable name="text">
    <xsl:text>&plaintext;</xsl:text>
  </xsl:variable>
...
```

We can use this trick for multiple entities within the stylesheet—the world of external files is now ours for the taking!

Typically we might use text from external files to check whether it has specific content (using, for instance, the contains() function), or to parse a set of lines and create some kind of markup from them. XSLT's text manipulation functions are fairly rudimentary, but they can be quite handy for short lists of lines, words, or phrases. With these tools in hand, and external files at our disposal, our stylesheets can now deal with just about everything in the world of text files, not just XML.

Creating Multiple Output Files (Requires XSLT Extensions)

Getting input from more than one file is easy enough in XSLT 1.0; sending output to more than one file in a single processing pass is not possible using the core instruction set. The only output file you can get is the one designated on the command line, and that's it.

That's pretty harsh, but that's the reality. The problem is fixed in XSLT 1.1 with <xsl:document> and in XSLT 2.0 with <xsl:result-document>,[7] but if we're stuck with XSLT 1.0, what other choices do we have? Sometimes there is no getting around the requirement of multiple output files from a single input document.

7. http://www.w3.org/TR/xslt20/#element-result-document

Sure, we could add a file splitter to our processing chain by creating something clever in Perl, C, Java, or what have you, but that takes us out of the realm of pure XSLT, where it's easy to do things like setting up system statements and validating the structure. (XSLT processors usually post an error if you try to output invalid XML.)

If we're given a 10,000-word document and we need to render it into bite-size chunks of HTML, we'll need to expand the scope of our instruction set to get it done. This is a case where the only possibility in XSLT 1.0 is to rely on XSLT extensions. XSLT extensions are tailored to specific XSLT processors, so it's not possible for me to say "just use this extension or that." But we can take a look at some of the more popular XSLT processors and what they support, with an example of each at work.

First, let's have a look at a specific problem. Let's say we have a long XML document of baseball statistics. It's a week's worth of statistic for pitchers and hitters for the American League. Additionally, there is a table with several fantasy league teams that shows which players belongs to each fantasy team. The following XML is a highly foreshortened excerpt:

```
<report week-number="12">
  <fantasy-league>
    <team name="Kelly Green Sox">
      <player position="3B">Miguel Cabrera</player>
      ...
      <pitcher>Max Scherzer</pitcher>
      ...
    </team>
    <team name="Walla-Walla Bing-Bangs">
      <player position="OF">Mike Trout</player>
      ...
      <pitcher>Cory Kluber</pitcher>
      ...
    </team>
    ...
  </fantasy-league>
  <mlb-players>
    <player name="Miguel Cabrera">
      <stats>
        <hits>14</hits>
        <home-runs>3</home-runs>
        <rbi>10</rbi>
        <stolen-bases>0</stolen-bases>
      </stats>
    </player>
    ...
  </mlb-players>
</weekly-report>
```

We would like to be able to create an HTML page for each team in the fantasy league (starting with my favorite, the Kelly Green Sox) and also a separate page for the league summaries.

In the following examples, we'll focus on how to send the output to multiple files rather than on how to create the contents of the files, but you're always welcome to do that part as an exercise. Just be careful who you show it to, or you'll wind up doing the stats for your fantasy league!

So let's have a look at Saxon's and Xalan's extensions for creating multiple outputs in XSLT 1.0. These two processors cover a lot of ground, and they both support extensions for creating multiple output files. We'll start first with Saxon, which offers the <saxon:output> instruction.Remember, when we use an XSLT extension, we need to include the extension namespace in the stylesheet's namespace declarations. The following code shows <saxon:output> at work.

The Saxon Solution to Multiple Output Files

stylesheets/fantasy-league-stats-saxon.xsl

```
<xsl:stylesheet xmlns="http://www.w3.org/1999/xhtml"
  xmlns:xsl="http://www.w3.org/1999/XSL/Transform"
  xmlns:saxon="http://icl.com/saxon" version="1.0">
  <xsl:template match="/report/fantasy-league/team">
    <saxon:output href="output-dir/{@name}.html" method="html">
      <html>
        <head><xsl:value-of select="@name"/></head>
        <body>
          <h1><xsl:value-of select="@name"/></h1>
          <h2>Hitters</h2>
          <xsl:for-each select="player">
            <xsl:variable name="player-name">
              <xsl:value-of select="."/>
            </xsl:variable>
            <xsl:value-of select="$player-name"/>
            <xsl:text>, </xsl:text>
            <xsl:value-of select="@position"/>
            <xsl:for-each select="/report/mlb-player/player[@name = $player-name]">
              (create the stat line for each player here)
            </xsl:for-each>
          </xsl:for-each>
          <xsl:for-each select="pitcher">
            (lather, rinse, repeat...)
          </xsl:for-each>
        </body>
      </html>
    </saxon:output>
  </xsl:template>
</xsl:stylesheet>
```

This stylesheet will only create one page per fantasy league team. We would need to restructure things slightly to also create the summary page.

In line 3, we've declared our namespace for the Saxon-specific extension elements. (Remember, we'll have to run the Saxon XSLT processor for this to work.) Then in line 5, we've used the <saxon:output> tag. The file name for the output files is given in the href= attribute; since we'll be creating multiple files, we've used a variable based on the fantasy league team name to create the file names. (One interesting thing about the href= attribute for this command is that it does not need single quotes around the string portions of the values, and a variable can be inserted in an attribute value template anywhere amongst the strings, as shown here.)

Notice that the open and close tags for <saxon:output> have to go around everything that will generate output for our alternative files. Otherwise, output outside the open and close tags will be directed to the standard output file.

What about the output for our standard XML output file? It looks like this stylesheet isn't generating anything that will go into that file—all the output is being sent to the alternate output files. As it happens, that's true in this case. (Maybe the standard output could contain our summary page.) But even though we aren't generating any output for it, we'll still need to specify an output file on the command line. An empty file will be created as part of the XSLT output—we can ignore this or clean it up with some other control process.

Also notice in line 5 that we've specified the method= attribute to be html. Does that look familiar? The last time we saw that attribute, it was connected to the <xsl:output> element. As it happens, <saxon:output> supports the same output attributes as <xsl:attribute> so we can control the output of our "splinter" file the same as we do our normal output.

And if you're wondering: no, we can't surround a <saxon:output> tag with another <saxon:output> tag. Sure, that would be a clever shortcut to use the same code to do a short version and a long version of the content, but it won't work.

The Xalan Solution to Multiple Output Files

In the Apache Xalan XSLT processor, the problem warranted creating an entirely new namespace for the solution: the redirect: namespace. This namespace includes three elements for sending content to external files: <open>, <write>, and <close>. In general, all we need is <write>, because the Xalan processor will hand the file open and file close for us automatically.

But if there's a need to open and close the files explicitly, the other tags are there.

Let's have a look at the solution we posted above, limiting ourselves to the XSLT elements where Xalan differs from Saxon:

stylesheets/fantasy-league-stats-xalan.xsl

```
1  <xsl:stylesheet xmlns="http://www.w3.org/1999/xhtml"
2    xmlns:xsl="http://www.w3.org/1999/XSL/Transform"
3    xmlns:redirect=" http://xml.apache.org/xalan/redirect" version="1.0">
4
5  <xsl:template match="/report/fantasy-league/team">
6   <redirect:write select="concat('output-dir/',@name,'.html'" file="no-team.html">
7     ...
8     [more XSLT code goes here]
9     ...
10  </redirect:write>
11 </xsl:template>
12 </xsl:stylesheet>
```

Line 3 shows the namespace declaration needed, and line 6 contains the markup for the <redirect:write> tag. There are a couple of significant differences from the Saxon version. In this example we have two attributes, select= and file=. It's required to have at least one of these two attributes.

Having both attributes is not required, but it is permitted. The select= attribute takes a normal XPath expression, which allows us to include a dynamic value. The file= attribute takes a string, which only allows for a static, pre-named output destination. If we use both attributes, the XSLT processor uses the select= attribute first. If it can't form a valid filename from the select= attribute, it uses the value in the file= attribute as the destination, if possible.

If you aren't able to use Saxon or Xalan, check whether your XSLT processor supports any other XSLT extensions. XSLT processors aren't required to support extensions, but many do.

What We Did

Congratulations! We've now covered most of the basic functionality available in XSLT 1.0. You've gone from being a stranger in a strange land to standing on top of a mountain peak, surveying all the territory we have covered. And now we've seen the possibility of connecting to other worlds of processing control and content.

In this chapter we've gone far beyond the confines of our simple stylesheet. First we looked at some of the global controls that we can apply to our stylesheets, concentrating our attention on global output controls for text,

HTML, and XML. We also took a look at attributes sets and talked about how they can be used to make our handling of attributes in the output more efficient.

Then we began opening the stylesheet to outside influences: first with external stylesheets called in by means of <xsl:include> and <xsl:import>, then with a short nod to the possibility of calling software languages outside of XSLT. We looked at different means of getting external file content into our processing by means of the document() function and unparsed XML entities. Finally, we saw that we could send content to multiple output files by means of XSLT extensions.

With this chapter, we've seen most of the XSLT functions that we are likely to need for basic XML processing. Of course, the adventure doesn't end here. There are always the "interesting" problems, which seem to come along more often than we'd like. XSLT is rich and flexible enough to be used for a wide range of problems. What we have seen in this book is just a starter kit for solving easy problem. As you find new problems in the wild, you will need a little creative thinking, a willingness to experiment, and, of course, plenty of research on the Internet. As you run into new problems...

Oh, wait. Problems?

Indeed, problems. After all, all you've done up to this point is read a book and try a few examples. It would be a miracle if you started programming XSLT and didn't screw up at least once. (Oh, come on, you're not THAT good!) So let's take a look at some troubleshooting techniques for XSLT programming. It's time to start cleaning up the campsite and get ready to head for home.

I looked hurriedly through the approaching gloom for a sign of Dejah Thoris, and then, not seeing her, I called her name. There was an answering murmur from the far corner of the apartment....

Edgar Rice Burroughs, A Princess of Mars

CHAPTER 11

Troubleshooting

Things inevitably go wrong, and XSLT can be infuriatingly terse in its feedback. There will be times when no matter what you do, nothing comes out, or a template gives utterly nonsensical results. I've seen grown programmers weep and fall to their knees over XSLT—including myself.

Fortunately, there are some reliable tools and strategies for finding the problems in our stylesheets. In this chapter, we're going to take a look at some of those methods, and we'll also look at some strategies for anticipating problems.

It Just Doesn't Work

This section covers what to do if you aren't getting any output at all. You may or may not be getting error messages, but you aren't getting an output file, or you're getting one but there's nothing in it.

Remember Murphy's Law? "If anything can go wrong, it will."[1] The number of things that can go wrong in XSLT is staggering. Given the relationships between the XSLT processor, the XML file, the XML structure, the XSLT stylesheet matching system, and the potential complexity of XPath statements, a lot of things can go wrong. Following Murphy's Law, we need to be prepared for a lot of unpleasant possibilities.

One of the most frustrating things when starting out with XSLT is that you run the processor and nothing happens. And if you read the questions people have, for instance, in stackoverflow.com you'll find that you're not the only one scratching your head.

There are a number of common issues you'll encounter when first learning XSLT. The good news is that we can identify and fix most of these fairly

---

1. http://murphyslaws.net/

rapidly. The following questions break down the XSLT process to help with understanding which part or parts of the process might be out of whack. The troubleshooting steps appear here in an order that follows the general order of the XSLT process itself. By testing in the order in which the XSLT process takes place, we eliminate some issues and move along to the next in a logical sequence until we arrive at (hopefully) a solution.

Is the XSLT processor executing?

The execution of the XSLT processor should be the first thing you check for. Different XSLT processors execute by different methods, so it's difficult to go into all the possibilities of why an XSLT processor would not execute. However, there are some basic things to check.

If you're using XSLT in a browser, does the browser software include an XSLT processor? If so, is the XML file you're processing recognized as XML? Does the XML file include a statement pointing to the XSLT stylesheet, similar to this:

```
<?xml-stylesheet type="text/xsl" href="caution1.xsl"?>
```

If you're using a command line or some other mechanism to invoke a standalone XSLT processor, the processor software may need some framework like Java or .NET to execute it. Is the execution environment set up properly? Do you get messages to the effect that Java or .NET is not a recognized command?

If the XSLT processor is not executing, you should see error messages from the command line or browser. If you get no error messages and still aren't confident that the processor is running, you will need to refer to the instructions for your particular XSLT processor and execution environment to ensure that it is working.

Is the XSLT processor attempting to run the stylesheet?

If you are opening an XML file in a browser, does the <?xml-stylesheet> tag's href= in the XML file point correctly to the XSLT stylesheet file you want to run? You can use a relative path or an absolute path; if using an absolute path, check that the path is preceded by the file:/// protocol identifier, like this:

```
<?xml-stylesheet type="text/xsl" href="file:///C:/Book/caution1.xsl"?>
```

Check the path to the stylesheet in the command line. Does it point to the stylesheet file correctly?

If you are running on a command line, do you see error messages in the terminal window like these?

```
Unable to access jarfile C:\Saxon\Saxon6-5\saxon.jar
Stylesheet file code\draft.xsl does not exist
```

The fix here should be fairly easy—get those paths straightened out! (See Chapter 3, *Installing, Testing, and Using a Stand-Alone XSLT Processor*, on page 31 for more information about setting up paths for the XSLT processor.)

If the paths are correct and you aren't getting error messages about the paths, chances are good that the XSLT processor is running the stylesheet. Move on to the next question.

Does the stylesheet parse properly?

With any luck, the XSLT processor posts a helpful error message if the stylesheet is malformed:

```
Error on line 7 of file:/H:/djkxsl/Book/code/stylesheets/draft.xsl:
  Error reported by XML parser: name expected (found " ")
Transformation failed: Failed to parse stylesheet
```

Well, sort of helpful. In this case, there is a space between a left angle bracket (<) and the name of the XSLT element. That won't fly.

Without an XML editor, preferably one that parses XSLT, tracking down these kinds of errors can become mind-numbingly tedious. And since the stylesheet fails at the first error, you could get yourself into a repetitive pattern of fix, run, fail, fix, run, fail, ad nauseum. An XML editor that speaks XSLT will be worth its weight in high-test espresso. I highly recommend one (the editor, not the espresso).

Does the XML source parse properly?

Is there an error in the command line window that begins:

```
Error reported by XML parser:
```

The source file is always parsed when it is opened: it must be valid XML. Here again, a good XML editor should provide guidance in fixing the source file if there is a problem.

In a pinch, you can troubleshoot by dividing the XML file in half and running it half at a time until you find the erroneous section. You can take out half the XML by deleting it or commenting it out (as long as there are no comments within comments). When you divide an XML file in half, though, you have to make sure it is still well-formed. Ending tags must be preserved, including for the root element.

If you are receiving invalid source files from an automated process, getting the XML fixed may be a lot more trouble than fixing it by hand, but fixing it by hand is almost never a good solution. You may have to push back on the people providing the source.

If the source is HTML, it's probably not up to XHTML standards. Plain HTML is not a valid input for XSLT processing. However, you might be able to transform the HTML to XHTML (which is a valid input because it's valid XML) using one of the numerous conversion utilities out there in the internet omniverse.[2]

If the source file is plain text, you won't be able to process it directly. Instead, use the trick in *Can I process text-only files if I don't need to process an XML file?*, on page 209.

Is the XML root being matched by a template?

If the stylesheet is being parsed and the source file is being parsed, the next step is determining whether the stylesheet is matching the root of the XML structure.

That should be simple: look through the templates and ensure that there is one with a `match=` whose value begin with either a forward slash (/) or the name of the top-level element in the XML source.

There should be only one template that matches on the root, at least for testing purposes.

If the match is to a complex XPath statement that includes the root, do yourself a favor and start simple. Start with a template that matches only the root or the root and root-level element. For example, if the root-level element of the source is `<XHTML>`, start with:

```
<xsl:template match="/XHTML">
  Hi there!
</xsl:template>
```

Your output file should say "Hi there!" right back at you. If it doesn't, check back though the earlier steps.

Make sure there is nothing in the template that tries to invoke other templates. We're just testing for whether we get top-level output. The root

2. http://tidy.sourceforge.net/#binaries, http://www.nuget.org/packages/HtmlAgilityPack, and http://corsis.sourceforge.net/index.php/Html2Xhtml, among others.

template should not contain any <xsl:apply-templates> or <xsl:call-template> tags. We just want something that will create output.

Also check whether the type of output you're creating is compatible with the output type specified for the stylesheet. If your stylesheet is creating text, and the output type is XML, the output might not be formed because it is not valid XML. Refer to *Output Controls*, on page 187 for details about setting the proper output format.

Is output being created? Is output being directed to the right file location?

Again, check the paths in your command line. If you're using a web browser as the processor and not getting output, try a command-line-based XSLT processor, or try to start with a simple, well-formed piece of output in the root-matching template.

If you're using relative paths, the base directory for the path to the output file will be the directory where the XSL stylesheet file is located. Look there to start your search for the output file.

If you're using a browser for processing, remember that no output file is produced. The only thing produced is the rendering in the browser. The browser does not provide a way to preserve this view—it has to be generated with the XML and XSL file each time. (You can do a screen capture like I did for this book, but that's not useful for very many purposes.) If you need a persistent output file, you'll need to process the file with a standalone XSLT processor.

Is the output encoding supported?

XSLT processors support only certain encoding types for output. If your stylesheet includes an <xsl:output> tag that references an unsupported encoding, the XSLT processor may not create output. In this case, it should give an error message. To check whether this is the problem, try changing the output encoding to a known supported encoding such as UTF-8.

I Get Output, But It's Not What I Want

Is it asking too much for output to contain all the required content in the proper order? Usually that's a *minimum* definition for success—so if it's not happening, let's see if we can fix it.

Once you start getting output, begin checking it for quality. Typically the questions to ask are:

- Is the content what you expect? Types of problems you might see are:
  - Upper-level content is okay, but some lower-level content is missing.
  - Content is repeated.
  - Content for an element appears correctly in some places but not in others.
  - The content appears in a form other than what you specified (that is, some kind of data manipulation is not working).
- Is the order of content correct?
- Is the output format correct? Typical problem types include:
  - Expected tags don't appear around all or some of the content.
  - Attributes don't appear in the output.
  - Whitespace and indentation are incorrect.

Let's take these questions one by one, then do a little more digging. This list contains some of the more common problems you're likely to encounter. Once you get beyond these, you may need to consult other resources, talk to colleagues, or just do what I do as a last resort—keep banging on it with different approaches until something works.

Is the content what you expect?

Upper-level content is okay, but some lower-level content is missing.

You're getting content from the template matching the root element, but content based on lower-level elements is missing. There are a number of possibilities here:

- Check whether the functioning, upper-level templates include an XSLT element that processes other elements. These include <xsl:apply-templates>, <xsl:for-each>, <xsl:value-of>, <xsl:copy>, and <xsl:copy-of>. These are required to process other elements from the context of the current XML node.
- Do the select= attributes (if used) match the correct paths to the elements that you want to process? XPath can be tricky. If necessary, simplify the select= and match= attributes to ensure that processing is taking place.

  If you're using <xsl:apply-templates>, you can omit the select= attribute altogether, although doing so may give more results than you want. But it's a start.

- Is there a chain of select= and match= attributes that complete the entire path to the missing content? In other words, if you have a hierarchy of elements like this:

```
<book>
  <chapter>
    <verse>
      <stanza>
        And in those days were giants...
      </stanza>
    </verse>
  </chapter>
</book>
```

  You can't just match on <book> and have that template include, say, <xsl:apply-templates select="stanza">. You might use select= and match= attributes to address the <chapter> and <verse> tags as well, or you might be fine skipping the content of <chapter> and <verse> with an XPath statement that includes only the content of <stanza>: <xsl:apply-templates select="chapter/verse/stanza"> or <xsl:apply-templates descendant::stanza>. In any case, you'll need an <xsl:template> with match= to match on the <stanza> tag. If you're only matching from the <book> element, you could use match="chapter/verse/stanza", or, if you might be matching <stanza> from the context of <book>, <chapter>, or <verse>, then you might be better off with a template for match="stanza".

- Are there templates to match the lower-level elements you are trying to process?

  If you're using the preferred method of creating the <xsl:apply-templates> tags without the select= attribute, and you want to catch all the elements for processing, you'll need a template to match every possible element that the XSLT processor might encounter within the current template's context element. Check your list of templates against the DTD or schema model for the current context.

  One trick for identifying missing templates is to create a catch-all template that flags untemplated elements. The template matches on the element wildcard (*), and produces a message with the name of the element that it processes. Following is an example of a catch-all template.

```
 <xsl:template match="*">
   <xsl:text>A template is needed for the element: </xsl:text>
   <xsl:value-of select="name()"/>
</xsl:template>
```

This template will output its text and the name of the problem element in the output.

Later in this chapter we'll see a way to output this information a little more discreetly so a reader will not see it if an unhandled element gets out into a production system.

- If the upper-level templates are set up properly, there's a template for the missing content's element, and that template appears to be addressed properly by upper-level templates, check whether the template for the missing content is actually producing content itself:
  - Place some arbitrary text or tag in the template so it will be emitted into the output. Does it appear in the output? If not, the template is not being invoked correctly, and you'll need to troubleshoot it with some of the preceding points.
  - Is there an XSLT instruction that produces content in the template? If so, does it point to the required data correctly, or perform its operations correctly? Simplify any XPath statements for testing purposes.
  - Is there conditional logic in the template? If so, test the instructions that produce output by pulling them out of the conditional logic. Troubleshoot the output statements, if necessary, then place them back in the conditional statements and troubleshoot the conditional logic separately.
  - Check the XML file to make sure the element and its content are where you expect them to be. (It happens.)

Content is repeated.

This condition can occur when there is more than one statement that retrieves or processes content for the same context. It's easy enough to retrieve the first element in a section for a section heading, then use a general `<xsl:apply-templates/>` to retrieve the rest of the elements in that section. But this would be wrong:

```
<xsl:template match="section">
  <section>
    <title>
      <xsl:value-of select="p[1]"/>
    </title>
    <xsl:apply-templates/>
  </section>
</xsl:template>
```

Line 6 is too general—it selects all the nodes in <section>, including the first paragraph, which we've already output. To fix this, we need to rewrite the templates so they don't match on the first paragraph. One way to do this would be to apply a selection in line 6 to omit the first <p>:

```
<xsl:apply-templates select="*[not(position() = 1)]"/>
```

Another way would be to put a qualifying predicate on the match for the <p> tag in the template that processes them:

```
<xsl:template match="*[not(position() = 1)]">
```

If you do it this way, though, you may find the default template creeping in to output the text of the first <p>. Some experts recommend against putting the limiting statement in the select= statement as we did in the first fix above, but I find it to be more precise. That way, the template for <p> remains available for general use.

One strategy I use when the content is repeated in the output is to begin eliminating instructions that might produce the extra output. Once you have determined where the multiple output sources are for the content, you can begin refining your code to make adjustments like the one above.

Content for an element appears in some places but not in others.
Inconsistent appearance of content for a given element usually points to a pattern in which the template for that element is being selected in some contexts but not in others. For example, if you have a <p> tag that can appear in several places, such as in <chapter>, <note>, and <cell>, check whether the templates for those elements have select= attributes or other instructions that are sufficiently inclusive to invoke the template for <p>. The template for <note> might look like the following because you expected <note> to contain only text, not tags:

```
<xsl:template match="note">
  <xsl:apply-templates select="text()"/>
</xsl:template>
```

In this case, the occasional <p> that comes through won't be processed. Remove the select= statement and tackle the next problem.

The content appears in a form other than what you specified
This is a situation in which some kind of data manipulation is not working. By data manipulations, we mostly mean numeric calculations, string manipulations, derivation of boolean values, and reordering of nodes.

This type of problem opens up numerous cans of worms that we can't cover in great detail in this book. However, there are some basic checks you can make when manipulating the data into other forms.

- Is the raw data for the calculations coming through? When debugging, create an output of each raw data item that you are using in your calculations or other processing.
- If using variables and parameters in your processing, create an output for each variable and parameter being used to see whether they give expected values.
- Are the XSLT manipulations doing what you think they should be doing? Create a test with a set of known values (static values rather than taken from the XML source) for all the inputs to the manipulations. Compare the output to the expected value.

  If the manipulation consists of several steps, create interim outputs to check that the output values for each step are as expected.

  Parameters can be tricky when you are handing them off from one template to another. When a parameter is first defined in a template, create a statement that shows the value of that parameter. Is the value what you expect?

When XSLT goes wrong, toss out any assumptions about earlier steps in the process. Create outputs for each template or even for each step within a template to ensure that you are working with the right values, the right templates, and in the expected order of events.

Is the order of content correct?

Changing the order of content can be achieved in a number of ways, which means it can go wrong in at least that many ways—squared. Or cubed.

Some of the troubleshooting steps in the preceding sections can help with this type of problem. But there are a few other general approaches for misordered content:

- If data is being retrieved within a template, are the paths correct?

  For example, suppose at the end of a paragraph in HTML we want to add a short list of related links for each `<keyword>` that appears in a `<p>` tag. The links will be formed by processing a separate glossary section of the XML, where each keyword contains an `id=` value to be used for the link. In the glossary section, a keyword is represented by a corresponding

Joe asks:
What if I can't figure out which template is creating output?

Sometimes when templates get complicated, it's difficult to understand which template is creating a given piece of output. In cases like this, I insert unique text for each template, and even for different sections within templates.

To indicate which template is at play, copy the entire match= attribute or template name into text immediately following the template and any parameters. If the template has a mode, include that in the text as well.

If there is output, use unique character strings on either side to show exactly its beginning and ending points. It makes for messy output during the testing phases, but it sure speeds up debugging. I favor strings like +!+ and !+!, and variants thereof. Use whatever you want just so long as you make it something unlikely to appear in the text of the input or output. (Try to keep it kind and gentle!)

You might add a reminder note using XML comment notation (<!-- -->) in the headers of your stylesheets so you remember to remove or suppress this text later.

<term> tag. To complete the link, we need to retrieve the id of the term from the glossary. We might start by constructing something like this:

```
Line 1 <xsl:template match="p">
-        <p>
-          <xsl:apply-templates/>
-         <span style="font-weight:bold;">
5           <xsl:for-each select="keyword">
-             <xsl:variable name="keyword-text">
-               <xsl:value-of select="."/>
-             </xsl:variable>
-             <a>
10              <xsl:attribute name="href">
-                 <xsl:value-of select="glossary/term[text() = $keyword-text]/@id"/>
-               </xsl:attribute>
-             </a>
-           </xsl:for-each>
15        </span>
-        </p>
-      </xsl:template>
```

All well and good, but check that XPath statement in line 11. Unless the <glossary> tag is located within the current paragraph, it will never return anything. The XPath needs to go up the tree and then back down to where the <glossary> tag lives, or, if you're certain there is only one <glossary> tag in the XML document, you could use select="//glossary/term[text() = $keyword-text]/@id".

- Locate the last template in which content comes out right, and also look at the template that should be processing the next bit of content. Look at the XPath statements (if any) in the instruction that invokes the next template, and look at the match= attribute in the template that isn't working. Are they aligned?

Cases of misordered data are most likely XPath issues, but also pay attention to where the instructions for invoking other templates appear within the current template.

Is the output format correct?

Typical problem types, and potential solutions, include:

- Expected tags don't appear around all or some of the content.
  - If all the text is coming out without tags, the <xsl:output> method= attribute may be set to text. Since the XSLT processor thinks the output should be plain text, it ignores the output of XML nodes other than text.
  - If that's not the problem, take a look at your templates and see whether the parts that create elements are properly formed.
  - If the elements are part of a namespace, be sure the namespace is specified properly in the namespace declaration in <xsl:stylesheet>.
  - If you are creating element nodes in variables, then placing the element nodes where you want by calling the variable, remember to call the variable with <xsl:copy-of> rather than <xsl:value-of>. The latter will only give you the text, while <xsl:copy-of> will give you the text and other nodes, like elements and attributes.
  - If you are copying elements from one document to another with the <xsl:copy-of> instruction, are you using select="." or select="*"? If you've matched on an element, the first select= will copy the current node (the element), while the second select= will only copy the children of the current node.
- Attributes don't appear in the output.
  - Check the points at which attributes are defined. Are they defined as the first instruction following an element?
  - Alternatively, are they defined within the scope of an element tag using attribute value templates? (See *Adding Elements and Attributes Dynamically*, on page 52.)

  - If the attribute names are defined with a namespace, is the namespace defined properly in the <xsl:stylesheet> tag?
- Whitespace and indentation are incorrect.
  - If the output has unexpected whitespace, check whether the <xsl:output> tag has indent="yes".
  - Check the settings of the <xsl:strip-space> and <xsl:preserve-space> instructions at the beginning of the stylesheet, if they exist. If they don't exist, could they potentially solve the problem?
  - Check the use of <xsl:text> in the templates to see whether they may be causing the problems—or whether they might be a solution. Whitespace, including line returns, inside an <xsl:text> tag are preserved in the output.
  - If unwanted whitespace is coming through in text, try placing the normalize-space() function around the value of the text. This function strips leading and trailing whitespaces and line returns, and removes extra spaces between other characters.

In theory, XML should be agnostic to whitespace, but in the real world, we often run into tags where whitespace needs to be preserved or removed for one reason or another. And when creating plain text files, depending on the function the text will serve, spacing may be crucial. XSLT output can seem a little hodge-podge, but there are a variety of controls available to manipulate the spacing as needed.

Building Debug Helpers

Locating problems in XSLT code can be difficult. The default error messages from XSLT processors may be helpful, but in many cases they are cryptic or even nonexistent. You might get a message saying an attribute on a specific line of your stylesheet has an invalid value—or you could get a rousing round of silence if the attribute value is valid but dysfunctional. Are there any tools that help us pin down the locations of errors in the code?

Two XSLT instructions fit the bill admirably: <xsl:comment> and <xsl:message>. Both create output at the location they occur within a template.

<xsl:comment> creates an XML or HTML comment in the output document. <xsl:message> sends its content to an output location that depends on the execution environment and the XSLT processor. In a command-line based

execution environment, the message typically displays in the processing output in the command window.

In both instructions, the content of the comment or message are determined by the contents of the instruction. Both can contain almost any XSLT instruction as well as text or tag-based output. Any XSLT instructions are evaluated within the context of the template where the <xsl:comment> or <xsl:message> appear. The contents do not need to be well-formed XML.

With all that in mind, how can we use these instructions to help with debugging our XSLT? Let's have a look at each individually.

<xsl:comment>

The nice thing about <xsl:comment> is that it creates a record in the output document that can be easily referenced. Since it forms part of the output, it also gives a surefire way to show the context of a given piece of output. You can easily include information about the XML source as well as the template that processed the content within the comment. You can also include other information, such as the values of variables and parameters that are in scope within the template.

One of the simplest uses for <xsl:comment> is to mark the template, to show that it's working:

```
<xsl:template match="p">
  <xsl:comment>I'm in the <xsl:value-of select="name()"/> template!</xsl:comment>
  <p><xsl:apply-templates/></p>
</xsl:template>
```

If the template executes, the comment <!--I'm in the p template!--> appears just before the <p> tag and its contents in the output document.

You can also place <xsl:comment> in conditional statements to determine what branch of a condition executed within a template.

Comment contents can consist of complex XSLT statements and logic. You can use this ability to test bits and pieces of logic that go into the larger workings of a template, and to test combinations of XSLT manipulations to determine whether they are giving expected results.

There's one useful trick to remember when using <xsl:comment>. If you use an <xsl:variable> to call a template to calculate or create a value, and you place the comment in the called template, you won't be able to see the comment if you get the value of the variable with <xsl:value-of>. Typically you want to use <xsl:value-of>, or use the value of the variable in an attribute template where the comment would not make any sense. It's a bit of an annoyance, but you can get around the problem by using the variable normally with <xsl:value-of> or an attribute template, and by displaying the variable's value a second time within a comment using the <xsl:copy-of> instruction. But don't just take my word for it—here's an example:

```
Line 1 <xsl:template match="/accounts">
     -    <xsl:variable name="new-id">
     -      <xsl:call-template name="id-gen"/>
     -    </xsl:variable>
     5    <xsl:copy-of select="$new-id"/>
     -    <accounts id="{$new-id}">
     -      <xsl:apply-templates/>
     -    </accounts>
     -    <xsl:value-of select="$new-id"/>
    10  </xsl:template>
     -  <xsl:template name="id-gen">
     -    <xsl:comment>I'm a little comment.</xsl:comment>
     -    <xsl:value-of select="concat('book-id-',generate-id())"/>
     -  </xsl:template>
```

Line 5 contains the <xsl:copy-of> tag to allow us to see the comment in the variable. The output of these templates (and others, from Chapter 3, *Installing, Testing, and Using a Stand-Alone XSLT Processor*, on page 31, applied to the XML we used in Chapter 3, *Installing, Testing, and Using a Stand-Alone XSLT Processor*, on page 31, is:

troubleshooting/comment-in-output.xml

```
Line 1 <?xml version="1.0" encoding="utf-8"?>
     - <!--I'm a little comment.-->book-id-d0e1<accounts id="book-id-d0e1">
     -   <account id="100007" name="Jorge Luis Borges">
     -     <transaction>
     5       <date>June 6, 1984 12:00:00</date>
     -       <amount>$14.99</amount>
     -       <product>B-5643A</product>
     -     </transaction>
     -     <transaction>
    10       <date>July 23, 1966 23:47:12</date>
     -       <amount>$12.95</amount>
     -       <product>A-2345B</product>
     -     </transaction>
     -   </account>
    15 </accounts>book-id-d0e1
```

But again we have a problem. In line 2, the id= value is returned along with the comment, which renders our output invalid. That may be okay for checking the function of the called template, but it's a pain for testing the stylesheet in general. Could we possibly put the <xsl:copy-of> in line 5 of the

XSLT example into its own comment, so both the comment and the id appear within a comment?

The answer, unfortunately, is no. Comments can't be embedded in comments. If we put the <xsl:copy-of> with the variable containing the comment into another comment, the interior comment is stripped out.

If we want our output to be valid during testing, we'll need some other mechanism to get a message out of the variable value. Fortunately, XSLT includes the <xsl:message> instruction to address this and other issues.

<xsl:message>

<xsl:message> directs output to the command line or other message output stream, so its content isn't affected by the need to make sense in our final document. We can put anything we want in it, including comments. In the preceding example, if we put the <xsl:copy-of> with the variable into an <xsl:message> and execute the stylesheet with the Saxon command line, we get the following output in the command window:

```
<!--I'm a little comment.-->book-id-d0e1
```

The problem is that the command line gives us no context for understanding the messages. If we put a simple message like this into a template for <p> and our document has a couple of hundred <p> tags, we'll get a couple of hundred messages. For this reason, <xsl:message> tends to be a less useful type of debugging tool. However, it does have the advantage of being able to get messages out of templates that create variables.

To use <xsl:message> effectively, add detail to the message to capture the context. Include information about the template and the location of the element in question.

If a message is in a named template used for recursion, we might want the message to show how many times the recursion has occurred. This indicator is especially useful for tracking end conditions in recursive templates. If one is not already present, we'll need a parameter to use for passing the count back into the recursive template when we call it. Figure 51, *Word substitution template with a useful message*, on page 233 shows an example of this type of message, in this case a template for parsing through text and substituting a given word for any instance of another specified word

Line 6 sets up the parameter. We include the select="1" attribute to ensure that the count starts at 1 to indicate the first time we come into the template. Line 7 then issues a message containing the current number of times the

```
1  <xsl:template name="word-swapper">
2    <xsl:param name="old-word"/>
3    <xsl:param name="new-word"/>
4    <xsl:param name="our-string"/>
5    <xsl:param name="new-string" select=""/>
6    <xsl:param name="count" select="1"/>
7    <xsl:message>Count: <xsl:value-of select="$count"/></xsl:message>
8    <xsl:choose>
9      <xsl:when test="contains($our-string, $old-word)">
10       <xsl:call-template name="word-swapper">
11         <xsl:with-param name="old-word" select="$old-word"/>
12         <xsl:with-param name="new-word" select="$new-word"/>
13         <xsl:with-param name="our-string"
14           select="substring-after($our-string,$old-word)"/>
15         <xsl:with-param name="new-string"
16           select="concat($new-string,
17           substring-before($our-string,$old-word),$new-word)"/>
18         <xsl:with-param name="count" select="$count + 1"/>
19       </xsl:call-template>
20     </xsl:when>
21     <xsl:otherwise>
22       <xsl:value-of select="concat($new-string,$old-string)"/>
23     </xsl:otherwise>
24   </xsl:choose>
25 </xsl:template>
```

Figure 51—Word substitution template with a useful message

template has been executed. As long as our string contains the unwanted word, the conditional logic takes the first branch, which includes line 18. In this line we bump up the count and pass the incremented parameter back into the template.

Note that this counting method can be used inside a comment as well as a message as long as the comment is not ultimately returned into a variable.

The terminate= Option

When we think about recursive templates, we also think about runaway recursion. We've already talked about setting up conditions for stopping runaway recursions (*Putting It All Together with Recursion*, on page 175). But wouldn't it be useful to generate a message at the same time? As luck (and the standards committee) would have it, the <xsl:message> instruction contains a single parameter than can help with control of runaway recursions, among other things.

The terminate= attribute is an option (also popular in thriller novels) that takes the value of *yes* or *no*, with the default being *no*. When received by the XSLT

Retrieving the Coordinates of Any Element in the Source

Sometimes we need to know exactly which element caused a given problem or message. What I call the coordinates of an element in the source is really just a list of all the element's ancestors, along with the number of each ancestor's position with respect to its peers in the hierarchy. With that information we can pinpoint the element precisely within the source.

Since this information is likely to be needed in more than one message, we place the following "coordinate labeler" code in its own named template and call it where we need it in a message.

```
<xsl:template name="coordinates">
  <xsl:for-each select="ancestor-or-self::*">
    <xsl:text> </xsl:text>
    <xsl:value-of select="name()"/>
    <xsl:text>(</xsl:text>
    <xsl:value-of select="count(preceding-sibling::*) + 1"/>
    <xsl:text>):</xsl:text>
  </xsl:for-each>
</xsl:template>
```

Now let's add this template plus a new line to our message in the templates for <accounts> in our example. To make the messages a little more interesting, we'll also add the same message to the template for <date>. (To do this, we'll also need to add the variable for new-id that calls the id-gen template.

Here are the results:

```
<!--I'm a little comment.-->book-id-d0e1 accounts(1):
<!--I'm a little comment.-->book-id-d0e21 accounts(1): account(1): transactions(2):
   transaction(1):date(1):
<!--I'm a little comment.-->book-id-d0e45 accounts(1): account(1): transactions(2):
   transaction(2): date(1):
```

The coordinates indicate precisely which element is generating a message.

processor, execution of the stylesheet stops, and whatever content the <xsl:message> tag contains is sent to the command line.

Using this feature, we can plant "terminators" throughout the templates to let us know when we've reached parts of the templates that we don't want to reach. For example, if we know we have created templates for all of the elements that *should* appear in the XML source, we can create a catch-all template for any elements that *shouldn't* be in the XML, like this:

```
<xsl:template match="*">
  <xsl:message terminate="yes">
    We've trapped a rogue element named <xsl:value-of select="name()"/>.
  </xsl:message>
</xsl:template>
```

The terminate="yes" option is also useful for testing invalid values, unwanted conditions, and XPath relationships that indicate malformed or unfavorable input.

In most cases it may be enough simply to post a message and keep going. That way we can see how many times the problem condition occurs within a document. But there are times when the detection of an error condition is enough to be worth stopping the process. You might be processing documents that run into hundreds or thousands of pages of text. The error might be enough to render the results completely invalid or misleading to processes or people downstream. You might be in the middle of developing code, and you don't really need more than one message to know that the XSLT code or the XML is *still* broken. In cases like these, take the terminate="yes" option.

What We Did

Even with a well-equipped toolkit for constructing a functional stylesheet, we discovered a few more tricks to help us along. Troubleshooting is not something we like to think about, but it's unavoidable. The rough guidelines in this chapter should help deal with a lot of the problems you're likely to encounter.

There are always exceptions, of course, and you'll probably find plenty of those. But think about the principles we covered in this chapter: break down the process in the order it occurs, and establish a test to make sure each step is working.

XSLT processing is highly serial, so following the order of processing can usually help you identify the breaking point. Even when we get to the more free-form templates, which can be executed in almost any order, the XSLT process still follows the XML structure in serial order, following the nodes of the XML tree as we saw way back in *XSLT Processing: Under the Hood*, on page 19. By using <xsl:comment> and <xsl:message>, especially with the trick we learned to tag the precise coordinates of the XML, we can pin down exactly what XML node and what XSLT template or instruction is causing problems.

Of course, as we said earlier, XSLT can go wrong in a number of ways. Pinning down the location of problems is one part of the trick to troubleshooting. Another is determining exactly what went wrong. You've been exposed to the basic principles of XSLT programming, and you'll need those tools to help go beyond the troubleshooting tips given in this chapter.

Congratulations!

You've reached the end of the book, and you're ready to jump into XSLT feet first. Hopefully we've covered enough of the basic concepts to keep you moving forward—there's a lot still left to learn. Sure, it will still be a challenge, but think of what you've accomplished. You probably started out this book barely knowing how to spell XSLT, and now you can program more than enough to get in trouble. And that's a good place to be.

XSLT goes far beyond the scope of this book. We covered the elements and functions of XSLT 1.0, along with some of the most important principles for putting the pieces together to solve meaningful problems. We saw techniques for processing XML, getting output, addressing any part of XML from any other part, rearranging contents, and using values to construct more logically complex units for conditional processing and recursion. We saw strategies for expanding XSLT beyond a single XML file and a single stylesheet, and we learned some strategies to help us troubleshoot our stylesheets.

Having gotten your feet on the ground with this introduction, you'll hopefully start constructing stylesheets of your own. And once you do, you'll begin running into questions that this book can't answer. At that point you'll probably go to the Internet for research, or purchase other, more comprehensive (and ponderous) tomes about XSLT. You'll begin to explore the possibilities of XSLT extensions, XSLT 2.0 and 3.0, and alternative XSLT processors for specific purposes. And in the process, you'll find problems and solutions that this book can't begin to touch.

My hope is that this book has given you a firm conceptual foundation for understanding the principles that make XSLT work. Yes, there is a lot still to learn, but with a firm foundation, you can continue to build your understanding, rising to even greater heights than I can imagine. If so, this book will have accomplished its purpose.

Pack lightly, dress warmly, head for the nearest interesting peak...

...and good luck!

APPENDIX 1

XSLT 1.0 Element Reference

This appendix provides a listing of the XSLT elements in three different ways: a simple alphabetical list, a list that groups the elements by their functions, and a list of the elements with their syntax.

What this appendix does not contain is a definition of all XSLT elements. The definitive word on XSLT element definitions is the XSLT 1.0 specification, http://www.w3.org/TR/xslt. Not everyone likes reading specifications, though, so here are some other sources for XSLT definitions:

- W3Schools: http://www.w3schools.com/xsl/xsl_w3celementref.asp
- Microsoft: http://msdn.microsoft.com/en-us/library/ms256058%28v=vs.110%29.aspx
- Wikipedia: http://en.wikipedia.org/wiki/XSLT_elements
- DevGuru: http://www.devguru.com/technologies/xslt/8389

Alphabetical List of Elements

xsl:apply-imports	xsl:for-each	xsl:processing-instruction
xsl:apply-templates	xsl:if	xsl:sort
xsl:attribute	xsl:import	xsl:strip-space
xsl:attribute-set	xsl:include	xsl:stylesheet
xsl:call-template	xsl:key	xsl:template
xsl:choose	xsl:message	xsl:text
xsl:comment	xsl:namespace-alias	xsl:transform
xsl:copy	xsl:number	xsl:value-of
xsl:copy-of	xsl:otherwise	xsl:variable
xsl:decimal-format	xsl:output	xsl:when
xsl:element	xsl:param	xsl:with-param
xsl:fallback	xsl:preserve-space	

Elements by Functional Category

The following table provides a column with the "official" category of XSLT elements (which indicates their structural place in the language), and another column with categories I've more or less invented, to indicate the types of things the elements do. The intent is to guide you toward the right set of elements when you need to accomplish certain types of actions.

XSLT Element	"Official" Category	Functional Category
xsl:choose	instruction	conditional control
xsl:if	instruction	conditional control
xsl:otherwise	instruction	conditional control
xsl:when		conditional control
xsl:attribute	instruction	output
xsl:comment	instruction	output
xsl:copy	instruction	output
xsl:copy-of	instruction	output
xsl:decimal-format	top-level element	output
xsl:element	instruction	output
xsl:message	instruction	output
xsl:namespace-alias	top-level element	output
xsl:number	instruction	output
xsl:output	top-level element	output
xsl:preserve-space	top-level element	output
xsl:processing-instruction	instruction	output
xsl:strip-space	top-level element	output
xsl:text	instruction	output
xsl:value-of	instruction	output/processing
xsl:apply-templates	instruction	processing
xsl:for-each	instruction	processing
xsl:key	top-level element	processing
xsl:sort		processing
xsl:template	top-level element	processing
xsl:variable	top-level element and instruction	processing
xsl:apply-imports	instruction	stylesheet management

XSLT Element	"Official" Category	Functional Category
xsl:attribute-set	top-level element	stylesheet management
xsl:call-template	instruction	stylesheet management
xsl:fallback	instruction	stylesheet management
xsl:import	instruction	stylesheet management
xsl:include	top-level element	stylesheet management
xsl:param	top-level element	stylesheet management
xsl:stylesheet		stylesheet management
xsl:transform		stylesheet management
xsl:with-param		stylesheet management

Syntax of the Elements

This section gives the syntax for XSLT instructions, their attributes, and their contents. Notation used in the following syntax list is described in *Syntax Notation*, on page 243.

xsl:apply-imports

```
<xsl:apply-imports />
```

xsl:apply-templates

```
<xsl:apply-templates select = "node-set-expression"
    mode = "qname">
  Content: (xsl:sort | xsl:with-param)*
</xsl:apply-templates>
```

xsl:attribute

```
<xsl:attribute name = "qname"
    namespace = "uri-reference">
  Content: template
</xsl:attribute>
```

xsl:attribute-set

```
<xsl:attribute-set name = "qname"
    use-attribute-sets = "qnames">
  Content: xsl:attribute*
</xsl:attribute-set>
```

xsl:call-template

```
<xsl:call-template name = "qname">
  Content: xsl:with-param*
</xsl:call-template>
```

xsl:choose

```
<xsl:choose>
  Content: (xsl:when+, xsl:otherwise?)
</xsl:choose>
```

xsl:comment

```
<xsl:comment>
  Content: template
</xsl:comment>
```

xsl:copy	`<xsl:copy`
	`use-attribute-sets = "qnames">`
	`  Content: template`
	`</xsl:copy>`

xsl:copy-of	`<xsl:copy-of select = "expression" />`

xsl:decimal-format	`<xsl:decimal-format name = "qname"`
	`    decimal-separator = "char" grouping-separator = "char"`
	`    infinity = "string" minus-sign = "char" NaN = "string"`
	`    percent = "char" per-mille = "char" zero-digit = "char"`
	`    digit = "char" pattern-separator = "char" />`

xsl:element	`<xsl:element name = "qname"`
	`namespace = "uri-reference" use-attribute-sets = "qnames">`
	`  Content: template`
	`</xsl:element>`

xsl:fallback	`<xsl:fallback>`
	`  Content: template`
	`</xsl:fallback>`

xsl:for-each	`<xsl:for-each select = "node-set-expression">`
	`  Content: (xsl:sort*, template)`
	`</xsl:for-each>`

xsl:if	`<xsl:if test = "boolean-expression">`
	`  Content: template`
	`</xsl:if>`

xsl:import	`<xsl:import href = "uri-reference"/>`
xsl:include	`<xsl:include` `href = uri-reference />`

xsl:key	`<xsl:key name = "qname"`
	`match = "pattern"`
	`use = "expression"/>`

xsl:message	`<xsl:message terminate = "yes" | "no">`
	`        Content: template`
	`</xsl:message>`

xsl:namespace-alias	`<xsl:namespace-alias`
	`stylesheet-prefix = prefix | "#default"`
	`result-prefix = prefix | "#default" />`

xsl:number	`<xsl:number`
	`level = "single" | "multiple" | "any"`
	`count = pattern`
	`from = pattern`
	`value = number-expression`
	`format = { string }`
	`lang = { nmtoken }`
	`letter-value = { "alphabetic" | "traditional" }`
	`grouping-separator = { char }`
	`grouping-size = { number } />`

xsl:otherwise	`<xsl:otherwise>`
	`Content: template`
	`</xsl:otherwise>`

xsl:output	`<xsl:output`
	`method = "xml" | "html" | "text" | qname-but-not-ncname`
	`version = nmtoken`
	`encoding = string`
	`omit-xml-declaration = "yes" | "no"`
	`standalone = "yes" | "no"`
	`doctype-public = string`
	`doctype-system = string`
	`cdata-section-elements = qnames`
	`indent = "yes" | "no"`
	`media-type = string />`

xsl:param	`<xsl:param`
	`name = qname`
	`select = expression>`
	`Content: template`
	`</xsl:param>`

xsl:preserve-space	`<xsl:preserve-space` `elements = tokens />`

xsl:processing-instruction	`<xsl:processing-instruction`
	`name = { ncname }>`
	`Content: template`
	`</xsl:processing-instruction>`

xsl:sort	`<xsl:sort`
	`select = string-expression`
	`lang = { nmtoken }`
	`data-type = { "text" | "number" | qname-but-not-ncname }`
	`order = { "ascending" | "descending" }`
	`case-order = { "upper-first" | "lower-first" } />`

xsl:strip-space	`<xsl:strip-space` `elements = tokens />`

xsl:stylesheet	`<xsl:stylesheet`
	`id = id`
	`extension-element-prefixes = tokens`
	`exclude-result-prefixes = tokens`
	`version = number>`
	`Content: (xsl:import*, top-level-elements)`
	`</xsl:stylesheet>`

xsl:template	`<xsl:template`
	`match = pattern`
	`name = qname`
	`priority = number`
	`mode = qname>`
	` Content: (xsl:param*, template)`
	`</xsl:template>`

xsl:text	`<xsl:text`
	`disable-output-escaping = "yes" | "no">`
	`Content: #PCDATA`
	`</xsl:text>`

xsl:transform	`<xsl:transform`
	`id = id`
	`extension-element-prefixes = tokens`
	`exclude-result-prefixes = tokens`
	`version = number>`
	`Content: (xsl:import*, top-level-elements)`
	`</xsl:transform>`

xsl:value-of	`<xsl:value-of`
	`select = string-expression`
	`disable-output-escaping = "yes" | "no" />`

xsl:variable	`<xsl:variable`
	`name = qname`
	`select = expression>`
	`Content: template`
	`</xsl:variable>`

xsl:when	`<xsl:when`
	`test = boolean-expression>`
	`Content: template`
	`</xsl:when>`

xsl:with-param	`<xsl:with-param`
	`name = qname`
	`select = expression>`
	`Content: template`
	`</xsl:with-param>`

Syntax Notation

The following notation is used in *Syntax of the Elements*, on page 239.

()* or * Zero, one, or more of what the asterisk follows or what is in parentheses is allowed.

| A logical OR

? or ()? Zero or one of what the question mark follows or what is in parentheses is allowed.

+ or ()+ One or more of what the plus sign follows or what is in parentheses is required.

char Almost any Unicode character. Some Unicode control characters may not be permitted.

expression An XSLT or XPath expression as defined in *Expressions*, on page 112.

ncname A name that will not and should not have a namespace associated with it. It cannot contain these XML special characters:

`&, :, %, /, +, @, $, ,(comma) and ;)`

It also can't begin with a numeric character, a period, or a hyphen (minus) character.

nmtoken A name that follows the rules for a qname, except it doesn't have to avoid numbers and special characters in the first position. Like a qname, it can't include whitespace.

qname A qualified name as defined for the XML namespace. You can find the formal definition of a QName at http://en.wikipedia.org/wiki/QName. If you don't want to look it up, just use an alphabetic character in the first position and alphnumeric characters in the remaining positions. If you want to get fancy with names—look it up.

A qname cannot include whitespace.

qnames A space-separated list of one or more QNames.

string A group of text characters.

string-expression An XSLT or XPath expression whose result is a string.

template A template consists of instructions, text, and comments, but not top-level instructions. In other words, it consists of everything you would put inside an <xsl:template> tag except for <xsl:param>.

token(s) Strings from which extra whitespace has been removed.

uri-reference A uniform resource identifier. Basically a URI scheme ("http", "mailto", "file", etc.) with a colon and a path or other information following. Again, for a formal definition, check out Wikipedia: http://en.wikipedia.org/wiki/Uniform_resource_identifier.

APPENDIX 2

Function and Expression Operator Reference

Alphabetical List of Functions

boolean()	id()	starts-with()
ceiling()	key()	string()
concat()	lang()	string-length()
contains()	last()	substring()
count()	local-name()	substring-after()
current()	name()	substring-before()
document()	namespace-uri()	sum()
element-available()	normalize-space()	system-property()
false()	not()	text()
floor()	number()	translate()
format-number()	position()	true()
function-available()	round()	unparsed-entity-uri()
generate-id()		

Functions by Return Type

Boolean functions (return true or false)

- boolean()
- contains()
- element-available()
- false()
- function-available()
- lang()
- not()
- starts-with()
- true()

Node-set functions (return a node or node set)

- current()
- document()
- id()
- key()

String functions (return a string)

- concat()
- generate-id()
- local-name()
- name()
- namespace-uri()
- normalize-space()
- string()
- substring()
- substring-after()
- substring-before()
- system-property()
- text()
- translate()
- unparsed-entity-uri()

Numeric functions (return a number)

- ceiling()
- count()
- floor()
- format-number()
- last()
- number()
- position()
- round()
- string-length()
- sum()

Summary of Functions

The following is a short description of the functional purpose of Functions in the XSLT/XPath 1.0 family. For more extensive descriptions, check out any of the following sources:

- w3schools: http://www.w3schools.com/xsl/xsl_functions.asp
- Microsoft: http://msdn.microsoft.com/en-us/library/ms256046%28v=vs.110%29.aspx
- Zvon: http://zvon.org/xxl/XSLTreference/Output/xpathFunctionIndex.html
- wikipedia: http://en.wikipedia.org/wiki/XPath#Functions_and_operators

Notation for the arguments given here use the same syntax notation given for elements in *Syntax Notation*, on page 243.

Note that although arguments are indicated here as being objects, strings, numbers, and so forth, the arguments can be in the form of variables, parameters, XPath expressions that point to nodes, and so forth, as long as they resolve to the correct data type for the argument.

For instance, a string could be a literal 'string' (that is, characters inside single quotes), a variable or parameter that represents a string (but the variable/parameter doesn't need to be in quotes), or an XPath to a node that contains a string (such as @string, which is an XPath pointer to the string= attribute inside the current element).

boolean(object)
Converts its object to a true or false value.

ceiling(number)
Returns an integer equal to the argument if the argument is an integer, or it returns the next largest integer if the argument value is between two integers.

concat(string, string, string*)
Returns a string that is the concatenation of its arguments.

contains(string, string)
Returns true if the first argument is contained in the second argument. If not, it returns false.

count(node-set)
Returns the number of nodes in the argument.

document(object, node-set?)
Returns a document tree (a node-set) if the document in the given location (the "object") contains a valid XML document.

false()
Returns the false value.

floor(number)
Returns an integer equal to the argument if the argument is an integer, or it returns the integer part of the argument if the argument value is between two integers.

id(object)
Returns an element or elements who have the id or ids specified in the argument.

key(string,object)
Returns a node-set using the key named in the string argument and the node-set derived from the object argument (which is supplied to the use= argument of the named key).

lang(string)

Returns true or false depending on whether the language specified in the argument matches the language that is active for the current node. If no language is active for the current node or any of its ancestors, this function returns false.

last()

Returns a number equal to the position number of the last node in the context of the current node.

local-name(node-set?)

Returns only the local part of a node's expanded name. If the node-set returns more than one result, only the first result with a local name is returned. If there is no local name, or if the node-set is empty, it returns an empty string.

name(node-set?)

Returns the expanded name of the node in the argument. Usually this is the name of the node in the document, but it may include a namespace if namespaces are in effect. If all you want is the name of the node in the document, `local-name()` is safer to use.

If the node-set returns more than one result, only the first result with a name is returned. If the node-set is empty, it returns an empty string.

namespace-uri(node-set?)

Returns the namespace URI (that is, the prefix) of the expanded name of the node in the argument. If the node-set is empty, if the URI of the expanded name is null, or if the first node in the specified node set doesn't have an expanded name, it returns an empty string.

normalize-space(string?)

Returns a string equal to the argument string but with leading and trailing whitespace stripped out and any contiguous groups of whitespace replaced with a single space character.

not(boolean)

Returns the boolean inverse of the boolean value of its argument. Anything true returns false, and anything false returns true.

number(object?)

Returns a number based on the value of its argument. See *Generated Values*, on page 165 for more details.

position()

Returns a number equal to the position (within its parent) of the context in which it is evaluated.

round(number)

Returns the integer that is closest to it in value. If the argument is an integer, it returns that integer.

starts-with(string, string)

Returns true if the first argument string starts with the second argument string. Otherwise, it returns false.

string-length(string?)

Returns the number of characters in the argument.

If the argument is omitted, the current context node is evaluated for its string value, and, if it has a string value, that string is used.

string(object?)

Returns a string based on the object in the argument. The following table shows what type of string is output for different types of arguments.

Argument is...	Output is...
A string	The same string
An empty node-set	An empty string
A single node	The string value of the node
A node set	The string value of the first node
NaN	NaN
Positive or negative zero	0
An integer	The integer
An integer with a decimal part	The integer with a decimal part
A negative number	The number preceded by a minus sign
A boolean true value	true
A boolean false value	false

substring-after(string, string)

Returns the portion of the first argument string that appears after the second argument string, if the second argument exists in the first argument. If the second argument doesn't exist in the first argument, the empty string is returned.

substring-before(string, string)

Returns the part of the first argument string that comes before the first appearance of the second argument string. If the second argument doesn't appear in the first argument, the empty string is returned.

substring(string, number, number?)

Returns the portion of the string in the first argument that is measured by the second argument and, optionally, the third argument. The returned portion of the string starts at the character position specified by the number in the second argument, with the first character being in position 1.

If there is no third argument, the returned string goes to the end of the original string. If there is a third argument, the returned string goes from the position of the second argument to the position of the third argument.

If the original string is not as long as the second argument, the empty string is returned.

sum(node-set)

Returns the sum of the numeric values returned by the node-set expression. In general, only number characters in nodes will return numeric values. Applying this function to nodes with alphabetical characters will probably not yield useful results.

translate(string, string, string)

Returns the string in the first argument with characters that are translated by a mapping of characters in the second argument string to characters in the third argument string.

This function is described in more detail in *Variation on a Theme #3: Using a Function to Uppercase the Text*, on page 66.

true()

Returns the true value. Always.

Expression Operators

The following operators can be used in XSLT and XPath expressions.

| (Union)

When used between node sets in an expression, gives a result that includes all the node sets.

Example: `ancestor::* | descendant::* | self::*` returns a node set consisting of all the ancestor and descendant elements of the current node as well as the current element itself.

+ (plus)

Gives the sum of two numbers. + can only be used between numbers.

Example: 2 + 4 + 6 = 12

- (minus)

Gives the difference between two numbers.

Example: 12 - 6 = 6

*** (multiplication asterisk)**

Gives the product of two numbers.

Example: 12 * 6 = 72

div (divided by)

Gives the quotient of two numbers, where the first number is divided by the second number.

Example: 12 div 6 = 2

= (equals)

Expresses the relationship between two values. The expression is true only if both sides have the same value, otherwise it is false. The values can be numbers, strings, or node sets.

Examples:

- 12 div 6 = 2 is true.
- 12 div 6 = 3 is false.
- 'Now is the time' = 'Now is the time' is true.
- 'Now is the time' = 'No time like the present' is false.

!= (not equal)

The expression is true only if both sides have different values, otherwise it is true. The values can be numbers, strings, or node sets.

Examples:

- 4 != 3 is true.
- 4 != 4 is false.
- 'One good turn deserves another' != 'Turn about is fair play' is true.
- 'One of us is a liar' != 'One of us is a liar' is false.

< (less than)

The expression is true only if the left side has a smaller value than the right side. The expression is evaluated in terms of numeric values.

Examples:

- 2 + 4 < 12 is true.
- 12 + 1 < 12 is false.

> (greater than)

The expression is true only if the left side has a larger value than the right side. The expression is evaluated in terms of numeric values.

Examples:

- 12 + 1 > 12 is true.
- 2 + 4 > 12 is false.

<= (less than or equal to)

The expression is true only if the left side is smaller than or equal to the right side. The expression is evaluated in terms of numeric values.

Examples:

- 2 + 4 <= 12 is true.
- 8 + 4 <= 12 is true.
- 12 + 1 <= 12 is false.

>= (greater than or equal to)

The expression is true only if the left side is larger than or equal to the right side. The expression is evaluated in terms of numeric values.

Examples:

- 12 + 1 >= 12 is true.
- 8 + 4 >= 12 is true.
- 2 + 4 >= 12 is false.

mod (modulus)

The remainder after a division operation between the left side and the right side of `mod`.

Example: 15 mod 7 = 1

Index

D

E

F

G

H

I

J

K

L

M

N

O

P

R

W

X

XSLT Jumpstarter

Please visit this book's web page:
https://pragprog.com/book/djkxsl
Resources include source code from this book, errata, and more.